M000111186

Good Meals

and

How to Prepare Them

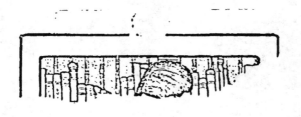

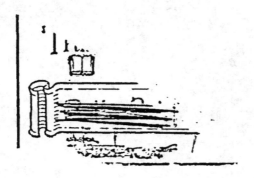

Dinner for a festal day with lighted candles, colorful glass and fragrant roses.

GOOD HOUSEKEEPING'S
Book of
Good Meals
How to Prepare and Serve Them

A Guide *to* Meal Planning
Cooking *and* Serving

GOOD HOUSEKEEPING INSTITUTE
KATHARINE A. FISHER, *Director*

Published by GOOD HOUSEKEEPING
119 West Fortieth Street, New York

SIXTH EDITION

Copyright, 1927, by
INTERNATIONAL MAGAZINE COMPANY, Inc.
NEW YORK, N. Y.

1st Edition Printed February, 1927.
2nd Edition Printed April, 1927.
3rd Edition Printed June, 1927.
4th Edition Printed October, 1927.
5th Edition Printed February, 1928.
6th Edition Printed August, 1928.

PRINTED IN U. S. A. BY JOHN F. CUNEO CO.

Contents

How Your Friends May Get This Book

Sooner or later your friends will learn that you possess this book. You will be having them in for dinner some evening, and they will express their enthusiastic admiration of your delightful hospitality— your attractive table settings—your gracious serving—and your delectable dishes. Then, glowing with their praises, you will in an unguarded moment reveal the fact that you possess a copy of this book.

And all will be lost. Then and there your friends will demand that you lend the book to them; or each one will come to you quietly and individually and simply insist that you let her have it first. And this cook book, that *was yours*, will become the common property of your entire circle; and you will be fortunate to be accorded the privilege of *"borrowing it back"* for very brief periods.

Of course you want to be kind to your friends. On the other hand, you want to keep this book for your own constant use and reference. So, may we suggest this:

Tell your friends that they also may have a copy of this book ABSOLUTELY WITHOUT COST by simply ordering Good House- keeping for two years for $4.50—a saving of $1.50 on the regular subscription price. This book, of course, cannot be bought any- where, at any price. It is published exclusively for Good House- keeping subscribers, and they may have it free.

Remember This Cook Book at Gift Time

For newlyweds, for Christmas, for birthdays—nothing makes such a delightfully appropriate gift as Good Housekeeping. Every month of the year it pleasantly reminds the recipient of the donor's good will and thoughtfulness. And, of course, when you order a two-year Gift Subscription to Good Housekeeping, you may also have a copy of this New Cook Book which you may use for another Gift. So the next time you are wondering what gift to buy a friend or relative, remember this page and send your order to—

Good Housekeeping

119 West 40th Street,   Dept. CB-427,   New York

To Our Readers

Good Housekeeping Institute has prepared this book as a gift to the readers of Good Housekeeping.

The material has been evolved in our own laboratories where every direction and every recipe have been submitted to careful and repeated tests. As with all material published by the Institute, the measures given are standard and level, thus insuring satisfactory results.

In planning this book, our aim has been to arrange it in such a way as to gather between the covers a thoroughly dependable and comprehensive guide to cookery and to meal preparation in general, which would, as nearly as possible, meet the needs of every one using it. With so much material to include this has not been a simple matter, but a glance at the table of contents will indicate the extent to which careful organization has accomplished this purpose.

The beginner and the inexperienced in housekeeping will find here most explicit directions for the best methods of cooking the simplest every day dishes, from the making of the breakfast cereal to baking a potato or broiling a steak or chop. Those searching for new dishes, for something that is different, or for an interesting and inviting menu for a festal day or special party will, we hope, find just the information they want.

The section on recipes by chart or schedule is unique as it gathers into a few pages in a very concise and ready-reference form all the interesting variations of the typical dishes on the basis of proper proportions and methods. The reasons why these proportions are used and certain methods followed are clearly presented, giving a new control over cookery processes.

The business of planning meals that will best suit various households, the keeping of these well balanced as to food values, for both grown-ups and children, the factors influencing meal costs, and much-asked-for information on table service have all been considered. Generous attention has been given to the effective use of modern equipment in meal preparation, with emphasis on methods of saving fuel and shortening the hours spent in the kitchen.

We have given a great deal of attention to the index, for to be really useful, all this material must be easily and quickly found. Every possible provision has been made for this. For example, most of the recipes are listed under a number of names. Baked Macaroni and Cheese is not only indexed under this name but also under Casserole Dishes, Cheese Dishes, Macaroni and Cheese and Cereals. Take every advantage, therefore, of such cross references in using this book.

5

The cover of this book should
only be wiped off lightly with
a damp cloth to remove soil.
Do not rub with soapy water
or an abrasive.

Fruits

I. FOOD VALUE

Fruit is an important source of body regulating and body building material. It also furnishes roughage, so necessary in keeping the intestinal tract clear. Fruits are often spoken of as foods that leave too much acid in the body, when in reality they practically all leave alkaline material. They are an appetizing beginning or ending for any meal, because of their flavor and acidity. They form the basis of many tempting salads and are much used as relishes for meat in the form of sauces and jellies.

II. SERVING FRUIT

Wash fruit thoroughly in cold water, but do not let it stand in the water. A colander is convenient for cherries, berries, etc. Do not dry grapes, plums, or peaches as one is apt to remove the bloom. In paring or cutting the fruit, use a stainless steel or glass knife as an ordinary steel knife discolors the fruit. Fruits will discolor if they stand after being cut, a point to be remembered in making raw fruit salads and desserts. Lemon juice will sometimes prevent this. Apples may be put in a weak salt solution to prevent discoloration.

1. **Dried Fruits.** They are usually stewed and served in a sauce dish with the juice in which they were cooked. Cluster raisins, pulled

7

figs, and dates may be washed and served in a large bowl or on individual fruit plates. They are also served cooked with a cereal for breakfast. Prunes may be soaked for one hour, the pits removed and stuffed with nuts, cream cheese or celery and served as confection or in a salad.

2. **Oranges.** a. Cut in halves crosswise. Place halves on a fruit plate with or without a doily between the fruits and the plate.

b. Orange juice. Strain and chill, serve in small glasses.

c. Orange sections. Pare an orange with a sharp knife; trim off the white membrane leaving the pulp exposed on the entire surface. Remove sections by carefully cutting toward center along the membrane which divides fruit into sections, first on one side of section, then on the other. Arrange sections on a fruit plate, around a small mound of powdered sugar if desired.

3. **Grapefruit.** To prepare a grapefruit after cutting, remove the seeds with a fork. Then, with a sharp knife, cut around each section, separating the flesh from the partitions. With scissors, cut down each partition from the edge to the core. Insert the knife again and separate the core from the fruit shell. With the scissors or finger tips lift the center, bringing the partitions with it and leaving the fruit sections intact.

4. **Fruit Cocktails.** They are prepared of fresh or canned fruit, either a single tart fruit or a combination. The combinations are innumerable, but they should always contain some tart fruit. All fruits are cut in pieces of serving size and no skin is left on except on cherries or grapes. The juice may be poured over the fruit and in this case it is eaten with a spoon; if no liquid is used, a fork is preferable.

GRAPES IN ORANGE JUICE COCKTAIL

California White Grapes   Red Tokays
Juicy Oranges

Rinse the grapes, cut them in halves, and remove the seeds. Squeeze the orange juice. Place in the refrigerator until just before serving. Allow one-third cupful of seeded grapes and one-quarter cupful of orange juice for each glass. Arrange the grapes in the glass and pour orange juice over them.

MINT GRAPE COCKTAIL

Pineapple, diced, canned   Grapefruit
Malaga Grapes   Red Grape Juice
Oranges   Sprigs of mint

Arrange in each cocktail glass two tablespoonfuls of diced, canned pineapple and two tablespoonfuls of seeded Malaga grapes. Over the top arrange three fleshy sections of orange cut in halves, and two fleshy sections of grapefruit cut in halves. Last, pour two tablespoonfuls of red grape juice over each and serve topped with a sprig of mint.

ORANGE COCKTAIL AU NATUREL

Oranges   1 cupful water
1 cupful sugar

Select oranges that have pronounced oil cells on the skin. Carefully remove a thin layer of the outside peeling, with none of the inner white skin. Chop this fine and measure two tablespoonfuls. Add the water and the sugar and simmer gently for ten or fifteen minutes or until the sirup is well flavored with orange. Chill. Meanwhile arrange fleshy sections of orange, cut in halves in the cocktail glasses. Pour over some of the orange sirup—about two tablespoonfuls for each serving.

PINEAPPLE COCKTAIL

Oranges   Grapes
Pineapple   Powdered sugar

Not always must a fruit cocktail be served in glasses. Pineapple Cocktail is attractive arranged on small glass plates. On each plate place a slice of canned pineapple, which has been cut in several places without losing its shape. Lay a smaller slice of orange, also cut in several places, on top of each slice of pineapple, and pile halves of seeded grapes in the center. Sprinkle lightly with powdered sugar and serve.

PIQUANTE FRUIT COCKTAIL

½ cupful powdered sugar   1 cupful canned stoned cherries
½ cupful orange juice   1 cupful canned cubed pears
⅓ cupful grapefruit juice   Chopped crystallized ginger

Mix together one-half cupful of powdered sugar, the orange juice, and grapefruit juice and chill. Remove pits from the canned cherries, either white or red, and cut canned pears in cubes of as even shape as possible. Place the fruit in cocktail glasses, fill with the liquid, and sprinkle each service with one-half tablespoonful of chopped crystallized ginger. Serves six.

5. **Other Fruits.** Apples, plums, pears, grapes, etc., are served piled in a large serving-dish or on individual fruit plates. Fruit knives should be supplied if necessary and finger bowls will save many spots on napkins. These should be removed with the fruit course.

III. GENERAL RULES FOR COOKING FRUIT

1. **Fresh Fruit.** a. Stewed: Wash fruit, pare or peel and cut in pieces or leave whole if small. Add enough water, hot or cold, to keep from browning. Cover and cook until tender. Add sugar to sweeten if necessary.

b. Compote cooked in sirup: Make a sirup using two cupfuls of water to one cupful of sugar. Put the prepared fruit in the hot sirup, cover closely and simmer until tender. A small amount of the fruit should be cooked at a time and drained out of the sirup. The same sirup may be used until all of the fruit is cooked, then poured over all.

c. Baked or Scalloped: Wash the fruit. If there is a core, remove with corer or cut fruit in half and scoop out the core. Lay in a baking-dish and sprinkle with sugar and spices if desired. Barely cover the bottom of the dish with boiling water. Bake at 400° F. until tender. Baste with the liquid in the dish several times during the baking. Add extra boiling water if necessary. Apples, quinces, etc., may be baked in a covered dish in less time, removing the cover for the last ten or fifteen minutes to brown.

d. Steamed: The steamer or the pressure cooker is excellent for cooking winter fruits.

2. **Dried Fruits.** They should be carefully washed in several waters and any hard parts removed. Soak six hours or overnight in cold water or for two hours in boiling water and cook in the same water until tender. Do not add sugar unless very tart. Dried fruits after soaking may be cooked by any of the methods used for fresh fruits.

3. **Fruit Whips.** Prepare one cupful of fruit pulp such as apple-sauce, sieved cooked prunes, or apricots, fresh or canned peaches; quince sauce, etc. Beat three egg whites until quite stiff, add sugar to taste and continue beating until blended. Fold the fruit pulp mixed with a little lemon juice, into the egg whites. Chill and serve with custard sauce. Or pour into greased pudding dish and bake at 300° F. for thirty minutes.

IV. SPECIAL FRUIT RECIPES

APPLE PORCUPINE

1½ cupfuls sugar	½ teaspoonful cinnamon
6 medium-sized apples	Blanched almonds
1 tablespoonful butter, fat or oil	Cream
2½ cupfuls water	

Cook the sugar and water together for three minutes. Pare and core the apples and cook them in the sirup until tender, but not broken, turning them frequently. Then drain them and place in a baking-dish. To the sirup add the fat and cinnamon and continue to cook until quite thick. Fill the cores of the apples and the surrounding space with the sirup and stick the apples with the blanched almonds lengthwise. Place in a 450° F. oven just long enough to brown the nut tips. Cool and serve with plain or whipped cream. Serves six.

BAKED APPLES GLACÉ

6 firm red apples	1 cupful sugar
1½ cupfuls water	3 tablespoonfuls sugar

Core and peel the apples about one-third of the way down from the stem end. Then place them in a deep dripping pan or casserole, which has a closely fitted cover. Meanwhile make a thin sirup of the one cupful of sugar and the water, boiling it for six minutes. Pour this sirup over the apples, cover them tightly and place in a 400° F. oven. Baste the apples occasionally until they are quite tender, but still whole and perfect. Remove the cover and place one teaspoonful of sugar in the cavity of each apple, also sprinkling sugar over the peeled surface. Then place the pan under the heat of the broiler, or in the top of a very hot oven until the sugar has melted, and the peeled section of the apple has taken on a very light delicate shade of brown. Baste once or twice during this process. Serve with plain or whipped cream. Serves six.

FRIED SWEETINGS

6 sweet apples	6 tablespoonfuls molasses
Fat	

Wipe and core the apples and cut each in three or four rings. Heat a little fat in frying-pan, lay the apples in, cover and cook slowly turning at the end of fifteen minutes. When both sides are brown pour one teaspoonful of molasses over each slice, cook five minutes longer and serve very hot. Serves six.

CRANBERRY SAUCE

4 cupfuls cranberries	2 cupfuls sugar
2 cupfuls water	

Wash cranberries carefully and pick out any soft ones. Put sugar and water in saucepan and bring slowly to boiling point. Boil about ten minutes until a thin sirup is formed. Add the cranberries, cover and simmer gently until clear and transparent, but not broken. Serves six to eight.

CRANBERRY JELLY

4 cupfuls cranberries   2 cupfuls sugar
1 cupful boiling water

Pick over and wash the berries carefully. Place in stewpan with the boiling water. Boil until all the berries have burst open, about ten minutes. Pour into a sieve and mash through as much of the pulp as possible. Add two cupfuls of sugar, return to fire and bring slowly to boil, stirring constantly so that all sugar is dissolved. Pour at once into wet mold or sterilized glasses. Serves six to eight.

DATE CREAM

2 cupfuls dates   1 tablespoonful lemon juice
1 cupful chopped walnuts   Whipped cream

Wipe dates carefully with a damp cloth and remove pits. Cut the dates in pieces and combine with nut meats and lemon juice. Arrange in sherbet glasses and top with a spoonful of whipped cream. Serves four to six.

SHREDDED DATES

Dates   Candied ginger
Milk   Whipped cream

Fill individual glass dishes with dates that have been stoned and shredded, mixing in a few bits of candied ginger. Pour into the dishes enough sweet milk to almost cover the dates and set in the ice chest to chill for an hour or two. Before serving put a little freshly whipped cream on top of each dish. This is an excellent nursery dessert.

ORANGES AND RAISINS

Raisins   Oranges

Wash and soak the raisins in water to cover for six to eight hours. Simmer gently until tender. Add some thinly sliced orange or orange sections and serve with cream.

STUFFED ORANGES

6 oranges   ½ cup shredded coconut
½ cupful stoned dates   1 egg white
½ cupful chopped walnut meats ¼ cupful powdered sugar

Cut a slice from the end of each orange and carefully remove pulp. Discard all tough membrane. Clean and chop the dates. Mix dates, nuts, orange pulp, and coconut together and refill orange shells. Beat egg white until stiff, add sugar gradually, continue beating. Pile on top of oranges. Brown at 300° F. Serve warm. Serves six.

PRUNE CRISPS

Rounds of bread   Stewed prunes
Fat   Whipped cream

Delicately brown rounds of bread in fat. While hot, cover with cold pitted stewed prunes. Top with whipped cream and serve at once.

PRUNE DELIGHT

1 cupful dried prunes   ¼ cupful sugar
1 cupful sugar   ½ teaspoonful lemon extract
4 eggs   ½ cupful browned almonds
¼ teaspoonful salt   3 cupfuls milk
             3 cupfuls cold water

Soak the prunes overnight in the cold water. Then simmer slowly until the prunes are very soft. Discard the pits and rub the prunes through a coarse strainer. Meanwhile melt the one cupful of sugar in a frying-pan until caramel in color. Pour one-half of it into the mold in which the custard is to be baked and the other half on a greased pan to harden. To the prune pulp add the milk and bring to the scalding point. Beat the eggs slightly, add one-fourth cupful sugar, the salt, lemon extract and the hot milk and prune mixture, adding the latter a little at a time while stirring constantly. Pour into the mold, place in a pan of warm water and bake at 325° F. for one and one-quarter hours or until firm when tested with a silver knife. Cool the custard slightly and turn out on a serving dish. Meanwhile remove the hardened caramel from the pan and together with the browned almonds, crush very fine. Sprinkle over the custard and serve either hot or cold. Serves six.

CINNAMON PRUNES

1 pound prunes   3-inch stick cinnamon
2 slices lemon or orange   Cold water

Wash the prunes carefully, cover with cold water and soak overnight. Add the cinnamon and slices of lemon or orange. Cook slowly in a covered utensil until tender. If cooked very slowly, no sugar will be needed. Serves six.

STEWED PRUNES

Wash prunes carefully. Cover with boiling water and let stand for half an hour. Place over low heat and cook slowly until tender. It is not necessary to add sugar with this method.

EPICUREAN RASPBERRIES

Raspberries   Cantaloupe
Powdered sugar

Pick over and wash firm raspberries and chill well.   Prepare halves of cantaloupe and chill.   Arrange raspberries in cantaloupes and serve with powdered sugar for breakfast or dessert.

RHUBARB AND BANANAS

4 cupfuls sweetened   2 large bananas
rhubarb sauce   ⅓ cupful sugar

Slice the bananas thinly in a serving-dish.   Sprinkle them with the sugar.   Pour the hot sweetened rhubarb sauce over the bananas.   Set aside to cool.   Serve cold.   Serves six.

BAKED RHUBARB

4 cupfuls rhubarb, cut small   ¼ teaspoonful cinnamon
2 cupfuls granulated sugar   12 whole cloves
½ teaspoonful mace   1 large orange

Place the ingredients all together in a greased casserole, adding the grated rind of the orange as well as the juice and pulp.   Cover and bake at 350° F. until the rhubarb is tender.   If very juicy, uncover during the last fifteen minutes of baking.   Serves six.

V. FRUIT PUNCHES (P. 183)

VI. FRUIT SALADS (P. 164)

Drinks and Beverages

Coffee

I. · GENERAL DIRECTIONS FOR MAKING AND SERVING

1. Buy coffee in reasonably small quantities, and keep in a tight container. If bought in the bean, grind as used.
2. Use two level tablespoonfuls of ground coffee to one cupful of water, regardless of the method.
3. Serve coffee as soon as made. If you must delay, keep it piping hot, but never let it boil.
4. Keep the coffee-making appliance very clean, and entirely free from odor of stale coffee. A solution of borax or baking soda and water boiled in the container keeps it odorless.
5. Serve plain or with cream. Pour cream or milk into cups before pouring coffee over it.

II. DRIP COFFEE

1. Preheat drip coffee pot by filling with boiling water a short time before using. Pour off this water just before making coffee.
2. Grind coffee to consistency of powdered sugar.

15

3. Place coffee grounds in proper compartment, allowing two table-spoonfuls for every cupful of boiling water.
4. Pour boiling water over coffee grounds, in the proper quantity, and allow to drip through. Remove the coffee-grounds container and cover the pot and serve at once.
5. If the coffee can not be served immediately, place the container in a pan of hot water, or over low heat.
6. If drip coffee pot, with a cloth bag for grounds, is used every day, let the bag stand in cold water each time, after washing.

III. PERCOLATED COFFEE
1. Grind coffee "medium."
2. Place coffee grounds in proper compartment allowing two tablespoonfuls for every cupful of boiling water.
3. Pour fresh, rapidly boiling water in proper amount, in bottom of percolator.
4. Percolate for seven minutes or until a deep golden brown. Then lift cover, remove strainer with coffee grounds, and serve.
5. If necessary to keep hot, set percolator in pan of hot water, or over low heat.

IV. BOILED COFFEE
1. Scald the coffee pot.
2. Grind the coffee "medium," and measure, allowing two table-spoonfuls to each cupful of cold water.
3. Beat one egg slightly, add one-half of the cold water, the crushed, washed egg shell and the ground coffee. Turn into coffee pot, pour in rest of cold water and boil three minutes. Then let stand on the back of the stove for ten minutes and serve.

V. ICED COFFEE
Fill tall glasses one-half full of chipped ice. Put two tablespoonfuls of cream in each glass and pour over freshly made hot coffee. Serve with powdered sugar and a bit of whipped cream.

Tea

I. GENERAL DIRECTIONS FOR MAKING AND SERVING
1. Store tea in an air-tight container.
2. Measure carefully. Use two teaspoonfuls of tea or one or two tea bags for each pint of boiling water.

II. HOT TEA

1. Scald the teapot with boiling water.
2. Add tea and pour over it boiling water in the proper quantity. Let stand where it will keep warm, not hot, from three to five minutes.

III. ICED TEA

1. Make hot tea as above, increasing the quantity of tea to four teaspoonfuls for each pint of water.
2. Fill iced-tea glasses about one-half full of chopped ice and over this pour the hot tea.
3. Serve with lemon in quarter or eighth sections or orange slices. One tablespoonful of lemon or orange juice may be added to the tea. The flavor is much finer by chilling the hot tea quickly.

Cocoa and Chocolate

I. FOOD VALUE

Cocoa and chocolate beverages differ from tea and coffee in that they contain nutriment as well as stimulant. Particularly is this true if the beverage is made of milk or nearly all milk. Theobromine, the stimulant in cocoa and chocolate, is almost identical with theine and caffein found in tea and coffee, in its composition and effects.

II. HOT COCOA

1 to 2 teaspoonfuls cocoa	¾ cupful scalded milk
¼ cupful water	1 to 2 teaspoonfuls sugar if
Few grains salt	desired
	2 drops vanilla

Combine the cocoa, water, salt and sugar. Boil two minutes. Add the scalded milk and heat well. Beat two minutes with an egg beater, when froth will form, preventing scum. This last process is known as "milling." Add the vanilla and serve. Serves one.

III. HOT CHOCOLATE

1½ teaspoonfuls grated choco-late	1 to 2 teaspoonfuls sugar if desired
¼ cupful boiling water	Few grains salt
¾ cupful scalded milk	2 drops vanilla

Melt the chocolate with the sugar and salt in a saucepan. Add the boiling water slowly and stir until smooth. Boil one minute, add the scalded milk and heat well. Beat two minutes with an egg beater, when froth will form preventing scum. Add the vanilla and serve. Serves one.·

IV. ICED COCOA OR CHOCOLATE

Fill tall glasses one-half full of cracked ice. Pour over freshly made hot cocoa or chocolate. Garnish each with one tablespoonful of whipped cream.

Punches

(See Chart for Punches on Page 183)

Egg Nog

Egg nog is made from milk or cream and beaten eggs, and has all of the nourishing features of these two valuable foods.

	Egg	Sugar	Fluid	Flavoring
Plain Egg Nog	1	¾ tbsp.	¾ c. milk or cream	1 tsp. vanilla or speck nutmeg or speck cinnamon
Coffee Egg Nog	1	1½ tbsp.	6 tbsp. milk or cream	6 tbsp. strong coffee
Fruit Egg Nog	1	2 tbsp.	¼ c. water, ¼ c. chopped ice	2 tbsp. fruit juice

Method I. Beat egg well. Add sugar and beat again. Add remaining ingredients and beat. Serve very cold in glass. This method is preferable for fruit egg nogs. Serves one.

Method II. Beat yolk of egg until thick and lemon colored. Add sugar and beat again. Beat white of egg to a stiff froth, mix with yolk and sugar, add milk, then coffee or fruit juice. Serve in glass on china plate with doily. Serves one.

Method III. Beat yolk of egg until thick and lemon colored. Add the sugar, beat again. Add the flavoring. Pour into glass and lay on top the stiffly beaten white. Serves one.

Malted Milk

For **Plain Malted Milk**, mix 3 tablespoonfuls malted milk powder with a little warm water to make a smooth paste. Add ¾ cupful hot milk and serve. For **Chocolate** Malted Milk, mix 2 tablespoonfuls malted milk powder with 1 teaspoonful cocoa, 1 teaspoonful sugar and a little warm water to make a smooth paste. Cook one minute, then add ¾ cupful milk. Serve hot or cold.

Milk Shakes

For Vanilla Milk Shake, add 2 teaspoonfuls sugar and ¼ teaspoonful vanilla to each cupful of milk. Shake well and serve at once. For Orange Milk Shake, substitute ¼ teaspoonful orange extract for the vanilla. Or omit vanilla and add 2 tablespoonfuls orange juice. For Coffee Milk Shake, add 2 tablespoonfuls of strong coffee. For Chocolate Milk Shake, add 2 tablespoonfuls chocolate sirup to ¾ cupful of milk and 2 tablespoonfuls of chopped ice. Shake well and serve. For the Chocolate Sirup, add 1 cupful of boiling water to 1 ounce of cooking chocolate. Stir well and then add 1½ cupfuls sugar. Boil 3 minutes until thoroughly blended, cool and add 3 tablespoonfuls of vanilla.

Eggs

I. FOOD VALUE

1. Eggs are protein or tissue-building food and may be used as a substitute for meat. They also contain a high percentage of easily digested fat, and are a good source of iron and vitamin A.

II. METHODS OF COOKING

1. Poached—Fill a frying-pan two-thirds full of water. Add one-half teaspoonful salt to each pint of water. Put in the greased muffin rings or egg poachers. Break eggs one at a time in a saucer and slip into the rings in the boiling water. Turn off heat entirely so that eggs will cook slowly. Cover pan or carefully baste tops of eggs to form white film. When whites are firm, lift out eggs carefully. Poached eggs may be served as a luncheon dish, by placing them on squares of buttered toast, and pouring over them a savory sauce, such as Cheese Sauce, Tomato Sauce or Hollandaise Sauce.

POACHED EGGS LAFAYETTE

Place rounds of buttered toast on hot, individual serving dishes; on these lay pieces of cooked ham quickly "frizzled" in a hot frying-pan. On the ham place a poached egg lightly sprinkled with salt and pepper. Pour over all Hollandaise Sauce (P. 184), to which one tablespoonful of minced parsley has been added for each cupful of sauce.

2. **Soft Cooked Eggs**—The albumin in the egg is toughened by a high temperature so that it is better to cook eggs below boiling. Allow one pint of water for one or two eggs and one additional cup for each additional egg. When the water is boiling, put in the eggs, **cover tightly** and turn off heat. Six minutes is sufficient time to produce a soft cooked egg; eight minutes for a medium cooked egg.

3. **Scrambled**—Break four eggs into a bowl and beat slightly, add two tablespoonfuls of milk, cream or water, one-half teaspoonful salt and speck of pepper. Melt two tablespoonfuls of butter in a frying-pan, add eggs, and lower the heat. When the mixture begins to set on the edges, stir it and lift from pan so that the uncooked portion will run under. When entirely set, remove from fire and serve at once. The eggs should be firm but not hard. This recipe may be varied by adding cooked vegetables, fish or meat, which have been chopped or diced, to the egg mixture just before removing from the fire. Serves four.

4. **Omelet, Plain**—Break five eggs into a bowl and beat just enough to blend yolks and whites. Add five tablespoonfuls of water, one teaspoonful salt, and one-eighth teaspoonful pepper. Melt two tablespoonfuls of butter into a frying-pan, and tip the pan to grease the sides and bottom. Pour in the omelet and cook until a film of cooked egg has formed on the bottom of the pan. Lift the edge of the omelet nearest you with a spatula, and at the same time, tilt the pan so that the uncooked egg mixture runs under the raised cooked portion. Allow the omelet to cook a minute longer and repeat the tilting process. Continue until all the mixture is cooked and the omelet is brown on the bottom. Loosen the omelet with a spatula, fold over like a jelly roll and slip from the pan to a hot platter. Spread with jelly before folding, if desired. Serves six.

PUFFY OMELET

Separate the yolks and whites of six eggs. Beat the yolks until thick and lemon colored. Add six tablespoonfuls of milk or water, three-fourths teaspoonful salt, one-eighth teaspoonful pepper. Beat egg whites in separate bowl until stiff and very dry and fold into the egg yolk mixture. Melt one and one-half tablespoonfuls of butter in an omelet pan or frying-pan and tip slightly to grease sides and bottom. Pour the omelet into the hot buttered pan spreading it evenly on the surface. If a regulation omelet pan is used, butter both sides and pour half the mixture in either side. Cook over a slow fire until the omelet is golden brown on the underside. Place the omelet in a slow oven at about 350° F. for five minutes to dry off top. Loosen from pan with spatula, fold and turn on to a hot platter. Serve at once. Serves six.

SPANISH OMELET

Prepare a puffy omelet and serve with the following Spanish sauce:

1 tablespoonful fat	1 teaspoonful chopped onion
1 tablespoonful chopped green pepper	½ tablespoonful flour
	¼ teaspoonful salt
¼ teaspoonful celery salt	Speck of pepper
3 chopped mushrooms	1 cupful tomatoes

Melt the fat, add green pepper, onion and mushrooms. Cook slowly for three minutes, add flour and seasonings. Mix well. Add tomato and simmer gently until thick. Serves six.

BREAD OMELET

5 eggs	1 teaspoonful salt
⅔ cupful milk	⅛ teaspoonful pepper
⅔ cupful bread crumbs	2 tablespoonfuls butter

Soak the bread crumbs in the milk for fifteen minutes. Make same as Puffy Omelet. Serves six.

5. Soufflés—See Chart on Soufflés (P. 188)

6. Hard Cooked Eggs in Variety

Allow one pint of water for one or two eggs and one additional cup for each additional egg. When the water is boiling, put in the eggs, cover tightly and turn off heat. Let stand covered sixty minutes.

CREAMED EGGS WITH SHRIMPS

2 tablespoonfuls fat	1 cupful thin cream
3 tablespoonfuls flour	½ cupful milk
¼ teaspoonful paprika	6 hard-cooked eggs
¾ teaspoonful salt	1 small can shrimps
½ teaspoonful prepared mustard	6 rounds toast

Melt the fat, browning slightly. Add the flour and seasonings stirring until the mixture is well blended. Pour in the cream and milk gradually, stirring until smooth and thickened. Chop the eggs coarsely; remove the viscera from the shrimps and cut in halves. Turn into the white sauce. When heated, serve on rounds of buttered toast. Garnish with parsley. Serves six.

CURRIED EGGS

6 hard-cooked eggs
2 tablespoonfuls flour
2 tablespoonfuls fat
1 cupful milk
½ teaspoonful salt

½ teaspoonful curry-powder
1½ cupfuls boiled rice
Few grains each pepper and
paprika

Make a sauce of the fat, flour, seasonings and milk. Bring to scalding point, and add the eggs quartered. Arrange a border of rice around the platter, and pour the egg mixture in the center. To prepare this in the chafing-dish, make the sauce in the blazer, add the rice, put the quartered eggs on top, and let all stand to become hot. Serves six.

EGGS AU GRATIN

8 eggs
2 tablespoonfuls fat
3 tablespoonfuls flour
1½ cupfuls milk

¾ teaspoonful salt
⅛ teaspoonful paprika
½ cupful grated American
cheese

Hard-cook the eggs. Meanwhile, prepare a white sauce as follows: Melt the fat and add the flour, stirring constantly. When smooth, and bubbling, add the milk, a little at a time, and stir until the sauce is smooth. Then add the salt and paprika. Shell the eggs, halve them lengthwise, and arrange in a greased baking-dish. Pour the white sauce over them and sprinkle the top with the grated American cheese and a little paprika. Bake in a medium oven of 350° F. for fifteen minutes or until thoroughly heated and browned on top. Serves six.

LUNCHEON EGGS

2 teaspoonfuls chopped onion
2 tablespoonfuls fat
1 cupful thin cream
1 cupful milk
3 tablespoonfuls flour
6 slices buttered toast

6 hard-cooked eggs
½ teaspoonful grated nutmeg
½ teaspoonful salt
½ teaspoonful paprika
1 canned pimiento

Cook the onion in the fat until it is yellow, but not brown. Add the flour, nutmeg, salt and paprika. When well blended together, add the cream and milk gradually, stirring constantly. Cook until smooth and thickened. Cut the eggs into quarters lengthwise and the pimiento into strips. Arrange the eggs on the toast, pour the sauce over all, and garnish with strips of pimiento. Serves six.

OEUFS GOURMET

6 hard-cooked eggs	Few grains pepper
½ cupful grated American cheese	Few grains mace
	Few grains paprika
5 tablespoonfuls tomato catchup	Olive oil
	Lettuce and stuffed olives
¼ teaspoonful salt	

Split the eggs in halves lengthwise. Remove the yolks, mash them, and combine with the cheese, seasonings, and catchup, adding olive-oil to moisten as necessary. Roll into oval balls, lay them in the whites of the eggs, and garnish each with half a stuffed olive. Serve in nests of lettuce with cheese straws. The cheese mixture alone or with the egg-yolks makes delicious sandwiches, or the whole may be served with mayonnaise as a salad. Serves six.

PRESSED EGGS

6 hard-cooked eggs	½ teaspoonful salt
1 green onion	1 tablespoonful prepared mustard
½ seeded green pepper	
2 tablespoonfuls stock	1½ cupfuls chopped ham

Chop fine the hard-cooked eggs, onion and green pepper. Mix together with salt and prepared mustard. Place half of the mixture in a small, greased loaf pan, press down, then add a layer of ham, chopped. Finish with the rest of the egg mixture. Pour on the stock to help bind it together, and press down well. Keep in the refrigerator until molded well enough to slice. Serve in place of cold meat or use as a sandwich filling. Serves six.

CREAMED STUFFED EGGS

6 hard-cooked eggs	2 cupfuls medium white sauce
1 teaspoonful salt	⅛ teaspoonful paprika
1 can Vienna style sausages	1 cupful buttered crumbs
⅛ teaspoonful pepper	

Cut the eggs in halves lengthwise, mash the yolks and mix half of them with ground sausages, seasoning with salt, pepper, and paprika. Refill the whites, and add the other half of the egg-yolks to the white sauce. Arrange the halved eggs in a baking-dish, cover with white sauce, and then with crumbs, making two layers of each, if necessary. Bake at 375° F. for twenty minutes. Garnish with parsley and whole sausage. Serves six.

STUFFED EGGS

Have ready cold hard-cooked eggs. Cut crosswise or lengthwise and remove yolks. Press yolks through a sieve; season well with salt and pepper; a little prepared mustard or mayonnaise or butter may be added. Finely chopped ham, or cooked chicken liver make a savory addition. Fill the egg whites with the mixture.

CREAMED POTATOES WITH EGGS (P. 108)

7. Baked Eggs or Shirred Eggs

1 cupful mashed potatoes	½ cupful minced, cooked ham
½ teaspoonful salt	¼ teaspoonful pepper
6 eggs	1 tablespoonful fat

Blend together the mashed potatoes, minced ham, salt and pepper; add one beaten egg and put in bottom of greased baking-dish. Break the remaining five eggs over the potato mixture, being careful to keep them equidistant and not to break yolks. Dot with fat and dust with salt and pepper. Bake in a medium oven of 375° F. until eggs are firm. Serves six.

III. EGG NOGS—See Drinks and Beverages (P. 18)

IV. MERINGUES FOR PIES AND PUDDINGS

Beat chilled egg whites to a stiff dry froth. Allow two tablespoonfuls of sugar for each egg. Add sugar, one tablespoonful at a time, beating the egg whites constantly until the meringue is stiff, but glossy and creamy in consistency. Flavor, allowing one-fourth teaspoonful of vanilla to two egg whites. Bake in a slow oven of 300° F. for fifteen minutes.

V. TIMBALES

Small portions of left-over fish, meat, or vegetables may be used in timbales. Chop the cooked vegetables or meat very fine. Fill slightly greased timbale molds with the vegetable or meat. Fill the interstices with a custard mixture, made by beating two eggs slightly with one cupful of milk, one-fourth teaspoonful salt, speck of pepper. Set molds in a pan of hot water and bake at 325° F. until set. Tip out carefully and serve with a sauce if desired.

Milk

I. PLACE IN THE DIET

Milk belongs to the group of protein or tissue-building foods. It is a liberal source of vitamin A, and is an important source of calcium. A child should have at least one quart of milk a day and an adult one pint.

GETTING MILK INTO THE MEALS

Soups	Creamed Vegetables and Meat Dishes	Milk Drinks
Cream of Potato Soup	Creamed Potatoes and	Milk Shakes
Cream of Lettuce Soup	Green Peppers	Chocolate
Cream of Mushroom Soup	Creamed Green Peppers	Vanilla
Cauliflower Soup	Creamed Carrots and Peas	Orange
Cream of Corn and	Creamed Cabbage	Coffee
Tomato Soup	Creamed Onions	
Pimiento Soup	Creamed Celery	
Cream of Watercress Soup	Creamed Brussels Sprouts	Egg Nog
Oyster Stew	Creamed Cauliflower	Coffee
Corn Chowder	Creamed Turnips	Fruit
Fish Chowder	Scalloped Cabbage	Nutmeg
Tomato Bisque	Scalloped Onions	Cinnamon
Cream of Celery Soup	Scalloped Celery	
Cream of Lima Bean Soup	Scalloped Cauliflower	Malted Milk
Cream of Pea Soup	Scalloped Potatoes	Plain
Cream of Spinach Soup	Scalloped Meats	Chocolate

Desserts	Desserts	Desserts
Junket	Soft Custards	Baked Custards
Vanilla	Vanilla	Vanilla
Caramel	Chocolate with	Caramel
Chocolate	Marshmallow	Coffee
Bread Pudding	Caramel	Date
Raisin	Coffee	Coconut
Caramel Nut	Coconut Orange with	
Banana	Meringue	Spanish Cream
Chocolate Nut	Pineapple	with Nuts
Maple	Lemon	with Fruit
Queen		Maple
Floating Island	Rice Pudding	Banana
Coffee	with Milk or Cream	Chocolate
with Sponge Cake	with Chocolate Sauce	Caramel
with Bananas	with Dates	Coconut
with Oranges	with Raisins	
with Peaches	Chocolate with	Cornstarch Pudding
Chocolate	Meringue	Vanilla
Coconut	Lemon	Chocolate
Tapioca Cream	Caramel	Coffee
Plain		Caramel
Date	Bread and Butter Pudding	with Fruit
Coffee	Plain	with Fruit Sauce
Chocolate	Marmalade	with Chocolate Sauce
		with Caramel Sauce

II. RECIPES FOR USE OF MILK

VANILLA JUNKET

Dissolve two junket tablets in one tablespoonful of cold water. Meanwhile, heat one quart of milk until lukewarm—not hot. If the milk is scalded, the junket will not "jelly." To the warm milk add three tablespoonfuls of sugar and one teaspoonful of vanilla and last, the dissolved junket. Stir one minute longer; pour at once into dessert glasses. Do not disturb until firm; then chill in the refrigerator. Serve plain, with whipped cream or with fruit sauces. For **Caramel Junket:** Dissolve two junket tablets in one tablespoonful of cold water. Meanwhile, melt four tablespoonfuls of sugar until caramel in color. Add six tablespoonfuls of boiling water and continue cooking until the sirup is clear and smooth. Add this to one quart of lukewarm milk, and one teaspoonful of vanilla and stir until mixed. Then add the dissolved junket, and pour at once into dessert glasses. Serves six. For **Chocolate Junket:** Mix four tablespoonfuls of cocoa, two tablespoonfuls of sugar and six tablespoonfuls of boiling water and simmer for four minutes. Then add gradually one quart of milk and heat until lukewarm. Add two junket tablets dissolved in one tablespoonful of cold water. Pour at once into dessert glasses and do not disturb until firm. Chill in the refrigerator. Serves six.

FLOATING ISLAND

Prepare a plain cooked custard as follows: Beat three egg-yolks slightly and add four tablespoonfuls of sugar and one-eighth teaspoonful of salt. While stirring, add two cupfuls of scalded milk which has been heated in the top of a double boiler. Return to the double boiler and cook, while stirring constantly until the mixture thickens and coats the spoon. Pour immediately into a shallow baking-dish. Beat up the egg-whites, add six tablespoonfuls of sugar and one-fourth teaspoonful of vanilla. Arrange the meringue by spoonfuls on the custard and put a bit of jelly in the center of each island. Brown at 300° F. for fifteen minutes. For **Coffee Floating Island:** Scald with the milk four tablespoonfuls of finely ground coffee. Strain through cheesecloth before pouring over the eggs. **Floating Island with Sponge Cake:** Arrange strips of sponge cake in dessert dishes; pour over them the hot custard combined with two sliced bananas. Top with meringue. For **Floating Island with Peaches:** Arrange slices of fresh or canned peaches in dessert dishes, pour the hot custard over and top with the meringue. For **Chocolate Floating Island:** Add two squares of melted chocolate to one-half cupful of scalded milk, then add the rest gradually. For **Coconut Floating Island:** Add one-half cupful of coconut to the custard. Serves six.

TAPIOCA CREAM

Scald two cupfuls of milk in the top of a double boiler. Add one and one-half tablespoonfuls of minute tapioca and cook until the tapioca is transparent—about twenty minutes. Then separate two eggs adding five tablespoonfuls of sugar and one-eighth teaspoonful of salt to the beaten egg-yolks. Pour the hot mixture slowly on the egg mixture, then return to the double boiler and cook until it thickens. Remove from the double boiler, add the beaten egg-whites and one teaspoonful of vanilla. **For Date Tapioca Cream:** Add one-half cupful of cleaned, stoned and diced dates. **For Coffee Tapioca Cream:** Scald the milk with three tablespoonfuls of ground coffee. Strain and proceed. **For Chocolate Tapioca Cream:** Melt two squares of chocolate and blend with one-half cupful of scalded milk. Beat until smooth; then add one and one-half cupfuls of scalded milk and proceed. Serves six.

III. USES OF SOUR MILK AND CREAM

Sour milk and sour cream are common articles of diet, being used a great deal in cookery. They add materially to the nutritive value of any dish of which they form a part. Sour whole milk and sour cream have much the same nutritive value as the original sweet products. Buttermilk, which is a by-product of the manufacture of butter, is often used in cookery instead of sour whole milk. Its nutritive value, however, differs from that of sour whole milk in that it contains little of the original fat content of the milk. It is always advisable to use milk and cream that have soured quickly, and are mild in acidity and of good flavor. If the souring process takes place slowly, the clabber may have a bitter and unpleasant flavor.

1. Sour Cream and Milk Recipes

CREAM SPICE CAKE

2 cupfuls brown sugar	3 eggs
½ cupful shortening	1 teaspoonful soda
2 cupfuls pastry flour	2 teaspoonfuls cloves
1 cupful sour cream	2 teaspoonfuls cinnamon
¼ teaspoonful salt	2 teaspoonfuls allspice

Cream the brown sugar and shortening together until thoroughly blended. Add the spices and beaten egg-yolks and beat well. Measure and sift together the pastry flour, salt and soda. Add to the mixture alternately with the cream. Last fold in the stiffly beaten egg-whites. Pour into a greased, floured cake pan and bake at 350° F. for 45 minutes. The yolks of five eggs may be substituted for the three eggs if desired.

STEAMED CABBAGE WITH SOUR CREAM DRESSING

1 small head cabbage	1 teaspoonful sugar
1 egg	1 teaspoonful salt
1 cupful sour cream	$\frac{1}{8}$ teaspoonful pepper
1 tablespoonful fat	$\frac{1}{8}$ teaspoonful paprika
2 tablespoonfuls vinegar	$\frac{1}{8}$ teaspoonful mustard
1 tablespoonful lemon juice	Few celery seeds

1 canned pimiento

Wash and shred the cabbage. Steam it until tender—about twenty-five minutes. Meanwhile place the sour cream in the top of a double boiler. Add the beaten egg, fat, vinegar, lemon juice, sugar, salt, finely chopped pimiento, pepper, paprika, mustard and celery seeds. Stir constantly until quite thick. Then pour immediately over the steamed cabbage which has been seasoned with salt, pepper, and butter. Serves six.

SOUR CREAM SALAD DRESSING

1 cupful sour cream	$\frac{1}{4}$ teaspoonful tabasco sauce
1 teaspoonful salt	1 teaspoonful sugar
2 tablespoonfuls lemon juice	2 hard-cooked eggs
$\frac{1}{8}$ teaspoonful pepper	$1\frac{1}{2}$ tablespoonfuls chilli sauce

$\frac{1}{2}$ seeded green pepper finely chopped

Whip the sour cream until quite stiff. Add the salt, lemon juice, pepper, tabasco sauce and sugar, continuing beating all the while. When smooth and well blended, add the finely-chopped green pepper, the chopped, hard-cooked eggs, and the chilli sauce. Chill well and serve on crisp, shredded cabbage, lettuce, or Romaine.

SOUR CREAM NUT JUMBLES

$\frac{1}{2}$ cupful shortening	$2\frac{1}{2}$ cupfuls pastry flour
1 cupful granulated sugar	$\frac{1}{2}$ teaspoonful soda
1 egg, well beaten	3 teaspoonfuls baking-powder
$\frac{1}{4}$ teaspoonful salt	1 cupful sour cream
1 teaspoonful vanilla	$\frac{1}{2}$ cupful chopped nut-meats

$\frac{1}{2}$ teaspoonful mace

Cream the shortening and sugar together until smooth. Then add the well-beaten egg and salt. Measure and sift together the flour, soda, baking-powder, and mace. Add to the shortening mixture alternately with the sour cream, beating constantly. Add the vanilla and nut meats and beat again. Drop by teaspoonfuls on a greased baking sheet and bake in a medium oven of 375° F. until golden brown on top and bottom—about twelve to fifteen minutes.

JAMES RIVER WAFFLES

2 cupfuls flour	3 eggs
¼ teaspoonful salt	2 cupfuls sour milk
2 teaspoonfuls baking-powder	6 tablespoonfuls fat
1 teaspoonful soda	

Separate the eggs and beat the egg-yolks until light. Then add one cupful of sour milk. Meanwhile measure and sift together the flour, salt, soda and baking-powder, add to the yolk mixture, and beat. Add another cupful of sour milk and beat again; then add the melted fat and last fold in the egg-whites, beaten stiff. The batter is then ready for use in the waffle iron. Serves six.

SOUR CREAM MUSHROOM SAUCE

1 cupful sour cream	¼ teaspoonful paprika
1 tablespoonful grated onion	¼ cupful diced mushrooms
½ teaspoonful salt	2 tablespoonfuls flour

In the top of a double boiler heat the sour cream with the grated onion and skinned, diced mushrooms. Meanwhile, make a smooth paste of the flour, salt, and paprika by adding two tablespoonfuls of cold water. Add to the hot cream mixture gradually while stirring constantly, and continue cooking until the mixture is thick. Serve with steak, Hamburg balls, chicken or the like.

DEVIL'S FOOD NUT CAKE

2 cupfuls brown sugar	2 eggs
2 squares chocolate	½ cupful sour milk
½ cupful cold water	1 teaspoonful soda
1 egg yolk	2 cupfuls pastry flour
1 cupful chopped nut meats	¼ teaspoonful salt
¼ cupful shortening	1 teaspoonful vanilla

Combine one-half cupful of brown sugar, the chocolate, cold water, and egg-yolk, and cook in the top of a double boiler, stirring constantly until thick. Then add the chopped nuts and set aside to cool. Cream together the shortening and one and one-half cupfuls of brown sugar. Add the eggs beaten until light. Measure and sift together the soda, pastry flour, and salt, and add to the cake mixture alternately with the sour milk. When well blended, add the vanilla and the chocolate mixture. Pour into a greased and floured cake pan and bake at 350° F. for forty-five minutes. Raisins may be added to this recipe if desired.

BUTTERMILK CHOCOLATE CAKE

1½ cupfuls sugar	¼ teaspoonful soda
½ cupful shortening	3 eggs
2 squares chocolate	2½ cupfuls pastry flour
¼ cupful hot water	½ cupful buttermilk
2 teaspoonfuls baking-powder	¼ teaspoonful salt

Cream together the sugar and shortening until thoroughly blended. Meanwhile melt the chocolate with the hot water and stir until smooth. Add to the sugar mixture. Beat the eggs until light and add the buttermilk. Measure and sift together the soda, pastry flour, salt and baking-powder. Add to the cake mixture alternately with egg-and-milk mixture. Beat well, pour into a greased, floured cake pan, and bake at 350° F. for forty-five minutes.

2. To Use Sour Cream in Place of Shortening

Sour cream may be used in the place of both fat, and sour milk, or buttermilk in some recipes.

Since one cupful of sour cream would be equivalent to one-third to one-half cupful of fat plus two-thirds to one-half of a cupful of sour milk or buttermilk, it is evident that sour cream should be substituted only when the proportion of fat to liquid called for in the recipe is at least one-third of a cupful of fat, three-fourths of a cupful of liquid and three to four teaspoonfuls of baking-powder; one and one-half cupfuls of a very thick cream would be the equivalent of both fat and liquid, and no additional fat would be required.

Sour cream should be treated as though it were sour milk, however in adding soda and baking-powder. Since one-half teaspoonful of soda neutralizes one cupful of sour milk or buttermilk, it will also neutralize one cupful of sour cream.

Cereals

I. FOOD VALUE

Cereals are an economical source of energy and protein but are more satisfactory in their mineral and vitamin content when the whole grain is used. In the whole grains, such as rolled oats, cracked wheat etc., the cellulose is very useful for bulk. Long slow cooking softens the cellulose and cooks the starch so that it is more palatable. It is important that this method be followed for children and invalids.

II. GENERAL RULES FOR COOKING CEREALS IN DOUBLE BOILER

Kind of Cereal	Quantity of Dry Cereal	Water	Salt	Time of Cooking
Granular Cereals				
Corn-meal	⅓ c.	2 c.	½ tsp.	1 hour
Farina	½ c.	2 c.	½ tsp.	½ hour
Hominy Grits	½ c.	2 c.	½ tsp.	2 hours
Flaked Cereals				
Rolled Oats	⅔ c.	2 c.	½ tsp.	3 hours
Rolled Wheat	⅔ c.	2 c.	½ tsp.	3 hours
Whole or Cracked Grains				
Rice	½ c.	2 c.	½ tsp.	1 hour
Scotch Oatmeal	½ c.	2 c.	½ tsp.	8 hours
Cracked Wheat	⅓ c.	2 c.	½ tsp.	3 hours
Pastes				
Macaroni	½ c.	2 c.	½ tsp.	½ hour

31

Method—Put the salt and water in the upper part of a double boiler. When the water is boiling, sprinkle in the cereal—gradually so that the water does not stop boiling. Only the fine grained cereals need stirring and they should be stirred as little as possible as it makes the cereal sticky and unpalatable. Cook directly over the fire until the cereal thickens. Draw a spoon across the bottom of the double boiler to be sure that the cereal does not burn on. Place in the lower part of the double boiler which should be one-third full of boiling water. Cook as specified above.

Quick Method for Cereals—Put salt and water in a saucepan. When the water boils, sprinkle in the cereal gradually stirring constantly. Simmer over a low flame from 3 to 20 minutes, stirring frequently. In some cereals the grains are cut before flaking or are ground very fine and partly cooked. This type of cereal may be cooked in 3 to 5 minutes. The directions for cooking which are given on the package of cereal should be followed carefully. Scotch Oatmeal, cracked wheat or other hard cereals can not be cooked by this method. When putting cereal away for the next day, cover top with a thin layer of water. Pour this off the next morning.

III. BOILED RICE

Wash rice in coarse strainer; hold directly under running cold water. Allow two quarts of boiling water for each cupful of rice and one tablespoonful salt. When the water is boiling rapidly, sprinkle in the rice slowly so that the water does not stop boiling. Continue rapid cooking until rice is tender, lifting the rice occasionally with a fork so that it does not stick to bottom of pan. When tender, drain the rice in a colander. Dry the rice in a warm oven. Stir the rice once or twice with a fork so that all the steam may escape. Serve hot with melted butter.

IV. BOILED MACARONI OR SPAGHETTI

Follow directions for boiling rice. It is not necessary to first wash the macaroni or spaghetti. When tender, drain in a colander and serve hot as a vegetable with melted butter.

V. SELECTED RECIPES

BAKED MACARONI AND TOMATOES

2 cupfuls cooked macaroni	¼ teaspoonful salt
1 can tomatoes	2 tablespoonfuls melted fat
Buttered crumbs	

Add fat and salt to the tomatoes, arrange in layers with macaroni in a greased baking-dish. Cover with buttered crumbs. Bake at 500°

F. for 12 minutes. If very cold, bake at 400° F. until heated through and crumbs are brown. Serves six.

MACARONI OR NOODLES IN BEEF STOCK

1 quart beef stock	1 tablespoonful fat
1 cupful macaroni or noodles	1 tablespoonful flour

Add macaroni or noodles to boiling stock and cook until tender. Melt the fat and combine with flour and use to thicken the stock. Serves six.

MACARONI AND CHEESE (P. 36)

ITALIAN MACARONI OR SPAGHETTI

½ pound spaghetti or macaroni	2 tablespoonfuls chopped green pepper
1 teaspoonful salt	1 pint canned tomatoes
¼ cupful salad oil	1 teaspoonful salt
2 medium-sized onions	1½ lumps loaf sugar
Grated Parmesan cheese	

Heat the salad oil in a saucepan, add onions and pepper; cook till half tender, then add tomatoes, salt and the loaf sugar. Cook slowly till the onions are tender, and the sauce is reduced one-third. Cook macaroni or spaghetti as directed above. Put into a heated dish, stir about two ounces of grated cheese through it, pour over the sauce, and serve at once. Serves six.

SPANISH RICE

2 cupfuls cooked rice	1½ cupfuls canned tomatoes
2 tablespoonfuls fat	1 tablespoonful sliced mushroom
1 tablespoonful chopped onion	1 tablespoonful capers
2 tablespoonfuls shredded green pepper	¼ teaspoonful salt
	Buttered crumbs
Few grains cayenne	

Add onion, green peppers, mushrooms, seasonings and capers to melted fat and cook until onion browns. Add tomatoes and cook until moisture is nearly evaporated. Arrange in layers with rice in greased baking-dish. Cover with buttered crumbs. Bake at 400° F. until heated through and crumbs are brown. Serves six.

SPOON BREAD

1 pint scalded milk	1 teaspoonful salt
½ cupful corn-meal	3 egg yolks
½ teaspoonful baking-powder	3 egg-whites beaten stiff
2 tablespoonfuls melted fat	

Stir corn-meal gradually into milk and cook in double boiler until of the consistency of mush. Add baking-powder, salt, fat and egg yolks. Fold in stiffly beaten egg-whites. Pour into a hot greased baking-dish and bake at 375° F. thirty minutes. Serve at once in dish in which it is baked. Serves six.

RICE PUDDING

4 cupfuls milk	½ teaspoonful salt
⅓ cupful rice	⅓ cupful sugar
Grated rind ½ lemon	

Wash rice, mix ingredients, pour into a greased pudding dish, set in a pan of hot water and bake for three hours at 300° F. Stir every 10 minutes during the first hour of baking to prevent rice from settling. Serves six.

INDIAN PUDDING

5 cupfuls scalded milk	1 teaspoonful ginger
⅓ cupful corn-meal	1 teaspoonful salt
½ cupful molasses	½ teaspoonful cinnamon

Pour milk slowly on to corn-meal, cook in double boiler twenty minutes. Add remaining ingredients. Pour into a greased baking-dish, set in a pan of hot water and bake at 350° F. for two hours. Serve with top milk. Serves six.

Cheese Dishes

I. FOOD VALUE

Cheese is valuable for its flavor as well as its food value. It supplies protein and fat to the diet, and is a cheap substitute for meat. It is also a good source of calcium and phosphorous. Cheese is a concentrated food and is better used to flavor such bland foods as rice, macaroni, or bread. If eaten in too large quantities, it may irritate the stomach.

II. GENERAL DIRECTIONS FOR COOKING

1. All cheese dishes should be cooked at a low temperature. To melt cheese for rarebit, etc., it should be placed over hot water, as it burns very easily and the protein is made tough by extreme heat, and so unpalatable and indigestible.

WELSH RAREBIT

1 lb. fresh American cheese	½ teaspoonful dry mustard
¼ teaspoonful salt	Few grains cayenne pepper
⅛ teaspoonful pepper	½ cupful cold water
¼ teaspoonful paprika	1 teaspoonful Worcestershire
Toast or crackers	sauce

Cut the cheese into small pieces in the top of a double boiler or chafing dish. Melt the cheese slowly. Keep the water beneath the cheese just under the boiling point. As the cheese melts, add seasonings. When completely melted, stir in gradually the cold water and Worcestershire sauce which have been mixed together. Cook until smooth, serve on salad crackers or crisp toast. Serves six.

WELSH RAREBIT WITH MILK

1½ cupfuls cheese	⅛ teaspoonful mustard
cubed or sliced	⅛ teaspoonful paprika
2 eggs	⅛ teaspoonful pepper
2 tablespoonfuls flour	2 cupfuls scalded milk
½ teaspoonful salt	2 tablespoonfuls fat
Toast or crisp crackers	

Melt cheese over hot water just under the boiling point, add flour, fat and seasonings. Add milk and beaten eggs gradually and cook until smooth. Serve on toast or crisp crackers. Serves six.

TOMATO RAREBIT

1 pint canned tomatoes	⅛ teaspoonful pepper
1 teaspoonful salt	Dash cayenne
1 teaspoonful sugar	1 tablespoonful chopped onion
½ pound cheese	1 teaspoonful fat
1 beaten egg	

Heat the canned tomatoes, add the salt, sugar, pepper, cayenne and chopped onion. When hot, melt in it the cheese cut in bits, adding it gradually while stirring constantly. When smooth, add the fat and the beaten egg, stirring all the while. Serve on slices of hot, buttered toast or hot crackers. Serves four to six.

ENGLISH MONKEY

1 cupful stale bread crumbs	½ cupful cheese cut in
1 cupful milk	pieces
1 tablespoonful fat	1 egg
½ teaspoonful salt	Few grains cayenne

Crisp buttered crackers

Soak bread crumbs fifteen minutes in milk. Melt the fat in top of double boiler, add cheese. When cheese is melted, add soaked crumbs, egg slightly beaten and seasonings. Cook three minutes and serve on crackers. Serves four.

2. Uses of Cheese Sauces   (See Chart for Sauces, P. 184)

MACARONI AND CHEESE

Cook three-fourths cupful macaroni (P. 32). When cooked mix with one and one-half cupfuls of cheese sauce and serve at once. Or put in greased pudding dish, cover with buttered crumbs and bake until crumbs are golden brown. Rice may be prepared and served in the same way. Serves six.

MACARONI WITH CHEESE AND TOMATO SAUCE

Cook three-fourths cupful of macaroni. To one and one-half cupfuls tomato sauce (P.184) add one cupful grated cheese and stir until cheese is melted. Pour over the cooked macaroni and serve at once, or bake as in Macaroni and Cheese. Serves six.

SAVORY TOAST

To the recipe for medium white sauce, add one-half cupful cheese cut in small pieces. Add a few grains of cayenne, and pour over slices of hot toasted bread. Surround with slices of broiled tomatoes, highly seasoned with salt and pepper. Serves four.

3. For Other Uses for Cheese Sauce

See Scalloped Vegetables with Cheese Sauce (P. 106)
Vegetable Sauces (P. 105)
Flounder Rarebit (P. 85)
Sardine Rarebit (P. 90)
Tuna or Crabmeat au Gratin (P. 91)

4. Selected Recipes

CHEESE DREAMS

Bread   Butter
Cheese

Cut slices of bread one-eighth inch thick, and butter.   Arrange thin
slices of cheese, either American or Swiss, on half of the slices.   Cover
each with a buttered slice.   Brown quickly on each side in a little
fat in a hot frying-pan.   Or toast them quickly in the broiler oven.
In this case, butter the outside of the sandwiches before toasting them
in the oven.

CHEESE FONDUE

6 slices stale bread	Speck cayenne
2 eggs	1 cupful fresh grated cheese
1 cupful milk	¼ teaspoonful mustard
¼ teaspoonful salt	⅛ teaspoonful paprika

Cut the bread in one-third-inch thick slices.   Cut off most of the crust
and cut in finger lengths.   Arrange in a greased baking-dish.   Mix
other ingredients together and pour over the bread.   Set in a pan of
hot water and bake at 325° F. until custard is set, about thirty minutes.
Cottage cheese may be substituted for the grated cheese.   Serves six.

CHEESE SAVORIES

6 rounds bread—3 in. in diameter	4 tablespoonfuls butter melted
⅓ cupful grated cheese	3 slices cooked ham

For each savory, dip a round of bread in melted butter and then in
the grated cheese.   Place plain side down on the buttered pan.   Prepare another round of bread in the same way and place it on the first,
plain side up, and with a slice of ham between them.   Brush the top
with melted butter and bake at 400° F. until a delicate brown—about
ten minutes.   These proportions serve three.   Tomato sauce may be
poured over these, if desired.

MEXICAN RELISH

½ pound soft American cheese	⅛ teaspoonful paprika
2 tablespoonfuls butter	½ teaspoonful sugar
1 seeded green pepper	Speck cayenne
1 red pepper	1 can kidney beans
¼ teaspoonful salt	2 tablespoonfuls catchup
	Buttered toast

Slice the cheese and melt over a slow fire in the fat, stirring
constantly.   Add peppers minced fine and seasonings.   Add beans

and catchup, beat thoroughly and serve on hot buttered toast. Serves six.

WOODSTOCK TOAST

6 thick slices bread	1 tablespoonful Worcestershire
½ small cream cheese	sauce
1 snappy cheese	¼ teaspoonful salt
¼ teaspoonful paprika	2 eggs
12 slices bacon	

Cut the bread three-fourths of an inch thick and trim the crusts sparingly. Cream together the cream cheese and snappy cheese and add the Worcestershire sauce, salt, paprika, and the eggs slightly beaten. Spread this on the bread generously, and place on each slice two slices of bacon cut very thin. Brown in a 450° F. oven ten minutes or until the bacon is crisp. Serves six.

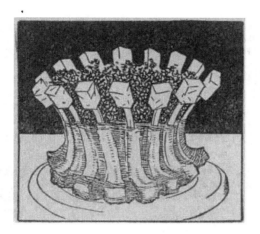

Meat

I. FOOD VALUE

The value of meat in the diet lies chiefly in the protein and fat supplied. The flavor is due to extractives which contain little nutritive matter but are a stimulus to the appetite.

II. METHODS OF COOKING THE TOUGH CUTS

The so-called tougher cuts of meat come from the muscles of the animal which are exercised most. Because the muscles are used so constantly the connective tissue becomes toughened and must be softened by long slow cooking, with moist heat.

1. Boiling—This method is suitable for mutton, veal, ham, chuck of beef, rump, flank, and shank of beef. The meat is left in one piece. Wipe with a damp cloth. Plunge into boiling water and boil for ten minutes. This forms a coating which prevents the escape of the juices. Reduce the heat and simmer gently until tender.

2. Stewing—This method is suitable for chuck, short rib, flank, rump, round of beef, mutton, lamb or veal. Remove skin and superfluous fat from meat, cut in pieces suitable for serving; dredge with flour and sprinkle with salt and pepper. For a brown stew, melt a little

39

fat in a kettle and sear the meat a delicate brown.   Cover with boiling water and simmer gently until tender, two to four hours.   Prepared vegetables may be added last hour of cooking.   Thicken the gravy with flour, stirred smooth with a small amount of cold water.   Parsnips and potatoes cut into dice are a delicious combination of vegetables not often used.   Serve with dumplings (P. 41).

STEWED ROUND STEAK

1½ pounds round steak cut thin   Bacon
Salt and pepper   Onions

Cut the steak into twelve pieces.   Pound them to make larger and to facilitate rolling.   Lay a small piece of bacon and a thin slice of onion on each piece of steak; dust with salt and pepper and roll, fastening together with toothpicks.   Proceed as for a brown stew (P. 39). Serves six.

STEWED VEAL

1 cupful pared and quartered potatoes
¾ cupful small whole mushrooms
½ cupful sweet green peppers cut in strings
1½ pounds shoulder of veal
2 teaspoonfuls salt
⅛ teaspoonful paprika
⅛ teaspoonful celery salt
1 bay leaf
4 tablespoonfuls flour
2 tablespoonfuls milk
2 cupfuls boiling water
Parsley
1 small onion, chopped fine

Prepare according to general directions for stewing.   Season with the salt, onion peeled and chopped, paprika and celery salt and bay leaf. After cooking two hours, thicken with the flour blended with the milk, and cook fifteen minutes longer.   Serve in a deep platter, garnished with parsley and surrounded with dumplings (P. 41).

HARICOT OF MUTTON

1 medium-sized onion
1 large green pepper
2 tablespoonfuls bacon fat
2 cupfuls water
1½ pounds lean mutton
2½ teaspoonfuls salt
⅛ teaspoonful pepper
1 can peas

Chop the onion and green pepper, fine.   Sauté in bacon fat until tender.   Then remove the onion and pepper.   To the fat add the lean mutton cut in chunks one and one-half inches square, and brown; then add the sautéd onion and pepper. Season with salt and pepper.   Then add the water, cover closely, and stew until tender — about one hour.   Add the peas, drained, and heat thoroughly before serving. Serves six.

3. Dumplings for Stews

2 cupfuls flour   ½ teaspoonful salt
3 teaspoonfuls baking-powder   1 tablespoonful fat
            Milk

Sift together the flour, baking-powder, and salt. Cut in the fat.
Add milk to make a soft dough, about three-fourths cupful. Drop the
dough by spoonfuls, from the tip of a spoon into the boiling stew.
Care should be taken to drop each one on a piece of meat or vegetable
so that it may not be immersed in the liquid. Cover the kettle closely.
Steam twelve minutes. Be sure that the liquid is boiling the entire
time. Do not remove the cover until the dumplings are cooked. The
dumplings may be rolled out on a well-floured board to one inch in
thickness and cut any desired size. Serves six.

4. Braising—This method is a combination of baking and steaming
suitable for rump, flank, short ribs, tongue, liver or chuck of beef, and
mutton. Wipe the meat, dredge with flour, salt, and pepper and brown
in a little fat. Arrange the meat on a trivet in a baking-pan and surround with any desired combination of vegetables. Whole spices may
be added. Add just enough water to cover well the bottom of the pan,
cover closely and bake four hours at 300° F., adding more water if
necessary. Turn after the second hour. Throughout the cooking, the
liquid should be kept below the boiling point.

5. Pot Roasting—This method is suitable for cooking round, rump,
chuck or plate of beef. Buy four to five pounds of beef, wipe with a
damp cloth. Dredge with flour, sprinkle with salt and pepper. Put
two or three tablespoonfuls of fat in a kettle and sear the meat well on
all sides. Add about one cupful boiling water, cover tightly and simmer gently. Do not let the water cook entirely away, but keep adding
a little at a time. Cook until very tender, about three hours. Prepared vegetables, such as potatoes, carrots, or string beans, may be
added the last hour of cooking. A Dutch oven or covered casserole is
excellent for cooking pot roasts.

POT ROAST WITH VEGETABLES

4 pounds beef   1 Spanish onion
4 tablespoonfuls flour   4 tomatoes
1 tablespoonful beef drippings   2 sweet green peppers
2 teaspoonfuls salt   1 cupful diced celery
¼ teaspoonful pepper   1 pint hot water

Prepare according to general directions for pot roasting (Page 41).
Serves six to eight.

BEEF À LA MODE

5 pounds pot roast	2 bay leaves chopped fine
¼ pound salt pork	½ cupful vinegar
1 teaspoonful salt	2 onions
⅛ teaspoonful pepper	1 tablespoonful fat
1 tablespoonful onion juice	5 carrots
1 teaspoonful thyme	2 turnips
1 tablespoonful chopped parsley	1 No. 3 can tomatoes

Mix the salt, pepper, onion juice, thyme, parsley and bay leaves. Cut the salt pork in thin strips and roll in the mixed seasonings. Cut gashes all over the meat one-half inch deep and insert the seasoned strips of pork. Roll the roast well in the vinegar and let stand overnight or from early morning until after luncheon. Chop the onions and brown in the fat. Put in the roast and brown on all sides. Add the cleaned carrots, the prepared turnips and the tomatoes. Cover tightly and simmer three hours. · Serves six to eight.

6. **Casserole Dishes**—Instead of stewing or pot-roasting on top of the stove, a convenient method that requires little attention is to cook in the oven in a casserole instead of in a baking pan. Being a serving dish as well, the casserole saves washing an extra pan and is an attractive method of serving.

CASSEROLE FLANK STEAK

1½ pounds round or flank steak	1 teaspoonful sage
3 medium onions	1 teaspoonful salt
½ cupful minced suet	¼ teaspoonful pepper
2 cupfuls stale bread crumbs	½ teaspoonful thyme
1 egg	Hot water
½ teaspoonful marjoram	2 tablespoonfuls drippings
	Flour

Select two slices of top round steak, cut a scant half-inch thick. Peel the onions and pour boiling water over them; let stand fifteen minutes; drain and chop finely. Add to the onions, the suet, bread crumbs, seasonings and egg. Mix together well and add sufficient hot water to make moist enough to spread. Lay the steaks flat, spread the bread mixture evenly over both, roll up and skewer, or tie securely. Roll in seasoned flour and sear quickly in a hot frying-pan in which drippings have been melted. Place in a casserole, add one-half cupful of hot water, cover, and cook one hour at 400° F. Remove to a hot platter, take off the skewers or string, and thicken the gravy in the pan. Serves six.

BAKED BANANA STEAK

2 pounds top round, 1½ inches Sprinkling of pepper
  thick   2 teaspoonfuls sugar
3 large bananas   Parsley
6 strips of bacon   3 tablespoonfuls water
            1½ teaspoonfuls salt

Split the steak through the center. Leave one end uncut and lay
it open like a book. Sprinkle with the salt and pepper. Cut the bananas lengthwise into rather thick slices, and place on one-half of the steak,
sprinkle with the sugar, add the water, then lay the other half of steak
over the banana-covered portion. Place strips of bacon across the top
and fasten the two portions together with skewers. Put in casserole
and bake at 400° F. for forty minutes. If desired rare, bake only thirty
minutes. Garnish with parsley. Serves six.

HUNGARIAN GOULASH

1 dozen onions   3 teaspoonfuls salt
Paprika to make pink (about ¾ 3 pounds stew meat, prefer-
  teaspoonful)   ably beef
            ½ cupful fat

Peel and chop the onions fine; cook them in the fat till they are well
browned. Cut the meat in pieces, but do not dry it after washing, so
that there will be enough moisture to make gravy. Add the salt and
paprika, put all in a casserole, and cook very slowly for two and a half
or three hours. Serves six.

SPRING LAMB STEW EN CASSEROLE

2 pounds lamb   2 tablespoonfuls tomato
¾ cupful diced carrots   ketchup
1½ cupfuls diced potatoes   1 teaspoonful Worcestershire
1 tablespoonful minced parsley   sauce
2 tablespoonfuls diced celery 1½ teaspoonfuls salt
1 cupful peas   ¼ teaspoonful pepper
Flour   2 onions

Cut the meat in cubes, after freeing it from fat as far as possible.
Roll in as much flour as it will take up, and put a layer in the bottom of
a casserole. Sprinkle with the vegetables, except peas, mixed together,
and a little of the salt and pepper, and continue in this way till all is
used. Cover with boiling water, put on the lid, and bake in a 350° F.
oven for an hour and three-quarters. If canned peas are used they

may be added with the Worcestershire sauce and ketchup ten minutes before serving time. If fresh peas are used, they should be added according to age, from twenty to sixty minutes, before the dish is finished cooking. Serves six.

7. Selected Recipes for Using Tough Cuts

HAMBURGER À L'ITALIENNE

2 peeled onions	1 teaspoonful salt
1 cupful salad oil	½ teaspoonful pepper
1 pound hamburg steak	¼ teaspoonful Worcestershire
2 cupfuls stewed tomatoes	sauce
1 cupful grated cheese	1 cupful egg noodles

Brown the onions, cut small, in the salad oil. Add the hamburg steak and brown, combine with the tomatoes, salt, pepper, Worcestershire sauce, and simmer slowly ten minutes. Cook the egg noodles in boiling salted water until tender, add to the meat mixture, and cook slowly thirty minutes longer, stirring frequently. One tablespoonful of water may be added if necessary to keep it moist. Serve on a platter surrounded with one cupful of grated cheese. Serves six.

HAMBURG BALLS, POTATOES AND TOMATOES

1½ pounds flank or round steak, chopped	2 tablespoonfuls horseradish
1 cupful suet	½ teaspoonful dry mustard
2 small onions peeled	2 tablespoonfuls green pepper, minced
2 teaspoonfuls salt	2 tablespoonfuls tomato catchup
2 tablespoonfuls Worcestershire sauce	Cooked potato
Tomatoes	1 egg-yolk

Hamburg Balls, Potato Vienna Style, and Spiced Tomatoes make a tasty combination for a one-plate meal. For the Hamburg Balls, chop together the flank or round steak, suet and onions. Add the salt, Worcestershire sauce, horseradish, dry mustard, minced green pepper, and tomato catchup. Form into balls and cook on all sides in a hot frying-pan. For the Spiced Tomatoes, wash good-sized tomatoes, remove the stem end, and make a cross cut in the top of each tomato. Place in a 400° F. oven and bake for ten minutes. For the Potato Vienna Style, left-over potato or freshly made boiled potato may be used. Beat the riced potatoes until light and creamy, and if necessary, add a little milk. Have the mixture dry rather than too moist. Shape into portions similar to a Vienna roll, with the ends tapering. Score each roll three or four times, and brush over with the yolk of an egg beaten and diluted with one tablespoonful of water. Set in a 400° F. oven to thoroughly heat and brown the surface of the roll. Place two Hamburg balls on each plate with a celery curl made by fringing the ends of a piece of celery three inches long and allowing it to stand in cold water before using. Place a Vienna roll and a spiced tomato on each plate; place a spoonful of mayonnaise dressing on the top of each tomato. Serves six.

HAMBURGER STEAK AND SPAGHETTI

⅓ cupful salad-oil
½ cupful fat
3 large onions, chopped fine
1 pound ground round steak
3 cloves of garlic
1 teaspoonful salt
½ teaspoonful pepper
1 quart can tomatoes
1 small can peeled green chillies or 6 green peppers
1 small can mushrooms
1 cupful olives (chopped)
1 pound spaghetti
1 bay-leaf
½ pound grated Parmesan or American cheese

Brown the peeled, chopped onions and steak in the fat and oil, then add the chillies and garlic minced, the tomatoes, salt and pepper, and simmer slowly for two hours. During the last half-hour, add the mushrooms and olives. The tomato liquor should be allowed to evaporate, to make the sauce thick and rich. In the meantime, cook the spaghetti with the bay-leaf in the boiling, salted water; when tender, drain. Pile on a platter. Cover with the cheese. Pour over the hamburger sauce, and let stand in the oven for a few moments. This is good even without the mushrooms and olives. Serves twelve.

HAMBURG STEAK WITH VEGETABLE GARNISH

Purchase one and one-half pounds of round steak ground with a small piece of suet. Season as desired and press into a single cake. Insert a slender stick of fresh suet to simulate the bone of a sirloin. Broil, place on a hot platter, dot with butter, and sprinkle with salt and pepper. Surround with alternate mounds of different vegetables, cooked, seasoned well, and buttered liberally—the whole very hot. Vegetable combinations are numerous; a good one is tiny onions, carrots cut in small fingers, turnips diced, small bits of canned string-beans, or diced beets. The mounds of vegetable may be separated with sprigs of parsley or cress. Peppers stuffed with any of the vegetables mentioned may also be used. Serves six.

MEAT BALLS

¾ pound lean beef	1 teaspoonful white pepper
½ pound lean veal	2½ teaspoonfuls salt
¼ pound bacon	2 tablespoonfuls chopped onion
¾ cupful milk	4 tablespoonfuls fat
1 or 2 eggs	2 tablespoonfuls Italian
¾ cupful dried bread-crumbs	tomato paste

Wash the meat. Cut into dice, together with the bacon, and put through the food-chopper three times. Beat the eggs, add the milk and bread-crumbs, and let stand until the crumbs are soft. Sauté the onion brown in a little of the fat, stir into the crumb mixture, and then work this into the meat, together with the seasonings. Form the mixture into small balls. Brown well in the fat, and add a cupful of boiling water. Cover the pan and let the balls cook through. This will take about fifteen minutes. Dilute tomato paste in three-fourths cupful of warm water, add to the gravy, and thicken it if desired with a little flour mixed to a paste. Serves six.

SPANISH MEAT BALLS WITH CORN-MEAL

1 pound chopped beef	1 tablespoonful flour
2 beaten eggs	1 minced onion
1½ teaspoonfuls salt	1 minced green pepper
¼ teaspoonful pepper	2 sprigs parsley
1 tablespoonful fat or	2 chopped tomatoes
drippings	2 quarts boiling water

Corn-meal

Mix together the meat, eggs, salt and pepper with enough corn-meal to make a stiff mass; shape into balls and roll in corn-meal. Melt the fat in a deep kettle, and add the flour, vegetables, the boiling water, and one teaspoonful of salt; drop in the meat balls, cover, and boil gently for forty-five minutes, taking care that the mixture does not stick, as the gravy is thickened by the corn-meal. Serves six.

SPANISH STEAK

Flank or round steak, about	¾ cupful chopped tomatoes
2 pounds chopped	1 tablespoonful fat
½ cupful chopped onion	Salt and pepper to taste
½ cupful chopped green peppers	

Season the chopped steak to taste, form into a single cake and broil. In the meantime, the fat should be melted, the vegetables added, and cooked slowly till tender, about twenty minutes. Season to taste with salt and pepper, and serve spread over the meat. Serves six.

8. Beef Loaf Recipes

The round, shoulder, chuck, rump or flank are suitable for a beef loaf.

BEEF LOAF

2 pounds ground beef	1 egg
Grated rind and juice of	Few drops onion juice
½ lemon	1 teaspoonful salt
1 tablespoonful chopped parsley	⅛ teaspoonful pepper
4 slices bacon, chopped fine	½ cupful bread-crumbs

Put all ingredients together in a bowl and mix well. Form into a loaf and put in a well-greased loaf pan. Bake at 400° F. for forty-five minutes. Serves six to eight.

FILIPINO BEEF LOAF

1 pound round steak, ground	1 cupful bread or cracker
1 teaspoonful salt	crumbs
2 cupfuls canned tomatoes	⅛ teaspoonful pepper
1 egg	½ onion, chopped fine

Mix all the ingredients together, make into a loaf, and place in a greased baking-pan. Bake in a 400° F. oven for forty-five minutes. Serves six.

SOMERVILLE MEAT LOAF

2 pounds beef, ground	2 eggs
¾ cupful suet	4 tablespoonfuls horseradish
2 small onions	1 teaspoonful dry mustard
2 cupful soft bread-crumbs	4 tablespoonfuls minced green
3 teaspoonfuls salt	pepper
4 tablespoonfuls Worcestershire sauce	¾ cupful tomato catchup

Mix well all ingredients except catchup. Pack in a greased bread pan. Cover the top of the loaf with tomato catchup and bake at 400° F. for forty-five minutes. This loaf may be made of left-over meat and is delicious hot or cold. Serves six.

9. Soups with Meat Stock Basis

As a basis for a variety of soups, strained meat stock is useful and may be kept stored in refrigerator for a day or two.

VEGETABLE SOUP

Cuts suitable for soup stock are the shank, plate, and neck of beef or the shank or breast pieces of lamb and veal. Wipe the meat and cut in pieces. Have bones sawed in small pieces. Sauté part of the meat a deep brown in a little fat. Add remainder of meat and bones. Cover with cold water, allowing one quart to two pounds of meat. Let stand one-half hour, return to fire; simmer six hours. Prepare a small onion, two stalks of celery, two carrots, or any other combination of vegetables and some parsley. Add during last two hours of cooking. Also add one small bay.leaf, three peppercorns, one teaspoonful salt, one-eighth teaspoonful pepper. Remove bones and cut meat in smaller pieces if necessary. If there is much fat on the soup, it is more easily removed by letting the soup get cold and removing the covering of fat. Reheat and serve.

SOUP FROM COOKED BONES

All bones from cooked meat roasts, chops, steaks, and fowls with or without fresh meat together with trimmings may be used for soup. Break bones up and start in cold water, cook for four or five hours. Strain, cool, and remove fat. This may be used as stock for sauces or fresh vegetables may be prepared and added as for vegetable soup.

BOUILLON

Bouillon is clarified beef stock, highly seasoned and served very hot or jellied with gelatine. Soak one tablespoonful gelatine in two tablespoonfuls of cold water. Add two cupfuls boiling stock and pour into cold wet mold. Serve cold cut in one-half-inch cubes.

TOMATO BOUILLON

Add one can of tomatoes, one tablespoonful chopped onion, one-half teaspoonful celery seed to one quart clarified stock. Cook twenty minutes, strain through cheese-cloth and serve very hot. This may also be jellied as directed above and served cold.

CONSOMMÉ

Consommé is usually a stock made of several kinds of meat, i. e. beef, veal and chicken. It is highly seasoned with vegetables and spices and always served clear and very hot.

To Clarify Stock: Beat one egg-white slightly and add with the shell to the stock. Bring to boiling point, stirring constantly. Boil gently ten minutes without stirring. Add one-half cupful cold water and let stand ten minutes. Strain through a cheese-cloth wrung out of hot water. Let stand until cold. Remove the crust of fat from the stock and wipe the top with warm damp cloth to get off extra bits of fat.

CREAMED VEGETABLE SOUP

1 quart strained meat stock or   3 tablespoonfuls fat
4 bouillon cubes and   4 tablespoonfuls flour
1 quart of boiling water   1 quart milk
1 cupful diced carrots   2 teaspoonfuls salt
1 cupful diced turnips   ⅛ teaspoonful pepper
½ cupful raw rice   1 teaspoonful Worcestershire
1 cupful canned peas   sauce
            1 cupful canned string-beans

Bouillon cubes may often be used instead of meat stock. Heat the stock or dissolve the bouillon cubes in the boiling water. Add carrots, turnips and rice and cook until tender; only a little liquid should remain. Add peas and string-beans. Melt the fat in a saucepan and add the flour. Add milk slowly, stirring constantly. Add cooked vegetables, rice, remaining stock and seasonings. Serves six.

ONION SOUP AU GRATIN

3 cupfuls strained meat stock   2 tablespoonfuls fat
1 cupful strained tomatoes   6 slices toast
4 peeled onions   6 quarter-inch cubes of cheese
            Grated cheese

Add tomatoes to stock. Slice the onions in a casserole and dot with fat. Cook in a slow oven of 350° F. until onions are brown. Add stock mixture. Lay toast on top of soup mixture in casserole and place one cube of cheese on each slice. Place under broiling flame. Melt cheese and brown slightly. Serve hot with a little grated cheese on top. Serves six.

HOTCH-POTCH

2 quarts of strained stock or   3 or 4 young onions
8 bouillon cubes and   1 head lettuce
2 quarts of boiling water   1 medium-sized cauliflower
4 white turnips   1 quart peas, shelled
4 medium-sized carrots   1 pint string-beans

This is between a stew and a soup. Chop fine the turnips, carrots, onions skinned, and lettuce. Add the string-beans cut in small pieces and boil in the stock for an hour. Twenty minutes before they are done, put in the cauliflower, thoroughly washed and separated in small pieces, and the peas shelled. Add seasoning if needed. Serves six to eight.

ITALIAN SOUP

4 cupfuls soup stock (veal or chicken)	2 cooked carrots
2 cupfuls tomato, strained	2 tablespoonfuls minced onion
1 cupful canned Lima beans	1 teaspoonful salt
¼ cupful cooked shredded cabbage	¼ teaspoonful pepper
	6 tablespoonfuls Parmesan cheese

¼ cupful rice

Bring the stock and tomato to the boiling-point; add the rice and cook until tender. Replace with hot water the liquid which boils away. Add the other ingredients except the cheese, allow to boil two minutes and pour into serving dishes. Sprinkle with cheese. Serves six.

LUNCHEON PEPPER POT

1 quart consommé, bouillon or any clear, strong soup	4 tablespoonfuls celery
1 pint water	Salt and paprika to taste
4 tablespoonfuls shredded carrot	Dash of cayenne
4 tablespoonfuls green pepper	4 rounds toast
	4 thin slices cheese

4 poached eggs

Place in a kettle the consommé, bouillon, or any clear strong soup. Add the water to allow for boiling away, and the shredded carrot, green pepper, and celery. Cook until the vegetables are tender and season highly to taste with salt, paprika, and a dash of cayenne pepper. Divide into four portions at serving time and put into individual casseroles or soup bowls. Have ready four rounds of toast, on each of which has been melted and lightly browned in a hot oven a thin slice of cheese. Lay one in each casserole, place a poached egg on each, sprinkle with salt, paprika, and pepper, and dot with butter. Serve at once. Serves four.

RICE AND CABBAGE SOUP

3 cupfuls shredded, half-cooked cabbage	2 quarts stock
Fat	½ cupful rice
	Parmesan cheese

Sauté the partially cooked shredded cabbage in fat until golden brown. Wash the rice and boil till tender in the stock, which should be very well seasoned. Add the cabbage, let them boil together for a few moments. Pass freshly grated Parmesan cheese when served. Serves six.

SOUP FROM ALSACE

6 cupfuls well-seasoned stock	2 tablespoonfuls flour
2 whole eggs	1 cupful cold water

Beat together the eggs and flour, adding the cold water very gradually until a smooth consistency is obtained. Pour the boiling stock over this mixture very slowly, so as to avoid lumps, stirring constantly, and cook for five minutes in a double boiler. This soup is most appetizing and makes a splendid dish to serve an invalid. Serves ten.

10. To use pressure cooker for meat (see P. 218)
11. The waterless cooker may be used for meat
12. To use electric fireless cooker for meat (see P. 216)

III. METHODS OF COOKING THE TENDER CUTS

The tender cuts of meat are sometimes called the "select" cuts because they are quickly cooked and are consequently in great demand. The tender cuts come from those parts of the animal that receive the least exercise and for this reason do not contain as much or as thick connective tissue. The food value is the same in both the tender and tough cuts of meat.

1. Broiling—The cuts of meat suitable to be cooked by this method are sirloin, porterhouse, minute or Delmonico steaks, tenderloin or filet of beef, pork chops or slices from ham or tenderloin, loin rib, or shoulder chops of lamb, and sausages. This is a quick method of cooking meat by direct heat. Wipe the meat with a cloth wrung out of cold water. Heat the broiler for ten minutes, and rub with a small piece of fat cut from the meat. Place the meat in the center of the broiler rack with the skin or fat side on the outside toward the front. Place the broiling pan as near the heat as possible without coming in actual contact with the flame. Broil the meat for two minutes on one side then turn and broil for two minutes on the other side; repeat this until the steak is done. From ten to fifteen minutes is sufficient time for a rare steak one and one-half inches thick. Cook longer if steak must be well done. Sprinkle with salt and pepper and serve at once. From eight to ten minutes broils a pork chop and a loin or shoulder lamb chop; six to eight minutes a rib lamb chop and fifteen to twenty minutes, sausages or a mutton chop one or two inches thick. In broiling by electricity follow the same directions as when using gas.

2. Pan Broiling—The same cuts of meat are suitable for pan broiling that are used for broiling. Heat a frying-pan of heavy-weight material till very hot. Place the steak in the hot frying-pan without any added fat. Sear quickly on one side while counting ten, turn quickly and sear on the other side. Repeat, then lower the heat

slightly and continue the broiling and turning until meat is done. Continually pour off the melted fat that may collect in the pan as this tends to dry up the juices and make the meat tough. Broil about the same length of time as when using the broiler. Sprinkle with salt and pepper. Dot with butter and serve at once.

3. **Sautéing Chops and Cutlets**—Crumbed veal cutlets or pork cutlets are suitable for cooking by this method. The cutlets may be cooked whole or cut in pieces, suitable for serving. Arrange a heap of fine dried bread-crumbs on clean paper or meat board. Add one table-spoonful water to one egg in a shallow dish and beat enough to mix yolk and white. Roll the cutlet in crumbs then in egg; be sure to cover entire surface with egg. Roll in crumbs again. Cover the bottom of a frying-pan with fat. Heat, put in cutlets, brown slightly on one side, turn and brown on other side. Continue cooking, turning frequently to prevent crumbs from burning.

Note: To prepare crumbs, put left-over pieces of dried stale bread with crusts removed through a food chopper, using fine knife or roll on pastry board, and sift. Use the crusts for brown crumbs for top of scalloped dishes, the white crumbs for croquettes or cutlets.

4. **Roasting**—The cuts of meat suitable for this method of cooking are: Sirloin roasts, porterhouse roasts, rib or whole tenderloin of beef, the loin, leg and rack of veal, the loin, tenderloin and ham of pork, the loin, shoulder or leg of lamb. Wipe the meat and trim if necessary. Dredge with seasoned flour. Lay a few pieces of fat over the meat if too lean. Place on a small wire trivet set in the roasting pan. In roasting the standard method is to sear the roast, thus retaining the juices, by starting it in an oven preheated to 500° F. The temperature is lowered to 400° F. after the searing operation. In general those meats which required long cooking either because of their size like large poultry or because of their nature like pork or veal are best cooked in a covered roaster with a vent. Uncover the roaster while searing the meat. The more tender cuts of beef are better in flavor and color when cooked in an uncovered roaster. If your oven will not heat up to 500° F., sear meat for fifteen minutes in the broiling oven first heated for ten minutes. When searing in broiling oven, turn every two minutes to expose top, bottom and sides, then put roast in oven that has heated in the meantime and roast for remainder of time at 450° F. For searing and roasting temperatures and the time required for roasting various meats, see Good Housekeeping Institute Cooking Temperature Chart, P. 252. Season with salt and pepper to taste. The round bake pot is a useful type of small top stove oven which may be used with kerosene, gas, or electric ranges. Aluminum pans of various shapes are supplied for baking or roasting. Real roasting is possible in using this device by preheating for ten minutes over a medium gas flame.

CROWN ROAST OF LAMB OR PORK

This requires six ribs from each side of a rack of lamb or pork. Trim the ribs in the same way that lamb chops are cut when "Frenched" only do not separate the ribs. Turn the sections of meat so that the bones are on the outside and fasten together in a circle. The butcher will prepare this roast upon request. The center may be filled with a bread stuffing, sausage if pork, or with a hot cooked vegetable when ready for serving. Cover the ends of the bones with greased paper to prevent burning. Roast according to directions given above.

5. Selected Recipes for Using Tender Cuts

DEVILED DRIED BEEF

4 eggs	1 teaspoonful prepared mustard
1 tablespoonful fat	1 tablespoonful vinegar
1 cupful shredded dried beef	Speck of cayenne
⅛ teaspoonful salt	

Melt the fat. Add the eggs, slightly beaten. Add beef and seasonings. Cook slowly, stirring, until eggs are set. Serve at once. Serves four to six.

FRIZZLED DRIED BEEF

½ pound dried beef   2 tablespoonfuls fat

Shred beef and remove gristle. Cover with boiling water, let stand five minutes. Pour off water. Sauté in the fat in a frying-pan until thoroughly heated and curled. Serves four to six.

ENGLISH CHOPS WITH ROQUEFORT CHEESE

6 English chops	½ teaspoonful beef-extract
2 tablespoonfuls fat	1 teaspoonful Worcestershire
¼ pound Roquefort cheese	sauce
½ cupful soup-stock	5 drops tabasco sauce

Arrange chops, which should be rolled with the kidney, in a baking-pan. Sprinkle with salt and pepper, dot with fat, and sprinkle with Roquefort cheese which has been put through a potato-ricer. Put a little water in the bottom of the pan, cover, and bake twenty-five minutes at 450° F. During the last five minutes, baste with a sauce made of the soup-stock, extract, Worcestershire, and tabasco mixed together. Remove from this, and thicken the sauce that remains with flour paste. Serve the chops with frills on the sticks with which they are fastened together. Serves six.

BAKED SLICED HAM

2 pounds sliced ham	2 teaspoonfuls minced parsley
2 tablespoonfuls minced onion	Juice ½ lemon to each slice

Order ham sliced one-half inch thick; remove fat nearly to the lean, and chop it fine. Mince the onion and parsley, mix with the fat, and spread over the ham, which should be put into a dripping pan. Squeeze over the lemon-juice, and bake till tender in a 400° F. oven, from thirty to forty minutes. A delicious brown or milk gravy can be made from the drippings in the pan. Serves six.

HAM À L'ITALIENNE

2 pounds sliced ham	4 small peeled onions
1 pint canned tomatoes	Black pepper

Order the ham sliced an inch thick. Put it in a covered frying or roasting pan. Slice the onions over the ham, then add the tomatoes, a generous sprinkling of pepper, and a half-cupful of water. Cover and bake one hour in a 400° F. oven, then remove ham to a platter, and make a gravy of the tomato-juice and drippings, adding a tablespoonful of flour mixed with a little water to a cupful of the gravy. Serves six.

HAM HAWAIIAN

1 thick slice ham, weight 1 pound	1 egg
2 large sweet potatoes	½ cupful flour
4 large slices pineapple	¼ teaspoonful salt
½ teaspoonful sugar	1 tablespoonful milk

Trim the fat from the ham, place the ham in a hot skillet and brown on both sides. Remove to a small roasting pan, cover with boiling water and place in oven registering 400° F. In the meantime, cook in boiling water until partially tender the sweet potatoes, remove the skins, and cut the potatoes lengthwise in thick slices. When the ham has cooked for one-half hour, place the potatoes in the pan with it and continue cooking for another half hour. Make a batter by sifting together the flour, salt, and sugar. Add the egg, well-beaten, and sufficient milk to make a batter. Dip the pineapple into the batter. Try out the fat which was trimmed from the ham and sauté the pineapple in it. Serve the ham surrounded by potatoes and pineapple, garnish with parsley, and sprinkle a little paprika over the potatoes. Serves six.

HAM PIQUANT

1 pound thinly sliced cooked ham	2 tablespoonfuls milk
4 teaspoonfuls dry mustard	¾ cupful Parmesan cheese
Dash Cayenne	¼ teaspoonful pepper

Mix the mustard to a paste with the milk and seasonings. Spread on slices of ham and sprinkle with cheese. Arrange slices one on top of the other in a brick form. Tie with a string and place in baking-dish. Bake at 400° F. for twenty-five minutes. Chill, remove string and cut in slices down through the layers. Serves six.

SCALLOPED HAM AND POTATOES

1 pound sliced ham	1 pint milk
1 quart sliced potatoes	1 tablespoonful fat
12 whole cloves	2 tablespoonfuls flour
2 small onions	¾ teaspoonful pepper

Purchase the ham in one slice. Cut it into six portions and stick two cloves in each.   Soak the sliced, raw potatoes in cold water for one hour; then drain and dry thoroughly with a towel. Make a white sauce of the fat, flour, and milk. To do this, melt the fat, add the flour, and cook till bubbling; then add the milk gradually, stirring constantly, and cook until smooth and slightly thickened. Place in a greased casserole a layer of the potatoes, using a third of them. Over these slice one onion and sprinkle with pepper. Lay on these three pieces of ham; repeat, placing the rest of the potatoes on top. Pour the white sauce over all and bake for one hour in a 350° F. oven, covering for the first half of the time. Serves six.

STUFFED HAM

2 slices ham	¼ teaspoonful pepper
2 tablespoonfuls flour	1½ teaspoonfuls sage
2 cupfuls stale bread crumbs	¼ cupful chopped walnuts
¾ cupful hot water	2 tablespoonfuls chopped olives
Salt to taste	½ cupful milk
½ cupful water	1 egg

Have the ham cut about one-fourth inch thick as for frying. Make a stuffing by moistening the bread crumbs with the hot water and adding the egg, seasonings, nut-meats, and olives. Rub flour over one side of each slice of ham. Turn, and on the other side of each spread the stuffing generously. Roll up and skewer with toothpicks. Place in a baking-dish with the milk and water and bake about one hour at 400° F., basting frequently. Make a gravy of the juices in the pan and serve with hot apple sauce. Serves six.

CURRIED LAMB WITH MACARONI

1 pound mutton or lamb, cut in small pieces	2 tablespoonfuls fat
½ pound macaroni	2 tablespoonfuls flour
2 cupfuls milk	2 tablespoonfuls curry-powder
	1 teaspoonful salt

¼ teaspoonful pepper

Select lamb as for stewing, brown it in a hot skillet, with a little fat, add a small amount of hot water, and cook until tender. Cook macaroni in boiling salted water till tender and drain. In a saucepan melt the fat, add the flour, curry-powder, salt, and pepper, and blend thoroughly. Add the milk gradually, stirring constantly; cook until a slightly thickened smooth sauce results. Into a greased casserole put a layer of macaroni, then a layer of lamb and curry sauce. Repeat till all is used. Cover and bake in a 350° F. oven about one hour. Serves six.

BAKED PORK CHOPS WITH TOMATO

6 good-sized pork chops	2 teaspoonfuls salt
1½ cupfuls sliced onions	⅛ teaspoonful pepper
1 cupful water	1 pint canned tomatoes

Flour the chops and pan-broil them till slightly browned; cover with the onion, pepper, and salted water, put on the lid and simmer for half an hour. Add the tomatoes and bake thirty minutes more in a 400° F. oven. Serves six.

BERKSHIRE PORK CHOPS

2 thick pork chops	1 small tart apple, cored
1 small onion	¼ teaspoonful salt
1 tablespoonful chopped parsley	1 tablespoonful flour

Pepper to taste

Place the chops in a covered casserole, cover with boiling water, and bake at 450° F. for one-half hour. Chop the onion, parsley, and apple rather fine, add pepper and salt, and heap the chops with this mixture. Return the chops to the oven and cook for one-half hour longer. When done, remove the chops and sauté on both sides in a hot frying-pan. Remove to serving dish and cover with apple and onion mixture. Thicken the liquor left in the casserole with flour, allowing one tablespoonful mixed to a paste to one cupful of liquid. Pour sauce over meat and garnish with parsley. Serves two.

PORK TENDERLOIN

The tenderloin is one of the best cuts. It may be split and broiled. If not very fat, brush with melted fat before broiling. The tenderloin may also be stuffed with a good bread stuffing and roasted.

SAUSAGE AND FRIED APPLES

Pan broil the required number of small sausages or cakes of sausage meat and as soon as fat collects, as many halved, cored, and unpeeled apples as required, first dipping them in flour to which a little sugar has been added. Sauté until soft and browned. Place on a hot serving dish with two small sausages on each half.

SAUSAGE AND SPAGHETTI IN TOMATO SAUCE

1 pound sausages	1 can tomato soup
½ pound spaghetti	½ cupful hot water

Prick the sausages thoroughly, place in a frying-pan, cover with boiling water, and simmer until they are thoroughly done and well-browned, about an hour. Break the spaghetti in small pieces, and cook in boiling salted water till tender. Drain. Combine the sausages and spaghetti in the frying-pan, add the soup diluted with the hot water, and let it stand till very hot. If desired this may be served from the chafing dish. Serves six.

SMOTHERED SAUSAGES

1 cupful sausage meat	2 tablespoonfuls tomato or
1 cupful diced celery	white sauce
1 egg	1 quart highly seasoned
	mashed potato

Sauté the sausage meat until tender, and to it add the celery cooked until tender. Mix and moisten with the tomato or white sauce. Add one-half of a beaten egg to the mashed potato. Form into a thick roll with the sausage mixture in the center, lay in a greased baking-pan, and brush with the rest of the beaten egg. Bake about twenty minutes at 400° F. or until the potato is golden brown in color. Remove to a hot serving dish, surround with white sauce or tomato sauce, garnish, and serve. For individual servings, line an ice-cream scoop with mashed potato, fill the center with sausage mixture, and spread a layer of mashed potato on top. Invert on a greased baking-pan and bake and serve as directed above. Serves six.

VEAL BIRDS

2½ pounds veal cutlet	½ cupful minced onion
2 cupfuls soft bread-crumbs	¼ cupful fat
⅛ teaspoonful pepper	1 teaspoonful salt

Brown the bread-crumbs in the fat, and season with the salt and pepper. Cut the veal into two-inch squares, and pound until thin and the pieces are as large as the palm of the hand; spread with the filling. Roll up and tie with cord. Make the birds as round as possible, browning them in a little fat and when thoroughly browned remove the cords. In the meantime make a stock from the onions, gristle, bones, etc. Make a gravy in the pan in which the birds were browned, using a tablespoonful of flour mixed to a paste to each cupful of stock. Add birds to gravy. Transfer to a baking-dish or casserole and bake gently for four hours in a 350° F. oven. This recipe is also well adapted to the fireless cooker. Serves six.

VEAL LOAF

1½ pounds ground uncooked veal	Juice of one lemon
	Grated rind ¼ lemon
1 cupful ground ham (raw or cooked)	1 cupful milk
	1 tablespoonful fat, melted
2 eggs	1½ teaspoonfuls salt
1 cupful dried bread-crumbs	¼ teaspoonful pepper
⅛ teaspoonful nutmeg	1 quart canned tomatoes

Mix ingredients in the order given, shape into a loaf, and place in a dripping pan. Sieve the tomatoes and pour over the loaf, basting it with the tomato as it bakes. Cook for forty-five minutes in a 400° F. oven, adding a small can of chopped mushrooms during the last half of the cooking if desired. The ham may be omitted. Serves six.

IV. METHODS OF COOKING THE ORGANS

BOILED TONGUE

For a fresh tongue wash in cold water, put into boiling water and boil ten minutes, reduce the heat and simmer gently until tender. Beef or sheep's tongue will require four to five hours. Lamb tongue requires three to four hours. For a corned tongue, if very salt, soak in cold water overnight. Put in a kettle of cold water and bring slowly to the boiling point. Boil five minutes, remove scum and simmer until tender, from three to five hours. Cool slightly in cooking water. Remove skin and trim off roots.

TONGUE IN TOMATO ASPIC

1 cooked tongue	4 cupfuls strained tomato-juice
1½ teaspoonfuls salt	½ teaspoonful beef extract
6 cloves	1 small onion
2⅔ tablespoonfuls gelatine	Pepper to taste

Simmer together the tomatoes, salt, pepper, cloves, and onion for twenty minutes. Add the beef-extract and the gelatine, which should have been allowed to soften for five minutes in cold water to cover. Wet a mold with cold water. Pour in a thin layer of the tomato aspic, and when it is almost set, put in the tongue, which may be whole if nicely trimmed, or may be sliced. Add the remaining tomato aspic if the whole tongue is used, or if sliced, put in another layer of the aspic, and then one of the tongue, continuing in this way until all is used. Serves six.

TONGUE WITH BLACKBERRY SAUCE

1 fresh beef tongue	1 glass blackberry jelly or jam
Cloves	1 cupful raisins
	Juice 1 lemon

Cook the tongue till very tender in salted water containing a table-spoonful of mixed pickle-spice, one or two extra bay-leaves, and a few dried celery tips. Allow time suggested above. When very tender, remove the skin, trim off the root-end and stick the solid meat full of cloves. Place in a greased baking-pan, dust with salt, pour over the jelly, beaten soft with a fork, and the raisins, which should be cooked till tender in a cupful of water. Add the lemon-juice and bake twenty minutes, basting often. Serve hot or cold. Serves six.

SCALLOPED SWEETBREADS

2 pairs sweetbreads	¼ teaspoonful salt
1 cupful mushrooms	⅛ teaspoonful paprika
2 tablespoonfuls fat	2¾ cupfuls top milk
2 tablespoonfuls flour	½ cupful dried bread-crumbs
2 tablespoonfuls butter	

Cut the sweetbreads in pieces, after they have been soaked in cold water for fifteen minutes and allowed to stand in boiling water for ten minutes. Wash, peel, and cut in quarters the mushrooms. Sauté them with the sweetbreads in the fat, add the flour, salt, and paprika and cook one minute longer. Then add the top milk, or half milk and half cream, and cook several minutes. Pour into a casserole dish and sprinkle the top with the dried bread-crumbs and the two tablespoonfuls of butter in small bits. Brown in a 500° F. oven for twelve minutes. Serves six.

SWEETBREADS

Soak the sweetbreads in cold water, then simmer for twenty minutes in water to which has been added one teaspoonful salt and two tablespoonfuls vinegar. Lift out of boiling water and plunge at once into cold water for one minute. Trim off all gristle. The sweetbreads may then be seasoned with salt, pepper, and lemon juice, egged and crumbed and sautéd or cut into pieces and mixed with a white sauce. Creamed sweetbreads are served on rounds of toast or in ramekin dishes covered with buttered crumbs and browned in the oven. Garnish sautéd sweetbreads with pieces of lemon and parsley.

SWEETBREAD CUTLETS

2 pairs sweetbreads	2 tablespoonfuls water
Bread-crumbs	Toast points
	2 beaten eggs

Clean, trim, and cook the sweetbreads in boiling, salted water until tender. Then drain and cut in neat, half-inch cutlets or slices. Dip the sweetbreads in finely sifted, dried bread-crumbs, then in two beaten eggs, to which the water has been added, then in fine crumbs. Fry in deep fat at 390° F. until golden brown on all sides. Lay on a hot platter, and garnish with toast points, and lemon or serve with a savory sauce. Serves six.

SWEETBREAD MOUSSE

2 sweetbreads, or 1 pair	3 egg-yolks, beaten light
½ cupful chopped English walnut meats	½ cupful cream, whipped
	¾ teaspoonful salt
1 tablespoonful gelatine	⅛ teaspoonful cayenne
1¼ cupfuls sweetbread liquor	pepper

Clean the sweetbreads, and simmer till tender in slightly salted water. Remove from the liquor and strain it. There should be one and one-fourth cupfuls of liquor. Add one-fourth cupful to the gelatine; combine the egg-yolks, salt, cayenne, and the remaining liquor in a double-boiler top, and cook over hot water until the mixture coats a spoon. Add the gelatine, and just before the mixture begins to set, add the nuts and whipped cream. Put the sweetbreads in a mold, pour over the mixture, and let stand in a cold place till solid. Slice and serve on lettuce-leaves with a garnish of mayonnaise and English walnut meats. Serves four to six.

HEART

Trim the heart, and wash in cold water. For beef's heart, soak in cold water one hour. Melt one to two tablespoonfuls fat in a kettle.

Chop one onion into small pieces and sauté in the fat. Add the heart and sear on all sides. Pour over boiling water to cover and boil ten minutes. Reduce the heat and simmer gently until tender. A lamb's or calf's heart will require one and one-half to two and one-half hours. Beef or sheep heart requires two to three hours. The heart will have a better flavor if some vegetables are cooked with it—one carrot minced, three tablespoonfuls minced celery, one tablespoonful tomato catsup or Worcestershire sauce, and a dash of cayenne. Thicken gravy with one tablespoonful flour mixed with two tablespoonfuls cold water.

CURRIED BEEF HEART

1 beef heart	1 tablespoonful curry-powder
1 onion	2 tablespoonfuls fat
1 pint boiling water	Salt
About ½ cupful flour	Pepper

Pour boiling water over beef heart and let stand for ten minutes. Trim off fat and arteries and cut up in small pieces. Try out enough of the fat which was cut off to make two tablespoonfuls. Chop the onion, and brown it in the fat together with the pieces of heart rolled in the flour. Add the water and cook gently until the meat is tender. Replenish the water, as it boils away. When done, add seasoning and curry-powder mixed with a little cold water. Thicken with flour if needed. Sufficient to serve eight.

RAISIN STUFFED HEARTS

Calf's heart about 1 pound	1 teaspoonful salt
2 cupfuls bread-crumbs	¼ teaspoonful pepper
1 teaspoonful fat	⅛ teaspoonful each paprika,
2 tablespoonfuls seedless raisins	powdered sage, onion salt,
1 peeled onion	and marjoram

Wash the heart thoroughly and remove veins and arteries. Soak about fifteen minutes in acidulated cold water. Soak the bread-crumbs in water to soften; then mix with the fat, raisins, and seasonings. Stuff the heart with one-half of this mixture. Sew the opening together. Sprinkle the heart with salt and pepper, dredge with flour, and brown quickly in a hot, greased frying-pan. Then remove to a covered baking-dish, into the bottom of which the onion has been sliced. Half-cover with boiling water and bake at 350° F. for two hours, basting occasionally. Place the remaining stuffing in a buttered dish and bake thirty minutes. Serve with the baked heart on a platter with a gravy made from the liquor in which the heart was cooked, poured over all. Serves four to six.

LIVER

Calf's liver is considered the best of the animal livers although beef and lamb livers are good if properly cooked. They are all cooked in much the same way except beef liver, which must be parboiled for five minutes after slicing before cooking in the usual manner. Wash in cold water and remove any membranes. Cut in slices one-half inch thick. Cover with boiling water and let stand five minutes. Drain, dredge with flour, salt, and pepper and sauté in bacon fat.

CALVES' LIVER AND BACON

1 pound calves' liver	1 teaspoonful salt
¼ cupful flour	¼ cupful corn-meal
¼ pound bacon	

Prepare liver as above. Roll it in the flour, corn-meal, and salt mixed well together. Put bacon on to cook; as soon as fat collects, add the liver and sauté until browned on both sides. The bacon will cook first; remove it to a hot platter, and later add liver. Serves four. Slices of ripe or green tomatoes sautéd until brown add zest to this dish. Steamed rice added makes an entire course and an attractive club-plate.

LAMBS' KIDNEYS AND MUSHROOMS

1 large onion	1 bay leaf
2 tablespoonfuls finely chopped parsley	6 lambs' kidneys
3 tablespoonfuls fat	1 pound mushrooms
3 tablespoonfuls flour	¼ cupful hot water
2 beef bouillon cubes	2 tablespoonfuls fat
2½ cupfuls boiling water	½ teaspoonful celery salt
	¼ teaspoonful pepper.

Mince the onion and sauté it, together with the finely chopped parsley, in the fat until the onions are tender and golden brown in color. Then add the flour and stir until well blended; add two and one-half cupfuls of stock, made by dissolving the beef bouillon cubes in the two and one-half cupfuls of boiling water, and stir well. Add the bay leaf, broken up fine. Cover, and simmer three minutes, or until smooth and slightly thickened. Then add the lambs' kidneys, which have been prepared as directed above. Meanwhile, clean, scrape, and skin the mushrooms and slice in halves lengthwise. Simmer them in one-fourth cupful of hot water, two tablespoonfuls of fat, the celery salt, and pepper until the mushrooms are tender. Then add them to the lamb-kidney mixture and combine thoroughly. Place a mound of well-seasoned, mashed potato in the center of a dish and sprinkle with chopped parsley. Arrange the mushrooms and kidneys in sauce around the mashed potatoes. The same mixture may be served on buttered toast for luncheon if desired. Serves six.

KIDNEY STEW

The kidneys of beef, veal, mutton and lamb are used. To prepare for cooking, wash in cold water, scald and remove skin. If beef or mutton, soak in salted water, one teaspoonful to one quart of water, two to three hours. Cut the kidneys in pieces, season and roll in flour. Sauté a light brown, cover with water and simmer ten minutes. Mushrooms may be added to the stew and strained tomato instead of part of the water. Thicken gravy with more flour if necessary. Serve with a border of vegetables garnished with parsley.

V. BACON

Using kitchen shears, trim off rind and inner smoked edge from thin slices. Place in a hot pan and cook slowly until fat is clear. Turn once and cook one minute longer. Serve at once. Another good way to broil bacon is under the broiler. Place thin strips of bacon on the broiler rack with the heat high. Turn the bacon every minute until brown. Pieces of cooked bacon are appetizing in scrambled eggs or omelet.

BAKED PEAS (P. 122)

PIGS IN BLANKET (P. 98)

VI. GRAVY

Make the gravy in the same pan in which the meat was roasted. Measure the fat. Place the pan over the fire, and when the fat is hot add an equal amount of flour. Blend well and stir until a light brown. Add three-eighths of a cupful of cold water for each tablespoonful of fat. Boil until perfectly smooth stirring constantly. The gravy may be colored with a little very dark caramel.

VII. SAUCES SERVED WITH MEAT (Chart for Sauces, P. 184)

VIII. USES FOR LEFT-OVER MEAT

BAKED CORNED BEEF HASH

3 cupfuls cooked corned beef, chopped	2 tablespoonfuls fat
1 medium-sized onion	1½ cupfuls milk
6 medium-sized potatoes	2 teaspoonfuls salt
	½ teaspoonful pepper

Grease a casserole, place in the bottom the chopped meat, add the onion minced, then slice on top the raw potatoes. Repeat seasoning each layer of potatoes with fat, salt, and pepper. Pour milk over all. Cover and bake at 400° F. until milk is absorbed and potatoes are tender. Serves six.

CREAMED MINCED HAM WITH MUSHROOMS

6 tablespoonfuls butter	3 cupfuls milk
1 pound mushrooms	1½ cupfuls minced cooked
6 tablespoonfuls flour	ham
Salt and pepper	

Clean and slice the mushrooms. Melt the butter, add the mushrooms and cook three minutes. Add flour and stir until smooth. Add milk and cooked ham and boil one minute. Season to taste and serve at once. Serves six.

HAM MOUSSE

1 cupful chopped cooked ham, ground very fine	1 tablespoonful granulated gelatine
1 cupful ham-stock	¼ teaspoonful salt
3 egg-yolks	Few grains paprika
½ pint cream, whipped	

Beat the yolks of the eggs and stir lightly into the ham-stock, add seasonings and cook in a double boiler like a custard. Just before removing from the fire, add the gelatine which has been allowed to soften in a little cold ham-stock. Pour this custard over the ham and stir over ice water till it begins to set, then fold in the whipped cream, turn the mixture into a mold, let stiffen, and serve garnished with parsley. Serves four to six.

MARBLED TONGUE

1 pound boiled tongue	½ cupful melted butter
2 pounds cooked veal	Salt
Pepper	

Chop veal and tongue separately until fine; add salt and pepper to taste. Pour over the veal the melted butter, mix thoroughly; then put alternate layers of each in a pan and put under a press or weight. Serve in slices with lemon or a garnish of green pepper. This will serve ten to twelve persons.

MEAT PIE

Cut remnants of cold broiled steak or roast beef or any cooked meat in one-inch cubes. Cover with boiling water, add one-half onion, and cook slowly one hour. Remove onion, thicken gravy with flour diluted with cold water, and season with salt and pepper. Add potatoes cut in one-fourth-inch slices, which have been parboiled eight minutes in boiling salted water. Put in a greased pudding dish, cool, cover with hot mashed potatoes, baking-powder biscuit mixture or pie crust. Bake in a hot oven of 450° F. for thirty minutes. If covered with pie crust, make several incisions in crust that gases may escape.

MEAT SANDWICH ROLL

2 cupfuls flour	4 tablespoonfuls shortening
4 teaspoonfuls baking-powder	About ⅔ cupful milk
1 teaspoonful salt	3 tablespoonfuls butter
1½ cupfuls chopped cooked meat	Seasoned gravy

Prepare a baking-powder biscuit mixture. Turn out onto a floured board and roll to one-quarter inch in thickness. Spread the dough with the chopped cooked meat which has been seasoned and slightly moistened with gravy. Roll the dough up like a jelly roll. Then with a sharp knife cut it into six or eight pieces as preferred. Place the individual rolls cut side down in a greased pan. Place a small piece of butter on top of each. Bake at 450° F. for fifteen minutes. Serve with brown gravy, tomato sauce or white sauce to which peas have been added. Serves six.

POTATO AND HAM CROQUETTES

1 cupful minced cooked ham	2 eggs
2 cupfuls mashed potatoes	Dry bread-crumbs

Combine the ham and beaten egg-yolks and barely heat while stirring constantly. Cool, make into eight small balls, and cover with the mashed potatoes. Roll in fine, dry crumbs and then in the egg-whites, slightly beaten, with one-fourth cupful of cold water, then in crumbs again. Fry at 390° F. in deep fat. Serves six.

RICE AND MEAT EN CASSEROLE

2 teaspoonfuls minced onion	1 egg
½ teaspoonful salt	¾ cupful stock or hot water
⅛ teaspoonful pepper	1 cupful cooked rice
2 cupfuls cooked meat, chopped fine	2 tablespoonfuls soft bread-crumbs

1 tablespoonful butter

Add the minced onion, salt, and pepper to the cooked meat chopped fine. Then add the egg, well beaten and the stock or hot water. Put a layer of rice in the bottom of a greased casserole, and then a layer of the meat mixture. Cover the top with the bread-crumbs and the butter in bits. Bake at 350° F. for twelve minutes, and serve hot with a medium-thick tomato sauce, made as follows: Melt two tablespoonfuls of fat, add two tablespoonfuls of flour and one teaspoonful of salt. Cook until blended, and then add gradually one and one-half cupfuls of strained, cooked tomatoes. Cook until the mixture thickens; then serve. Serves six.

VEAL IN BROWN SAUCE WITH DUMPLINGS

3 tablespoonfuls fat	2 cupfuls diced cooked veal
4 tablespoonfuls flour	½ cupful sliced dried mush-
1 teaspoonful salt	rooms
¼ teaspoonful pepper	1 green pepper
1½ cupfuls stock	Dumplings

Melt the fat, add the flour, salt and pepper, and stir until well blended. Add the stock and bring to a boil. Slice the mushrooms, which
have been soaked in cold water for several hours. Discard the seeds
from the pepper and chop it. Add the veal, mushrooms, and green
pepper, cover, and cook over a low fire twenty minutes. Serve with
steamed dumplings around it. Serves six.

IX. CANNED MEATS

There is an infinite variety of canned and preserved meats on the
market that are very delicious and that offer a good selection for the
emergency shelf. Potted tongue and other potted meats are particularly good for sandwiches and for after-theatre suppers.

Poultry

FOOD VALUE

The food value of poultry does not, so far as i. known, differ in any important respect from that of other meats. Its chief value is as a source of protein. The light meat, such as the breast, is composed of more tender fibers than the dark meat, and usually contains less fat. For these reasons, the white meat is apt to be more rapidly digested.

Chicken

I. BROILED

1. Season—From May to September or October is the best season for broilers. They average in weight from one and one-half to two pounds and are usually from two to four months old.

2. General Preparation. a. Have the broiler dressed, drawn and cleaned by the butcher, if possible.
b. If you are doing it yourself, lay the bird on a meat board, breast side down. Cut down the back, on either side of the backbone from the neck, the entire length, thus cutting out the rump, backbone and the neck. Slightly raise the backbone and loosen the entrails from the back on both sides. Then loosen them from the breast; and remove the entire mass including the backbone, neck, rump and entrails. Carefully scrape and push the flesh from the breast bone and remove it. Remove the rib bones, cut off the legs at the second joint and cut through the sinews at all joints.

67

3. **General Cooking.** a. Broilers may be broiled directly under the broiler heat or in the baking oven. Spread them apart and wipe on both flesh and skin side with a damp cloth. Dry thoroughly. Sprinkle with salt and pepper, and rub the inside of each broiler with melted butter or oil. Sprinkle with finely chopped parsley and the juice of one lemon. Let stand in refrigerator one hour.

b. If broiling oven is used, preheat it for ten minutes with broiler rack in position. Then grease the rack, and place the broilers on it, skin side down, or place the broilers in a heated roasting pan. Sear quickly on one side, turn and sear the other side. Then reduce the heat and broil slowly, turning once or twice while basting with melted butter. Broil about twenty minutes or until tender. Since the skin side browns very quickly, most of cooking should be done on the flesh side. When done serve at once.

c. If a broiler oven is not available, bake the broilers in a roasting pan at 450° F. for thirty minutes, or until tender, turning frequently. Baste with butter frequently. Gravy may be made from drippings in roasting pan.

d. In carving broilers, insert the fork in the breast bone and cut each broiler in halves and then in quarters.

II. SAUTÈD OR "FRIED"

1. **Season.** From June to October is the best season for Frying Chickens. They average in weight from two and one-half to three pounds, and are usually about six months old—slightly older and larger than broilers.

2. **General Preparation.** a. Have butcher dress, draw, clean and cut up the chicken.

b. If you must clean the chicken yourself, prepare as follows: Singe, remove tendons, then neck, viscera and oil sack on tail. Wash body cavity.

c. Disjoint the chicken as follows:
To remove drumsticks and second joints cut through skin close to body between legs and body, and bend back the leg to snap the hip joint. Cut through flesh to remove leg from body. Separate "second joint" (upper part of leg) by cutting through flesh and then bending back to snap joint.

Cut through skin between wings and body and bend back to snap joint.

Separate back from breast by cutting through skin at middle line on side of body just where the ribs end. Bend back to snap joints attaching breast bone to back. Cut through middle of back and bend to break joint, dividing back into two pieces.

Cut off the tail piece and remove oil sack.

The wish-bone may be cut off by cutting through skin where it joins breast bone. Bend back to snap joint.

Cut off neck close to body.

3. **Cooking.** a. Wash and dry the pieces of chicken and roll each piece in seasoned flour entirely coating the surface, or dip in cracker crumbs or corn-meal, then in beaten egg and again in crumbs.

b. Melt fat or oil in a frying-pan, and when hot, place in it the pieces of floured chicken and sprinkle with salt and pepper. Brown one side, then the other.

c. Reduce the heat, tightly cover the frying-pan and continue to sauté slowly until the meat is tender—about twenty-five or thirty minutes. If it is not tender at the end of this time, add a small quantity of hot water, recover and simmer until tender.

d. If desired, brown gravy may be made from the fat left in the frying-pan, using milk or water as the liquid. (P. 63.)

SAVORY CHICKEN

Shaved ham	Sautéd mushrooms
Rounds of toast	Tomato sauce (P. 184)
Fried chicken	Parsley.

Fry small individual servings of shaved ham until crisp. Place each serving of ham on a large round of toast and lay on each a neat, boneless piece of fried chicken, having the pieces of chicken and ham nearly uniform in size. Top each with a mushroom. Arrange the servings on a platter or chop plate, and just before taking to the table, put a tablespoonful of highly seasoned tomato sauce carefully around the ham on the toast. One cupful of tomato sauce is sufficient for six servings. Garnish the dish with parsley and serve at once, very hot.

III. FRICASSEED CHICKEN

1. **Season.** Fowl weighing four to five pounds are generally used for fricassee and are seasonable the year round. This method of cooking is particularly excellent for rather tough birds.

2. **General Preparation.** Order the fowl dressed, drawn, cleaned and cut up as for Fried Chicken.

3. **General Cooking.** a. Put the cut-up chicken in a kettle, cover with boiling water and cook slowly until tender adding salt, about two teaspoonfuls, during the last half of the cooking.

b. When tender, remove from the stock and coat with seasoned flour. Sauté in fat until golden brown on all sides.

c. Simmer the stock until reduced to two and one-half cupfuls. Thicken with three tablespoonfuls of flour which have been mixed to a smooth paste with cold water. About ½ cupful of sweet or sour cream added to this makes a delicious gravy.

d. Arrange the pieces of chicken on a platter in this manner: Neck and tail in center, breast pieces and wish-bone on top of these, second joints at one end of dish, and legs crossed at the other, with wings on either side. Then pour the hot sauce over all. Garnish with halves of hot biscuits or dumplings.

IV. STEWED CHICKEN

Follow directions for preparation and cooking of Fricasseed Chicken, only do not brown by sautéing it. (P. 69.) Serve with or without Dumplings or hot biscuits.

V. STEAMED CHICKEN

Order the chicken dressed, cleaned and drawn. Cook in a steam pressure-cooker (P. 219), or use steamer large enough to hold chicken, sprinkle bird with salt, then steam until tender.

VI. BOILED CHICKEN

1. Order the chicken dressed, cleaned and drawn.

2. Place in deep kettle, cover with boiling water and cook slowly until tender. One bay leaf, one small onion sliced and a few peppercorns may be added to the water during the cooking, if desired. When serving cold, let chicken stand in liquor until cool.

VII. ROAST CHICKEN

1. Stuffing (For Recipes, see Page 81).

a. Stuff the cavity of a dressed, drawn and cleaned chicken until the body is plump, allowing some space for the swelling if crackers are used. Likewise, fill the space from which the crop was removed, inserting the stuffing through the slit in the neck. Thread a long darning needle with heavy white thread and sew up the slit in the neck, as well as the one in the body.

2. Trussing. a. After the bird is stuffed, it should be trussed. First draw thighs close to body and secure them by a skewer inserted through one thigh, in through body cavity and out through the other thigh. Draw the wings close to body and secure them in the same

manner.   Fold the neck skin back to wings and skewer in place.   Cross the drumsticks and with a string about two feet long, tie them down to the tail.   Then turn the bird on its breast, cross the string attached to the tail and wind one end around each end of the lower skewer which holds the thighs in place.   Again cross the string and draw it, one end around each end of the upper skewer which holds the wings in place. Holding the string taut, secure it with a knot and cut off the ends.

3. Roasting. a. Place the stuffed and trussed chicken on a trivet in a roasting pan, preferably a covered roaster.   Sprinkle lightly with flour, salt and pepper.

b. Roast according to Cooking Temperature (Chart P. 252), opening vent in cover of roaster last fifteen minutes.   If cover has no vent, remove the cover itself for the last fifteen minutes.

c. Remove chicken and make chicken gravy (see P. 63).   For Southern Giblet Gravy, follow directions for gravy making (see P. 63), with the following changes: Wash, skin and slice one pound of mushrooms and simmer five minutes in the fat before adding the flour.   Proceed as directed, adding the giblets, cooked tender and chopped, just before serving the gravy.   Remove skewers and string from chicken and arrange on platter.

VIII. BRAISED CHICKEN

1. Dress, clean and truss a fowl, as this method is more suitable for fowl than chicken.

a. Braise in waterless cooker or in Dutch oven.

a. Braise in oven as follows: Try out three slices of fat salt pork cut one-quarter inch thick.   Remove scraps and to the fat add two large carrots, scraped and diced, one small onion chopped, one bay leaf and one sprig parsley.   Cook three minutes.   Brown the bird on all sides in this fat mixture.   Then place on a trivet in a deep pan, pour over the fat, and add two cupfuls of boiling water.   Cover tightly and bake in a 350° F. oven for two and one-half to three hours or until the meat is tender.   Baste often, replenishing the water when necessary.   Serve the chicken with gravy made from the fat in the pan.

IX. CREAMED CHICKEN

Divide cold cooked chicken into large pieces.   Add to the white sauce made from all milk or half milk and half chicken-stock (See Schedule for Sauces, Page 184).   Serve in ramekins with buttered breadcrumbs or light mashed potatoes on top.   Or serve on squares or rounds of buttered toast.

X. SPECIAL CHICKEN RECIPES, INCLUDING USES FOR LEFT-OVER CHICKEN

CASSEROLE OF LEFT-OVER CHICKEN

About 3 cupfuls cooked chicken-meat
¼ pound fat salt pork or bacon, diced
1 tablespoonful minced parsley
1 teaspoonful celery-salt, or ½ cupful minced celery
1 cupful canned tomatoes, or 2 fresh tomatoes, quartered
1 cupful rice
1½ pints of chicken-stock (made from bones)
Salt and pepper

Put the bacon or salt pork in a casserole and brown it. Add the parsley, celery, tomatoes, and chicken-meat, together with a little salt and pepper. Mix well. Over this put the rice, and pour on the chicken-stock. Cover closely and bake gently in a slow oven of 350° F. one hour and a half; then stir together, adding a little onion-juice, Worcestershire sauce, or any extra desired seasoning. Sprinkle with chopped parsley before serving. Serves four to six.

CHICKEN À LA KING

2 cupfuls diced chicken-meat (white preferred)
5 tablespoonfuls salad oil
3 tablespoonfuls chopped pimientoes
6 tablespoonfuls chopped green peppers
1 tablespoonful capers
1 can or 1½ cupfuls fresh mushrooms
½ teaspoonful salt
3 cupfuls rich cream
2½ tablespoonfuls flour
1 tablespoonful fat
2 egg-yolks
Paprika

Cook mushrooms five minutes in the salad oil, then add the mixture to the chicken, capers, peppers, and pimientoes, and add a dash of paprika and salt. Prepare a white sauce of the fat, flour, and cream, beating the two egg-yolks, and pouring the sauce into them when it is done. Add the chicken mixture, heat thoroughly, and serve on diamond-shaped slices of buttered toast. Serves four to six.

CHICKEN CROQUETTES

See Meat Croquettes (Page 133)

CHICKEN CURRY

Cut up the remnants of a roast or boiled chicken into two-inch squares. Dredge with flour and brown in a little hot fat together with one medium-sized onion chopped fine.   For one pint of cubed meat, prepare one pint of gravy, to which add one teaspoonful of curry powder mixed with two tablespoonfuls of cold water.   Add this gravy to the chicken, and last of all introduce the beaten yolk of an egg and serve immediately in a mashed potato border.   Serves four to six.

CHICKEN MOUSSE

1 cupful white meat of chicken, cooked and ground very fine
1 cupful chicken-broth
3 egg-yolks

1 tablespoonful granulated gelatine
¼ teaspoonful salt
Few grains paprika

½ pint cream, whipped

Beat the yolks of the eggs and stir lightly into the broth, add seasonings, and cook in a double boiler like a custard.   Just before removing from the fire, add the gelatine, which has been allowed to soften in a little cold chicken-broth.   Pour this custard over the chicken-meat and stir over ice water till it begins to set, then fold in the whipped cream, turn the mixture into a mold, let stiffen, and serve garnished with parsley.   Serves six.

CHICKEN NEPTUNE

2 cupfuls cooked, white chicken meat, diced
2 dozen large oysters
2 dozen fresh shrimps
1 small can crab meat
1 pint cream
1½ teaspoonfuls salt

6 fresh mushrooms, sliced
½ green pepper, chopped fine
½ pimiento, chopped fine
4 tablespoonfuls butter, fat or oil
2 tablespoonfuls flour
¼ teaspoonful paprika

¼ teaspoonful pepper

Wash the shrimp and cook for twenty minutes in boiling water; shell, and remove the viscera.   Wash the oysters, cook slowly in their own juice until the edges curl.   Carefully clean the crab meat.   Combine the sliced mushrooms and green pepper, chopped, and sauté for three minutes in two tablespoonfuls of butter.   Meanwhile prepare a white sauce by placing two tablespoonfuls of the butter in the top of a double boiler.   When melted, add the flour gradually, stirring constantly. When smooth, add the cream slowly and the seasoning, still stirring the mixture, and cook until thoroughly blended.   Then combine with the diced chicken, oysters, shrimp, crab meat, mushrooms, green pepper, and pimiento, using a fork.   Heat thoroughly and serve on small slices of toast.   This quantity will serve ten persons.

CHICKEN SCRAPPLE

Carcass of roast or boiled fowl	¼ teaspoonful celery salt
1 teaspoonful salt	½ teaspoonful sweet marjoram
¼ teaspoonful pepper	½ teaspoonful thyme
¼ teaspoonful paprika	1 cupful white corn-meal

Crack up the carcass of a roast or boiled fowl, cover with cold water, and let simmer for several hours. When the liquor is reduced to one quart, strain and add any bits of meat from the bones, cut fine. Add the salt, pepper, paprika, celery salt, sweet marjoram, and thyme. Return to the fire and add the white corn-meal slowly. Cook in a double boiler for one hour. Then pour into a greased, shallow pan to cool. Cut in slices, roll in seasoned flour, and sauté until brown in a little hot fat. Farina or hominy grits may be used in place of the meal. Serves six.

CHICKEN AND RICE

1 fowl	1 teaspoonful lemon-juice
2 cupfuls medium white sauce	Cooked rice (P. 32)
(P. 184)	Parsley
1 beaten egg-yolk	

Cook the fowl until very tender and cut into neat, attractive servings, rather small, using the white meat only, if you wish it particularly delicate in appearance. Meanwhile, prepare the white sauce, using equal parts of milk and chicken broth. Just before removing the sauce from the fire, gradually add the beaten yolk of egg and lemon juice, stirring it rapidly. Combine with the chicken which has been reheated in a double boiler with four tablespoonfuls of the white sauce, lay on a hot, deep platter or chop plate, and surround with a ring of cooked rice. Pour a little more of the sauce over it and serve, garnished with sprigs of parsley among the rice or with finely minced parsley, sprinkled over the rice. Serves six.

JELLIED CHICKEN

1 five-pound fowl	2 pimientoes, chopped fine
1½ teaspoonfuls salt	1 green pepper, seeded and
1 bay leaf	diced
1 teaspoonful celery seed	¾ cupful stoned green olives
¼ teaspoonful pepper	⅓ cupful chopped pecan meats
1 tablespoonful gelatine	½ cupful finely diced celery

Cover the fowl with cold water to which the salt, bay leaf, celery seed, pepper have been added. Cook until the meat falls from the bone, replenishing the water when necessary. Remove the fowl from the broth, and when cool remove the bones and skin. Return the bones to the broth and boil for twenty minutes longer.   Meanwhile cut the chicken up in small pieces and combine it with the pimientoes, chopped fine, green pepper seeded and diced, stoned green olives, chopped pecan meats, and finely diced celery.   Season with salt and pepper to taste. Strain the hot broth and remove as much fat as possible.   Measure two and one-half cupfuls of broth.   Soak one tablespoonful of gelatine in one-fourth cupful of water for five minutes.   Then add the hot broth, and when the gelatine has dissolved, combine with the other ingredients. Place in a cold wet mold to stiffen.   Serves at least eight.

QUICK CHICKEN STEW

2 cupfuls cold potato	2 cupfuls thickened chicken
1 cupful bits or diced chicken	gravy
½ teaspoonful salt	2 cupfuls boiling water
⅛ teaspoonful paprika	1 onion minced fine
1 tablespoonful parsley	

Dice the cold potato, and add the chicken, salt and paprika.   Meanwhile, dilute the chicken gravy with the boiling water, add the onion, minced fine, and simmer until the onion is tender.   Then add to the chicken, heat thoroughly, and serve, sprinkling with the parsley just before serving.   Peas, tiny carrots, or a few cooked string-beans may be added to the stew.   Or dumplings may be made and arranged around the edge of the platter, if desired.   (P. 41.)   Serves six.

CHICKEN PIQUANT

2 large slices salt pork	2 minced sweet peppers
2 minced onions	1 pint canned tomatoes
1 five-pound fowl	2 cloves
Flour	1 teaspoonful salt
Salt	¼ teaspoonful pepper
Boiling water	

Put the salt pork through the meat-chopper and sauté in a hot skillet until the fat is tried out and bits of pork are dry and brown.   Skim out the pork and fry the minced onions in the fat until a light brown. Then remove the onions.   Joint the fowl, dredge with flour and salt, and brown in the fat, turning frequently.   Then put back the pork scraps and onions, add the sweet peppers minced, canned tomatoes, cloves, salt, pepper, and enough boiling water just to cover the chicken. Cover and let simmer one hour, stirring carefully that it may not stick. Then bake in a 400° F. oven for two hours or until very tender.   Uncover the last half-hour of the time, that the sauce may become thick and rich.   When ready to serve, remove the chicken and thicken the sauce slightly if it needs it.   Pour around the chicken and garnish with parsley, tiny biscuits, or cooked potato balls.   Serves six to eight.

SAVORY CHICKEN

1 six-pound chicken or fowl	2 medium-sized carrots
1 dozen small onions	1 teaspoonful salt
3 stalks celery	3 cupfuls strained tomatoes
1 tablespoonful butter	

Select a six-pound chicken or fowl, cut into neat pieces. Dredge with well-seasoned flour and sauté in fat or drippings until well browned on both sides. Lay in a deep casserole and place around it the onions which have been peeled, celery cut into inch pieces, and carrots sliced. Sprinkle all with the salt and then pour the strained tomatoes over the top. Dot the surface with the butter, cover tightly, and cook in a 350° F. oven until the chicken and vegetables are tender, the time required being from two and one-half to three hours. Serve with cooked rice. Serves six to eight.

SORRENTO CHICKEN PIE

1 large tender cooked fowl (5 pounds)	5 tablespoonfuls water
	Celery salt
2½ cupfuls cooked diced potatoes	Onion salt
1½ cupfuls small cooked onions	Paprika
1½ cupfuls cooked carrots	Rich baking-powder biscuit
1 cupful small canned peas	dough (P. 174)
8 tablespoonfuls flour	

Cut one large, tender, cooked fowl in neat servings. Add the cooked diced potatoes, onions, carrots cut in narrow strips, and peas. Strain the chicken broth left from cooking the chicken and cook it down to five cupfuls. Thicken this with the flour, mixed to a smooth paste with the five tablespoonfuls water. Add celery salt, onion salt, and paprika to taste. Nearly fill two casseroles with the chicken and vegetables. Add the hot sauce. Cover the top of each dish with rings of small biscuits cut from rich baking-powder biscuit dough. Brush the tops with milk and bake at 450° F. for fifteen to eighteen minutes or until the biscuits are done. Serves six to eight.

Turkey

I. SEASON

Turkeys are at their best from October to January. However, it is possible to get cold-storage birds that are excellent. Turkeys weigh from eight to twenty-five pounds.

II. ROASTING

1. Clean, stuff and truss as for chicken (see P. 70).
2. Roast, following Cooking Temperature Chart, (Page 252).

III. USES FOR LEFT-OVER TURKEY

CREOLE TURKEY

1 medium-sized white onion	1 teaspoonful salt
2 green peppers	1 teaspoonful sugar
1 tablespoonful fat	6 small skinned mushrooms
1 can tomato soup	½ teaspoonful chopped parsley
1 tablespoonful flour	½ teaspoonful chopped chives
Turkey slices	

Make a sauce as follows: Slice very fine the onion and peppers. Heat thoroughly in a frying-pan with the fat and brown for three minutes. Add the tomato soup and flour. Season this with the salt and sugar. When this is all blended together, add the mushrooms sliced, chopped parsley, and chopped chives. Slice the turkey as evenly and as attractively as possible. Place a row of slices overlapping each other in a flat baking-dish, moisten with a little melted butter, and heat thoroughly. On a platter put a sauce-boat and fill with the sauce. Arrange the turkey slices around the sauce-boat, garnishing with celery leaves and pimiento strips. Serves four to six.

TURKEY COUNTRY STYLE

Turkey meat	2 tablespoonfuls flour
1 carrot, quartered	2 tablespoonfuls fat
2 medium-sized peeled potatoes	1½ teaspoonfuls salt
12 small white onions	½ teaspoonful celery salt
2 quarts water	⅛ teaspoonful pepper
Left-over gravy and stuffing	Speck cayenne
1 teaspoonful chopped parsley and celery	

Trim off all the meat left from the turkey, leaving in as large pieces as possible. Put the bone and skin in a saucepan, add the carrot cut in quarters, peeled potatoes, and onions. Add the water, the left-over stuffing and gravy, and cook well covered for about an hour. Strain the broth off, leaving the vegetables. Thicken the broth with the flour and fat rubbed together. When the thickened broth comes to a boil, add the onions, the turkey, and the potatoes cut in small pieces. Season with salt, celery salt, pepper, and cayenne and pour into a deep dish. Add the chopped parsley and celery and serve. This dish will use the last of the turkey and will make a luncheon or supper main dish.

TURKEY BOMBAY

1 tablespoonful fat	2 cupfuls consommé
1 minced green pepper	½ cupful strained tomato
Minced hearts two white onions	juice
½ chopped apple	1 teaspoonful salt
1 cupful raw washed rice	⅛ teaspoonful pepper
2 cupfuls diced turkey meat	2 beaten egg-yolks
2 tablespoonfuls grated Parmesan cheese	

Cut the meat from the turkey in one-half-inch pieces. Heat the fat, add the minced green pepper and the minced hearts of the two white onions, brown a few minutes, and add one-half chopped apple, the rice, consommé, strained tomato juice, salt and pepper. Then add the turkey, mix well, put in a covered casserole in a 400° F. oven, and bake for forty-five minutes. Remove and add to the hot mixture the beaten egg-yolks and grated Parmesan cheese. Mix lightly, put all in a greased mold, and steam for twenty-five minutes. Unmold and serve hot with reheated gravy. Serves four to six.

Duck

I. SEASON

Roasting ducks may be purchased all during the year, but are best in winter. They weigh from three to six pounds, but do not have as much meat as chicken or turkey.

II. ROASTING

1. Have the bird carefully drawn, singed, cleaned and washed.

2. Fill cavity three-quarters full of chopped tart apples. Do not serve this stuffing as it is used merely to remove the strong flavor of duck. Or fill cavity with well-seasoned mashed potatoes adding one egg, one teaspoonful sage, one-half a small finely chopped onion, one-quarter cupful of melted butter and two tablespoonfuls of chilli sauce to every two cupfuls of mashed potatoes.

3. Truss—Draw thighs close to body and hold them by a skewer inserted under the middle joint and running it through the body so that it comes out under the middle joint on the other side. Place wings close to body and hold by inserting a second skewer through the wing, body and wing on the other side. Wind a string twice around the bone of one leg, then around the other so that there is a one-inch space between legs. With both ends of string, draw the legs close to the back, then cross the string under the back, around the lower skewer, cross again, fasten around the upper skewer and tie in a knot. Draw the neck skin under the back and fasten with a small skewer.

4. Dredge the trussed bird with flour and tie two slices of fat salt pork over the breast of the bird. Place on a trivet in a covered roaster. Roast in a very hot oven of 550° F. for twenty minutes and complete the cooking at 400° F. Allow fifteen minutes to the pound. Remove salt pork at end of first thirty minutes. Make gravy (P. 63.)

Goose

I. SEASON

Geese are best from October to March and generally weigh from four to eight pounds.

II. ROASTING

1. Singe, remove pinfeathers, wash and scrub the goose in hot soapsuds. Then remove the entrails and wash and rinse the bird in hot soda water, using one teaspoonful soda to each quart of water. Dry thoroughly, and rub inside with a mixture of salt, thyme and marjoram, or sprinkle inside and out with lemon-juice, or rub it with an onion cut in half. Stuff, truss and roast like Duck (see P. 78), allowing twenty minutes to pound. (P. 252.)

Squabs, Partridges, Pheasant, Etc.

These small birds are usually broiled as chicken (P. 67). Singe, remove feathers, wash, remove head and feet, and draw as for broilers. Lay birds open by beginning at neck and cutting down the back along spine.

Game

Rabbits

I. FOOD VALUE

The flesh of the tame rabbit is a highly nutritious and desirable food, closely resembling poultry in food value.

RABBIT BAKED IN MILK

1 rabbit	1 teaspoonful sage
⅓ cupful flour	3 tablespoonfuls fat
1 teaspoonful salt	3 strips bacon
4 cupfuls thin white sauce	

Dress and clean one rabbit and disjoint in pieces for serving. Mix the flour, salt and sage in a bowl. Thoroughly coat the rabbit with this mixture; then sauté in the fat until brown on all sides. Place the rabbit in a casserole and lay the bacon over the surface. Pour the thin white sauce over and around the rabbit. Bake in a moderate oven of 375° F. for two hours or until the meat is tender. Serves six to eight.

RABBIT SALAD

1 cooked rabbit	Stuffed olives
Diced celery	Salad dressing
Chopped green pepper	Salt

Paprika

Steamed or boiled rabbit is better for this than roast rabbit, because it is not so dry. Remove the meat from the bones in as large pieces as possible. Remove the skin and fat and cut into even cubes of one-fourth inch. To each cupful of diced rabbit add one-half cupful of diced celery, one-fourth cupful of chopped green pepper, and three stuffed olives, sliced. Mix with one-fourth cupful of salad dressing, one-fourth teaspoonful of salt and a dash of paprika. Arrange on lettuce leaves and serve. Serves eight.

RABBIT STEW

1 three-pound rabbit	2 teaspoonfuls salt
6 small onions	2 cupfuls diced carrots
1 bay leaf	3 potatoes
½ cupful chopped celery	3 tablespoonfuls flour

1 tablespoonful finely chopped parsley

Dress and clean a rabbit weighing about three pounds. Disjoint it in pieces for serving. Place in a kettle with the onions, bay leaf, chopped celery and salt. Cover with cold water and allow to cook slowly until almost tender—about two hours. Then add the diced carrots, potatoes, pared and cut into quarters. Continue cooking until these vegetables are tender. Moisten the flour in a little cold water and add to the stew. When slightly thickened, add the finely chopped parsley and serve at once. Serves six to eight.

RABBIT SUPREME

1 young jackrabbit	6 sprigs parsley
6 tablespoonfuls fat	1 sprig mint
½ clove of garlic	1 can condensed tomato soup
6 medium-sized onions	2 teaspoonfuls salt

Flour

Soak the jackrabbit in salted water overnight, after it has been cleaned and disjointed. Then pour off the water and dry each piece of rabbit carefully. Place the fat in a kettle, together with the clove of garlic, onions chopped fine, parsley and one sprig of mint. Cook until lightly browned, then add the condensed tomato soup and mix well. Place the rabbit in the kettle and cover with boiling water. Add the salt and cook until the rabbit is tender—about one and one-half hours or longer. Replenish the water when necessary. When the rabbit is tender, remove it to a hot platter. Thicken the gravy, allowing one tablespoonful of flour to each cupful of broth. Pour the gravy over the rabbit and serve with boiled rice and currant jelly. Serves six to eight.

Stuffings

BREAD STUFFING

4 cupfuls medium coarse bread-crumbs	½ cupful melted fat
1 cupful boiling water	1 small onion, finely minced
1 egg	1 teaspoonful finely minced parsley

As a first step, prepare the medium coarse bread-crumbs. Bread which is at least one or two days old is most suitable for this purpose. Place the measured crumbs in a mixing bowl and pour over them one cupful of boiling water or enough to moisten them well and set aside to soak from twenty to thirty minutes. At the end of that time, carefully squeeze all excess moisture from the crumbs, leaving them light, yet slightly moist. Then add the egg, beaten lightly, together with the melted fat. Have ready the onion finely minced and the finely minced fresh parsley and combine with the bread-crumb mixture. One cupful of chopped celery may be added if desired. This quantity is sufficient for a six-pound bird.

GIBLET STUFFING

Follow the directions given above for the plain Bread Stuffing, adding the finely minced cooked giblets, and using the stock in which the giblets were cooked, instead of the hot water called for to moisten the stuffing.

MASHED POTATO STUFFING

2 cupfuls riced potatoes	¼ teaspoonful white pepper
3 small onions	¼ teaspoonful paprika
2 tablespoonfuls chopped salt pork	Few grains cayenne pepper
½ teaspoonful marjoram	1 tablespoonful chopped parsley or
1 teaspoonful salt	1 teaspoonful dried parsley

1 tablespoonful melted fat

Pare potatoes and cook them until tender in salted water. To two cupfuls of riced potatoes, add onions which have been chopped and cooked with chopped salt pork, marjoram, salt, white pepper, paprika, cayenne pepper, chopped parsley or dried parsley and melted fat, in the quantity given above. Mix all well together. This stuffing is especially good in chicken but can be used in any variety of poultry. It is sufficient for a five-pound bird.

Fish and Shell Fish

I. FOOD VALUE

Fish and shell fish may be regarded as interchangeable with the ordinary meats in the diet, their principal use being as a source of protein. Sea foods, however, have another significance because of their high iodine content and of the vitamin D in the oily fishes. The variety offered by fish is a constant source of joy to the menu-maker.

II. METHODS OF COOKING FISH

1. Broiling—Wash fish carefully. Remove scales, if any, by drawing a knife over fish, beginning at tail and inclining knife slightly toward you. Wipe thoroughly inside and out. Sprinkle with salt and pepper. Rub the less oily fish with melted fat. Grease wires of broiler. Split fish should be broiled on the flesh side first, then turned and broiled until the skin is brown and crisp. It requires five to eight minutes for small fish, fifteen to twenty-five for large. Large fish are cut in one-inch slices, and broiled in the same way. They require from five to fifteen minutes. The fish is cooked when it will flake easily or the flesh separates from the bone.

2. Boiling—Prepare the fish as for broiling. A long kettle with a rack on which to place the fish is useful. The fish may be placed on a plate and the whole tied in a cheese-cloth. To each quart of water, add one tablespoonful vinegar and two teaspoonfuls salt. Lower fish into boiling water and simmer until the flesh flakes easily from the bones. The time for boiling a thin fish is about five minutes per pound, for a thick fish, eight to ten minutes. Serve with a well-seasoned sauce. (See Chart for Sauces, P. 184.) Salt codfish should be flaked, covered with cold water and brought slowly to the boiling point. This water is then poured off.

3. Steaming—Prepare the fish, tie in cheese-cloth and put in the steamer. The test is the same as for boiling; the flesh flakes from the bone. This method requires about ten to twenty minutes per pound according to thickness of the fish.

4. Baking—Clean a four or five pound fish, sprinkle with salt, inside and out, and stuff and sew. For dry fish such as haddock and cod, cut five diagonal gashes on each side of the backbone and insert narrow strips of fat salt pork, having gashes on one side come between gashes on the other. Shape with skewers in form of letter S and fasten skewers with small twine. Place on a greased fish sheet in a dripping pan. Sprinkle with salt and pepper and dredge with flour. Bake one hour at 425° F., basting every ten minutes. Serve with drawn butter or egg sauce. (See P. 184.) For a baked split fish, split the fish as for broiling

and remove the bones if desired.   Place on a greased baking sheet, skin side down and dust with salt and pepper; dot with bits of fat.   Bake according to Cooking Temperature Chart (P.251).   For stuffing (see P. 81.)

5.   Sauteing—Prepare fish, dry carefully.   Dredge with flour or dip in eggs and crumbs and sauté slowly in a small amount of hot fat until well browned.   This requires about twenty-five minutes.

6.   Scalloped Fish—Use one cupful flaked cooked fish, one cupful medium white sauce (see P. 184) and one-half cupful buttered crumbs. Mix the fish and white sauce together, pour into a greased baking-dish. Cover with crumbs and bake at 500° F. for twelve minutes.   Raw halibut, cod, or haddock may be cut in one-inch pieces, and used in place of the cooked fish.   This should be baked at 350° F. for thirty minutes.

7.   Deep Fat Frying—Clean fish or shell fish and dry carefully, egg and crumb (see Breaded Veal Cutlet, P. 52) and fry in deep fat (see Cooking Temperature Chart, P. 251).   Fish steaks may be cut into fillets, rolled, skewered and breaded.   Small fish are cut in half, boned and skinned for frying.

III.   SELECTED RECIPES FOR FISH

FINNAN HADDIE AND SPAGHETTI

½ pound spaghetti	2 cupfuls cooked finnan haddie
¼ cupful butter, fat or oil	1 tablespoonful chopped onion
4 tablespoonfuls flour	2 cupfuls milk
1½ teaspoonfuls salt	½ teaspoonful paprika
⅓ cupful pimientoes	2 tablespoonfuls grated cheese

Cook the spaghetti and line thickly the bottom and sides of a greased baking-dish.   Cook together for five minutes the fat and onion.   Add the flour and stir until well blended; then add the milk, salt, and paprika. When the mixture thickens, add the flaked fish and the pimientoes cut into strips.   Pour the fish mixture over the spaghetti and bake at 500° F. for five minutes; then sprinkle the cheese over the top and replace it in the oven until the cheese is melted.   Serves six.

FINNAN HADDIE SAVORY

1 finnan haddie	2 tablespoonfuls chopped
1 small onion	parsley
1 green pepper	¼ teaspoonful paprika
1½ cupfuls milk	4 tablespoonfuls butter, fat
¾ teaspoonful salt	or oil

Clean the finnan haddie carefully and dry.   Place in a large baking pan and dot over with the fat.   Then sprinkle with the onion and seeded green pepper, chopped fine, the chopped parsley, paprika, and salt.   Cover with the milk and bake at 375° F. for one hour, basting frequently as the milk evaporates.   Serve at once.   Serves four to six.

FISH PIE

2 cupfuls flaked, cooked fish	2 tablespoonfuls minced
3 cupfuls mashed potatoes	parsley
1½ cupfuls medium white sauce	1 cupful grated cheese
(see P. 184)	

Grease a baking-dish and line it with mashed potatoes, allowing the potatoes to come about one-half inch above the dish on sides.   Put in a layer of fish which has been broken into small pieces, then a layer of white sauce with parsley thoroughly mixed in, and then half of the cheese, another layer of fish and white sauce, finishing with the cheese. Bake at 425° F. for twenty minutes, or until the cheese is brown.   Left-over fish of all kinds can be used in this recipe.   Serves six.

FISH VEGETABLE STEW

5 tablespoonfuls butter, fat or oil	2 tablespoonfuls chopped parsley
3 medium onions	1 pint hot water
2 cupfuls diced potatoes	1 pint fish chunks
1 tablespoonful flour	2 cupfuls hot milk
2 cupfuls diced carrots	1 tablespoonful Worcestershire
2 cupfuls diced celery	sauce
1 bay leaf	1½ teaspoonfuls salt
¼ teaspoonful pepper	¼ teaspoonful paprika
2 cupfuls diced turnips	

Place four tablespoonfuls of fat in a kettle, and when melted add the onions, chopped fine.   Allow these to cook for five minutes, turning frequently to prevent burning, until the onions are a golden brown. Then add the potatoes, diced into one-half inch cubes, the diced carrots, turnips, and celery, the bay leaf and chopped parsley.   Add to the onions together with the hot water, Worcestershire sauce, salt, pepper, and paprika and simmer gently until the vegetables are half done. Then add the fish, simmer ten minutes and add the milk.   Thicken the stew slightly with one tablespoonful of fat and the flour, blended together.   Cook the stew from three to five minutes longer and serve. Serves six to eight.

FROGS' LEGS, SAUTÉD

Frogs' legs	Butter, fat or oil
Flour	Onion juice
Lemon-juice	Buttered toast
Salt	Pepper

After drying the frogs' legs thoroughly, roll them in flour and sauté them in fat to which a few drops of onion and lemon juice have been added.   When done, place on slices of thin, hot, buttered toast and dust with salt and pepper.

FLOUNDER RAREBIT

1 teaspoonful butter, fat or oil	3¼ teaspoonfuls lemon-juice
2 tablespoonfuls flour	½ teaspoonful salt
¼ teaspoonful paprika	1 cupful cold milk
·¾ cupful finely cut or grated cheese	1 cupful flaked cooked flounder
1 egg	Crackers

Melt the fat, add one-fourth teaspoonful of lemon-juice, the flour, salt, paprika, and enough of the milk to moisten it. Add the rest of the milk and the cheese, and when the latter is melted, add the fish. Stir in the egg, well beaten to which one tablespoonful of lemon-juice has been added. Serve hot on crackers, thin slices of toast, or toasted croùtons. Serves four.

FROGS' LEGS, BROILED

Frogs' legs	Salt
Butter, fat, or oil	Pepper
Butter sauce	

Select large frogs' legs. After they have been dressed, wash them, dry between towels, and pass the joint of one leg through the muscle of the other, thus holding them in good shape. Brush them over with the fat, dust lightly with salt and pepper and broil till a delicate brown and tender. Serve with a butter sauce.

HALIBUT AURORE

2-pound cut of halibut	1 tablespoonful mushroom catchup
1 tablespoonful flour	
1 tablespoonful butter, fat, or oil	1 tablespoonful tarragon vinegar
1 cupful milk	
1 tablespoonful minced parsley	1 tablespoonful capers
Juice 1 lemon	2 teaspoonfuls salt
¼ cupful water	1 teaspoonful vinegar

Place fish in baking-dish, with the water, the vinegar, and salt, and bake at 425° F. for thirty minutes or until tender, but not broken. Remove to a large dish and allow to cool. In one saucepan make a sauce of the fat, milk, flour and parsley. Meanwhile, in another, heat the mushroom catchup, tarragon vinegar, lemon-juice and capers. When the white sauce has cooled a little, blend the two, beating well, and pour over the fish. Serve very cold, garnished with cut lemons and sprigs of parsley. This may also be served hot, if desired. Serves six.

HADDOCK À LA CREOLE

4 pounds haddock	2 tablespoonfuls butter, fat or
2 medium-sized onions	oil
1 tablespoonful cold water	2 tablespoonfuls flour
¼ teaspoonful pepper	3 teaspoonfuls salt
3 cupfuls canned tomatoes	Dash of paprika

Select a fish suitable for baking, remove the head, tail and clean thoroughly. Place the fish in a baking-dish and partially cover with boiling water. Cook until the fish is almost tender; then remove from the pan and drain off all the water. Prepare a tomato sauce of the remaining ingredients. Place the fish in an uncovered dish, pour the sauce over it, and bake for twenty-five minutes at 400° F. Cooked rice may be served with the fish. Serves six.

HALIBUT, BAKED WITH TOMATO SAUCE

2½ pounds sliced halibut	⅛ teaspoonful pepper
6 slices onion	1 can condensed tomato soup
1½ teaspoonfuls salt	6 slices fat salt pork
2 tablespoonfuls flour	

Lay half the salt pork and half the onion on the bottom of a heatproof dish. Place the halibut over this, sprinkle with salt and pepper, and dredge slightly with the flour. Lay the remaining salt pork and onion on this, pour in hot water to the depth of half an inch, and bake at 450° F. about thirty-five minutes. Pour over the soup and finish cooking. Serves six.

MACKEREL, BAKED SPANISH

1 medium-sized mackerel	½ teaspoonful minced green
2 cupfuls bread-crumbs,	pepper
medium stale	¼ teaspoonful summer savory
½ small onion, minced	3 slices bacon
1 tablespoonful bacon, minced	⅓ teaspoonful salt
Few grains pepper	

Mix together the bread-crumbs, onion, chopped bacon, green pepper, and seasonings, and lay on the fish, which should be dressed for broiling. Place a slice of bacon on this and fold over the fish so that the dressing shows. Place on a fish-rack in a baking-pan, lay the remaining bacon on top of the fish, and bake thirty minutes in a 425° F. oven, basting frequently with the fat in the pan. Serve on a platter decorated with alternating rings of green pepper and sliced lemon. Accompany with the following sauce: Mix together two teaspoonfuls of chopped green pepper, four tablespoonfuls of mayonnaise, and three tablespoonfuls of chilli sauce, and use at once. Serves six.

SALMON AND SPAGHETTI, BAKED

3 cupfuls cooked spaghetti	½ teaspoonful pepper
1 cupful canned salmon	¾ teaspoonful paprika
1½ cupfuls milk	½ green pepper
1 teaspoonful salt	½ cupful dry bread-crumbs

2 tablespoonfuls butter, fat, or oil

Melt one tablespoonful of fat in a baking-dish, cover with half the bread-crumbs, then with alternate layers of spaghetti, salmon, green pepper, chopped fine, and seasonings, until all are used. Add the milk, sprinkle with the rest of the bread-crumbs, dot with fat, and bake at 500° F. for twelve minutes. Serves six.

SALMON CUTLETS

1 pound canned salmon	⅛ teaspoonful pepper
2 cupfuls mashed potatoes	2 cupfuls medium-thick white
1 egg	sauce
1½ teaspoonfuls salt	1 cupful canned peas

Dried bread-crumbs

Remove bones and skin from salmon and mash the flesh with a fork. Add potatoes, salt, pepper, and egg well beaten. Mix thoroughly and form into cutlets. Crumb, egg, crumb again, and fry in deep fat at 390° F. (See P. 133.) Arrange on a platter, and surround with the peas which have been heated in the white sauce. Serves six.

SALMON, MOLDED

1 can salmon or	¼ cupful vinegar
2 cupfuls flaked, fresh cooked	½ teaspoonful salt
salmon	1 teaspoonful granulated
½ tablespoonful flour	gelatine
Few grains cayenne pepper	1 teaspoonful mustard
2 egg-yolks	1½ tablespoonfuls melted
¼ cupful cold water	butter, fat, or oil

¾ cupful milk

Make a cooked salad dressing of the flour, mustard, pepper, egg-yolks, fat, milk, vinegar, and salt. In the meantime soak the gelatine in cold water to cover and add it to the salad dressing mixture when it is done. Then stir in the salmon. Pour into a mold and when stiff and cold, serve with the following sauce: Beat one cupful of heavy cream until stiff, slowly add one-fourth teaspoonful of salt, a few grains of cayenne pepper, and three tablespoonfuls of vinegar; just before serving, combine with one medium-sized cucumber, pared, chopped, and drained. Serves six.

SALMON PIQUANTE

1 can salmon	2 cupfuls cold water
1 onion	1 teaspoonful salt
2 tablespoonfuls butter, fat or oil	¼ teaspoonful chilli powder
3 tablespoonfuls catchup	7 tablespoonfuls flour
	Toast

Cut the onion in slices and sauté in the fat. Sift together the flour, chilli powder, and the salt; add to the sautéd onions, blending well. When slightly browned, add the cold water and the catchup gradually, stirring constantly until smooth. Heat thoroughly, then add the salmon and reheat. Serve on squares of hot, buttered toast. This will make six full-sized luncheon portions or twelve portions of a size suitable for a tidbit to be accompanied by a salad.

SMOKED SALMON CASSEROLE

1 cupful smoked salmon	1 cupful cooked onions
1 cupful cooked celery	1½ cupfuls dried bread-crumbs
2 hard-cooked eggs, sliced	¼ teaspoonful salt
2 cupfuls thin white sauce	¼ teaspoonful paprika
¼ teaspoonful pepper	2 tablespoonfuls butter
2 cupfuls cooked peas	

Freshen the fish and cut into shreds. Have ready the vegetables and white sauce to which the seasonings have been added. In a greased casserole place a thin layer of crumbs; on this place layers of salmon, peas, celery, eggs and onions until all have been used. Leave enough crumbs for the top. Pour white sauce over all, cover with the rest of the crumbs, dot over with the butter and bake at 500° F. for twelve minutes. Serves six.

SALT CODFISH BALLS, PERFECTION

1 cupful shredded codfish	1 tablespoonful butter, fat or oil
2 cupfuls mashed potatoes	
⅛ teaspoonful paprika	⅛ teaspoonful curry powder
Dried bread-crumbs	1 teaspoonful minced onion
2 tablespoonfuls water	1 egg

Scald and drain the codfish and add to the mashed potatoes and fat. Season with curry powder, paprika, and minced onion. Make in balls or croquettes, roll in the egg, slightly beaten and mixed with the water, then in fine bread-crumbs; place in refrigerator till morning if possible. Fry quickly in deep fat at 390° F. These may be rolled in flour instead of egg and crumbs, and then fried. Serves six.

SALT CODFISH PIE

1 cupful salt codfish	1 egg
2 cupfuls riced potatoes	½ cupful milk
½ cupful cracker crumbs	2 tablespoonfuls butter, fat or oil
¼ cupful grated cheese	Parsley

Shred the codfish and soak in lukewarm water for fifteen minutes. Drain, add the potatoes and milk, and put in a greased baking-dish. Spread with the egg beaten lightly. Cover with the crumbs, mixed with the melted fat, and sprinkle with the grated cheese. Bake at 500° F. for twelve minutes. Serve garnished with parsley. Serves six.

SARDINES AND RICE, SCALLOPED

¾ cupful rice	¼ teaspoonful pepper
1 tablespoonful butter, fat, or oil	1 can sardines
	1 tablespoonful flour
1½ cupfuls strained tomato juice	¼ teaspoonful paprika
	1 teaspoonful salt
⅓ cupful fine bread-crumbs	

Cook the rice until tender. Open a can of sardines canned in tomato sauce. Remove the bones and flake coarsely. Prepare a tomato sauce, using the tomato juice, fat, flour, salt, pepper and paprika. In a greased baking-dish, place alternate layers of rice, sardines, and tomato sauce until all are used. Cover with the bread-crumbs and bake for twelve minutes at 500° F. Serves six.

SHAD ROE

1 shad roe	Toast strips
4 tablespoonfuls butter, fat or oil	½ cupful dried, grated bread-crumbs
2 tablespoonfuls lemon-juice	1 teaspoonful chopped parsley
Yolks 2 hard-cooked eggs	⅛ teaspoonful pepper
1 teaspoonful salt	

Clean the shad roe and cook in boiling salted acidulated water for twenty minutes. Drain, plunge into cold water, drain, remove the membrane and separate the roe into pieces. Chill thoroughly. Meanwhile melt the fat in a saucepan and add the lemon-juice. Mix and add the shad roe. Break up lightly with a fork, add the hard-cooked yolks, mashed fine, the bread-crumbs, chopped parsley, salt and pepper. Stir until all is well blended and serve very hot with the toast strips. Serves six.

SARDINE RAREBIT

2 tablespoonfuls butter or fat
1 tablespoonful flour
¼ teaspoonful salt
1 cupful top milk or half
   milk and half cream

2 teaspoonfuls mustard
¼ teaspoonful paprika
1 cupful cheese
6 sardines
Toast

Prepare a white sauce with the fat, flour, salt and top milk. Then add the cheese cut in small pieces, and stir until the cheese is melted. Add the sardines which have been skinned and boned, the mustard and paprika, heat well, and serve on hot, buttered toast. Serves six.

TUNA FISH À LA KING

1 pound can tuna fish
3 tablespoonfuls flour
1 pint hot cream or rich milk
1 tablespoonful diced pimientoes
Buttered toast
Few grains cayenne

3 tablespoonfuls butter, fat or
   oil
½ tablespoonful diced green
   peppers
1 teaspoonful salt
½ bay leaf

Parsley

Melt the fat, add the peppers, and one teaspoonful of chopped onion, if desired. Cook these in the fat until tender, then add the flour. seasonings and gradually the milk, stirring constantly. Put in the bay leaf and let it stand in the sauce till it is ready to be used. Flake the tuna fish with a fork, stir carefully into the hot sauce, arrange on the toast, and garnish with parsley. Serves six.

TUNA LOAF

2 cupfuls canned tuna fish
1 cupful cold cooked rice
¾ cupful milk
1 teaspoonful salt
½ teaspoonful paprika
Few grains nutmeg

About ¼ cupful dry crumbs
1 tablespoonful butter
1½ cupfuls medium-thick
   white sauce
¼ teaspoonful lemon-juice
2 eggs

Turn the tuna fish into a strainer and pour cold water quickly through it. Then mince it and mix it with the rice, one whole egg, and the white of the other; add the seasonings and milk. Turn into a well-greased loaf pan, cover with dry crumbs and dot over with butter. Bake at 400° F. for about one-half hour. Serve with well-seasoned white sauce, to which the other egg-yolk and the lemon-juice have been added just before serving. Serves six.

TUNA FISH AND CAULIFLOWER, SCALLOPED

1 cupful tuna fish
1 to 2 cupfuls cooked cauliflower
¼ cupful cracker-crumbs
1½ cupfuls milk
¼ teaspoonful pepper

2 tablespoonfuls butter, fat, or
   oil
2 tablespoonfuls grated cheese
2 tablespoonfuls flour
1 teaspoonful salt

Make a white sauce of the fat, flour, seasonings, and milk. Combine the tuna fish broken apart and the cauliflower. Add the white sauce, pour into a greased baking-dish, and sprinkle the crumbs and cheese over the top. Bake at 500° F. for twelve minutes. Serves six.

TUNA AND CRAB MEAT AU GRATIN

1 large can crab meat or
2 cans shrimps
1 small can tuna fish
4 tablespoonfuls butter, fat
   or oil

1 teaspoonful salt
¼ teaspoonful pepper
1½ cupfuls milk
¼ cupful Parmesan cheese
3 tablespoonfuls flour

Prepare a white sauce with the butter, flour, seasonings, and milk. Cover the bottom of a greased baking-dish with a thin layer of white sauce thus made, add a layer of crab meat, cover with white sauce, then a layer of tuna, and continue alternating layers until dish is filled. Cover with cheese, dot with fat, using the remaining two tablespoonfuls and bake at 500° F. twelve minutes or until cheese has browned nicely. Serves six.

TUNA FISH AND RICE LOAF

3 cupfuls boiling water
5 beef bouillon cubes
2 tablespoonfuls granulated
   gelatine
½ cupful cold water

1 large can tuna fish
½ cupful chopped celery
1½ cupfuls cold cooked rice
Grating of onion

Soak the gelatine in the cold water for five minutes; add the boiling water and the bouillon cubes; stir until thoroughly dissolved. Set aside to cool. Flake the tuna fish and add to the rice, celery and onion. When the first mixture has begun to set, add the tuna fish and rice mixture, pour into a cold, wet mold and put in a cold place to harden. More seasoning may be added if needed, but the cubes and the rice previously cooked in salted water will usually furnish sufficient seasonings. Serves six.

TUNA FISH WITH CAPER SAUCE

1 large can tuna fish	⅛ teaspoonful pepper
5 tablespoonfuls butter, fat or oil	3 tablespoonfuls capers
	1 hard-cooked egg
2 tablespoonfuls flour	1 tablespoonful minced
1½ cupfuls cold milk	parsley
1 teaspoonful salt	

Place the tuna fish and two tablespoonfuls of fat in the top of a double boiler. Heat thoroughly. Prepare a white sauce with the remaining fat, flour, and milk. Add the salt, pepper, capers, and egg chopped fine. Turn the heated tuna fish out on a platter and dust with the parsley. Pour the hot sauce over the fish and serve at once. If desired, any boiled, flaked fish such as cod, haddock, or halibut may be substituted for the tuna. Serves six.

SMOKED WHITEFISH

3 whitefish	¼ cupful butter, fat or oil
1 cupful stale bread-crumbs	⅛ teaspoonful cinnamon
⅓ cupful raisins	2 tablespoonfuls oil
⅛ teaspoonful nutmeg	

Steam the whitefish, which should weigh about one-half pound each, until tender, not more than five to ten minutes being needed. Remove the backbone from each and stuff with the following dressing: Mix the raisins, fat, nutmeg and cinnamon with the bread crumbs. Skewer the fish together or tie with strips of oiled cheese-cloth, place in a baking-pan, baste with the oil and bake at 450° F. for twenty minutes or until crisp and brown. Serves six.

IV. PREPARING LOBSTERS

1. **Boiling.** Lobsters should be alive up to the time of boiling. They should be plump and a mottled bluish green in color. Add one tablespoonful of salt to six quarts of water and have it boiling vigorously. Grasp the lobsters by the back, and plunge them head first into the boiling water, immersing the entire body. Be sure to have enough water to cover the lobsters completely. Boil the lobsters for five minutes; then allow them to cook slowly for twenty-five minutes. Remove, and lay them on their claws to drain.

As soon as the lobsters are cool enough to handle, remove the flesh thus: First, break off the two large claws and the four pairs of small claws. Then separate the tail from the body at the joint where they come together. Holding the tail in the left hand with the hard shell side next to the hand, cut a single slit through the center the entire length of the tail. Break away the flesh from the shell and remove it in one piece. Run a sharp knife lengthwise through the center of this tail piece of flesh and remove the intestinal tract which is embedded in it. Next, hold the body shell firmly in the left hand and with the first two fingers and the thumb of the right hand, draw out the body, leaving in the shell the stomach, which is called "the lady," and is not edible, and also some of the green part which is the liver. The sides of the body itself are covered with the lungs, which are discarded. Break the body in several places and pick out the flesh surrounding the bones in the bony part of the body. The coral substance which is the roe of the lobster is used as a garnish.

Break open the large claws, using a small hammer or nut cracker, and remove in whole pieces, if possible, the flesh they contain. The small claws are usually used for garnishing.

2. Broiled Live. To split the lobster cross the large claws and hold firmly with left hand. With sharp pointed knife held in right hand, begin at the mouth and make a deep incision and with a sharp cut draw the knife quickly through body to the tail, being careful not to cut the back shell. Open lobster, remove intestinal vein, liver, and stomach. Crack claw shells with a mallet. Some markets will prepare the lobster for broiling if this is designated when the order for the lobsters is given. After cleaning place the lobster in a greased wire broiler. Broil eight minutes on flesh side, turn and broil six minutes on shell side. Serve with melted butter. The liver may be mixed with bread crumbs and seasonings and put back in the lobster just before broiling.

LOBSTER AND MUSHROOMS EN CASSEROLE

1 pound mushrooms	1½ cupfuls milk
5½ tablespoonfuls butter fat, or oil	½ cupful bouillon stock
3 tablespoonfuls flour	2 cupfuls canned or fresh lobster meat
1 teaspoonful salt	½ cupful cream
⅛ teaspoonful paprika	⅓ cupful dried bread-crumbs
2 egg-yolks	

Wash, peel, and cut the mushrooms in pieces. Sauté them in four tablespoonfuls of fat. Add the flour, salt and paprika. Cook about five minutes. Then add gradually the milk and bouillon stock. Cook three minutes. Then add the lobster meat, cut in pieces, and the cream. Beat the egg-yolks well and add. Pour into a greased casserole dish, cover the top with the dried bread-crumbs and one and one-half tablespoonfuls of fat in bits. Bake at 500° F. for ten minutes. Serves six.

LOBSTER NEWBURG

2 pounds lobster	Slight grating nutmeg
¼ cupful butter	1 teaspoonful lemon juice
½ teaspoonful salt	½ cupful cream
Few grains cayenne	Yolks 2 eggs

Remove lobster meat from shell and cut in slices. Melt butter, add lobster, and cook three minutes. Add seasonings and lemon juice, cook one minute, then add cream and yolks of eggs slightly beaten. Stir until thickened. Serve with toast. Serves six.

LUNCHEON LOBSTER

2 cupfuls diced lobster meat	2 tablespoonfuls butter
½ cupful heavy cream	fat, or oil
4 hard-cooked egg-yolks	Red and white pepper
Patties, buttered toast, or timbale cases	

Sauté the lobster in enough fat to keep it from sticking; add the cream, cook over hot water for a few moments, and then add the egg-yolks blended with the butter. Season to taste with the pepper and serve in the cases. This can be pressed through a coarse sieve, diluted with equal parts of hot cream and milk beaten in, and served as a bisque. Serves six.

7. PREPARING CRABS

1. **Boiled Hard Shell Crab.** Crabs should be alive up to the time they are cooked. A lifeless crab should not be used. To prepare hard shell crabs for use, place in a kettle, cover with rapidly boiling water; add one tablespoonful of salt and one teaspoonful of mustard for each quart of water. Cook until the crabs are a deep red.

When cooked, remove the crabs from the liquid and wash thoroughly in cold water. Break off the claws close to the body, crack them with a hammer or a nut-cracker, and extract the meat. A nut pick or an oyster fork is admirable for this purpose. There is a slight projection forming the tail of the crab's shell, sometimes called the "apron"; insert the fingers between this projection and the body, and with a slight effort the shell may be removed. There will be found a soft spongy substance, commonly called "fingers," adhering to the body on both halves. This should be removed, as well as the spongy material and the fat found in the cavity between the halves. With a small fork pick out the meat from the sections, being careful to exclude any part of the structural frame of the crab.

2. **Soft Shell Crabs.** Soft shell crabs are dressed with safety while still alive. To clean a soft shell crab, lift up the pointed ends of the shell and remove the spongy substance, then take out the eyes and the

feelers. The crab should be rinsed with cold water, and it will then be ready for use.

Canned crab meat has made a permanent place for itself in the markets, and if fresh crabs or fresh crab meat are not available, the canned variety may be substituted.

Soft shell crabs are usually served fried. After they have been cleaned, sprinkle with pepper and salt, roll in cracker crumbs and egg, and fry in deep fat at 390° F. for from three to five minutes, according to the size of the crab. Serve on toast accompanied by tartare sauce.

CRAB CROQUETTES

1 pound shredded crabmeat	Cayenne pepper
1 teaspoonful grated onion	2 tablespoonfuls butter, fat
1 teaspoonful Worcestershire	or oil
sauce	3 tablespoonfuls flour
Juice ½ lemon	Beaten egg
Cracker-crumbs	3 tablespoonfuls chopped
1 cupful mayonnaise	cucumber

1 cupful milk

Combine the crabmeat, grated onion, Worcestershire sauce, lemon-juice, and cayenne pepper. Make a white sauce, using the fat, flour and milk as the basis. Season the white sauce to taste and add the crab mixture to this. Put in a pan to the depth of two inches and place in an ice-box to stiffen. When ready to be used, cut the mixture into two-inch squares, roll in cracker-crumbs and beaten egg and sauté until golden brown on all sides. Serve with mayonnaise to which the chopped cucumbers have been added. These make an excellent entrée. Makes about eight croquettes.

CRAB, JAPANESE

1 can crab meat	1 cupful milk
½ lemon	1 small can mushrooms
1 teaspoonful Worcestershire	1 teaspoonful grated onion
sauce	⅛ teaspoonful paprika
Few grains cayenne	2½ teaspoonfuls salt
1 tablespoonful butter, fat, or	1 tablespoonful flour
oil	3 hard-cooked eggs

Combine the canned crab meat or an equal quantity of fresh meat with the mushrooms. Add the lemon-juice, onion, Worcestershire sauce, salt, paprika, and cayenne. Make a white sauce from the fat, flour and milk, and add to it the crab mixture and the hard-cooked eggs which have been cut in small pieces. Cook until thoroughly heated and serve on toast. Or fill greased ramekins and sprinkle with grated cheese and cracker-crumbs and bake for twelve minutes at 500° F. Serves six.

CRABMEAT IN MUSHROOM SAUCE

2 cupfuls fresh or canned   2 cupfuls white sauce (P. 184)
   crabmeat   ½ pound mushrooms

Pick over the crabmeat and heat in the top of a double boiler. Meanwhile, wash, skin and dry the mushrooms. Slice and cook five minutes in the butter used for making white sauce, before continuing with the recipe. Pour the mushroom sauce over the crabmeat and serve. Serves six.

VI. OYSTER COOKERY

Oysters are nutritious and easily digested, especially when eaten raw. They should be cooked at a very low temperature as a high temperature makes the oyster tough and indigestible. To prepare oysters, run each one through the fingers, using extreme care to remove every particle of shell. Place the oysters in a wire strainer, pour cold water through them. Oysters may be served raw on the half shell or on oyster plates garnished with lemon.

OYSTER CHOWDER

1 slice pork   1 quart raw potatoes, sliced,
2 minced onions   or cut in dice
1½ teaspoonfuls salt   ¼ teaspoonful pepper
1 quart milk   1 tablespoonful butter, fat or
1 tablespoonful flour   oil
        1 pint oysters

Cut the pork in small dice and fry until a light brown in the kettle in which the chowder is to be made. Remove from the stove and add the potatoes, onions, salt, and pepper. Cover with boiling water and simmer until tender, about one-half hour. Be careful that the potato slices do not break. Then add the hot milk and thicken slightly with the fat and flour blended together. Then add the oysters and cook a very few minutes only, until the edges of the oysters begin to curl. Accompany this chowder with tiny home-made pickles or cold slaw and hot crackers. Serves six.

OYSTER CASSEROLE

4 cupfuls of celery   4 tablespoonfuls butter, fat or
4 tablespoonfuls flour   oil
¼ teaspoonful white pepper   1½ teaspoonfuls salt
1 cupful milk   ¼ teaspoonfuls paprika
1 No. 2 can oysters   ½ cupful celery stock
½ cupful oyster liquor   ¼ cupful buttered crumbs

Cook the diced celery in sufficient boiling water to cover until tender. Drain, reserving one-half cupful of the celery stock. Melt the fat in a saucepan, then add the flour, salt and pepper, and paprika. Add the milk, celery stock, and the oyster liquor drained from the oysters, gradually, while stirring constantly. Cook until smooth and creamy; then add the cooked celery. In a greased casserole, place a layer of creamed celery, then a layer of drained oyster. Repeat until the ingredients are used up, having the celery on top. Cover with the buttered crumbs and bake at 500° F. for fifteen minutes. Serves six.

OYSTER DELIGHT

2 cupfuls cooked; white chicken meat, diced
2 dozen large oysters
2 dozen fresh shrimps
1 small can crab meat
1 pint cream
1½ teaspoonfuls salt
6 fresh mushrooms, sliced
½ green pepper, chopped fine
½ pimiento, chopped fine
4 tablespoonfuls butter, fat, or oil
2 tablespoonfuls flour
¼ teaspoonful pepper
¼ teaspoonful paprika

Wash the shrimps and cook for twenty minutes in boiling water; shell, and remove the viscera. Wash the oysters, cook slowly in their own juice until the edges curl. Carefully clean the crab meat. Combine the sliced mushrooms and green pepper chopped, and sauté for three minutes in two tablespoonfuls of the fat. Meanwhile prepare a white sauce from the remaining fat, the flour, cream and seasonings, and combine with the diced chicken, oysters, shrimp, crab meat, mushrooms, green pepper, and pimiento, using a fork. Heat thoroughly and serve on small slices of toast. This quantity will serve ten persons.

OYSTERS IN GOLDEN SAUCE

1 pint oysters
2 tablespoonfuls butter
1 teaspoonful salt
Few grains cayenne
Pepper
¼ teaspoonful nutmeg
2 beaten egg yolks
¼ cupful top milk or thin cream
1 teaspoonful lemon juice

Simmer oysters, after being carefully picked over, in the butter until plump and the edges begin to curl. Add the salt, cayenne, pepper, nutmeg, beaten egg yolks, and milk. Just before serving, add lemon juice, stirring rapidly. Serve on toast or crackers, garnished with parsley. Serves six.

OYSTERS, PAN-ROASTED

1 pint small oysters, drained	⅛ teaspoonful cayenne pepper
2 tablespoonfuls butter, fat or oil	½ teaspoonful salt
	1 cupful milk
½ cupful tomato catsup	1½ tablespoonfuls flour

1 tablespoonful Worcestershire sauce

Melt the fat, add the catsup, Worcestershire, cayenne, and salt. Mix the flour with a little cold water, add to the milk, and let boil up; then combine with the catsup mixture, stirring it in slowly. Turn in the oysters, let stand until the edges curl, and serve on very hot toast. Serves six.

CREAM OF OYSTER SOUP

1 pint oysters	1 tablespoonful flour
½ cupful water	1 tablespoonful butter, fat, or oil
1 pint milk	
2 teaspoonfuls salt	1 pint diced celery

¼ teaspoonful pepper

Wash oysters, and put on to cook with the water. Watch carefully, and when the edges curl, remove from stove and drain. Strain the broth through a fine strainer, add the milk, hot but not boiling, and the salt and pepper. Thicken with the flour and fat blended together. Add the oysters and the celery which has been stewed until tender, let boil up and serve. The thickening may be omitted, if preferred, but the creamy consistency is most delicious. If a thinner stew is desired, twice the quantity of milk may be used. In this case, double the amount of thickening also. Serves six.

PIGS IN BLANKETS

Thin bacon slices	Parsley
Oysters	Toast

Cut thin slices of bacon in halves. Dry the desired number of oysters thoroughly and wrap each one with a piece of bacon, fastening the ends together with a wooden tooth-pick. Lay on a towel till just before sautéing to thoroughly dry them. Brown very quickly in a hot frying pan and put two "pigs" on each square of hot toast. There will be a delicious thin gravy in the frying pan. Pour a little on each piece of toast. Garnish with parsley and serve immediately. Serves six.

SCALLOPED OYSTERS

1 pint oysters	1 cupful cracker crumbs
½ cupful oyster liquor	½ cupful melted butter
2 tablespoonfuls milk or cream	Salt
½ cupful white bread crumbs	Pepper

Mix bread and cracker crumbs and stir in butter. Put a thin layer in the bottom of a greased baking dish cover with oysters and sprinkle with salt and pepper. Add half oyster liquor and cream. Repeat and cover top with remaining crumbs. Bake thirty minutes at 400° F. Serves six.

VII. CLAMS

Clams are served raw, or are cooked very much like oysters.

STEAMED CLAMS

Clams for steaming should be bought in the shell and always be alive. Wash the clams with a brush, changing the water several times. Put in a large kettle and add one-half cupful boiling water to four quarts of clams; cover closely and steam until shells partially open. Serve with individual dishes of melted butter. The broth should be strained through a cheese cloth and served hot in cups.

CLAM CHOWDER

See Chowders (Page 127)

CLAM FRITTERS

1 dozen hard clams	½ teaspoonful baking-powder
1 egg	½ tablespoonful minced
1 cupful bread flour	parsley
½ cupful clam juice or milk	¼ teaspoonful salt
⅛ teaspoonful pepper	

Mix and sift the flour, baking powder, salt, and pepper together. Add the clam juice if it is not too salty, otherwise use milk, and the egg well-beaten. Mix together well and stir in the clams which have been washed and cut in small pieces, and the parsley. Drop by tablespoonfuls into deep fat heated to 360° F. Fry until a golden brown on all sides. Drain on crumpled paper. This recipe will make eight to ten small fritters.

DEVILED CLAMS IN RAMEKINS

25 fresh or canned clams	½ teaspoonful salt
2 cupfuls milk	1 minced green pepper
4 tablespoonfuls fat	¼ teaspoonful celery seed
4 tablespoonfuls flour	½ pound sliced, fresh mush-
1 teaspoonful finely chopped	rooms
onion	¾ cupful dry bread crumbs

If the clams are fresh, clean them and separate the hard parts, chopping them rather coarsely. Melt three tablespoonfuls of fat, add the minced green pepper, finely chopped onion, and hard portions of the clams and cook slowly for ten minutes. Then add the mushrooms and cook three minutes longer. Add slowly the salt, celery seed, and flour and cook until smooth. Gradually add the milk while stirring constantly, and when smooth, add the soft parts of the clams, or whole clams, if canned. When thickened, pour into well-greased ramekins and cover with the bread crumbs which have been mixed with one tablespoonful of melted butter. Brown in a 500° F. oven or under the broiler heat. This recipe serves six to eight, depending upon the size of the ramekins.

FRIED CLAMS

Clean the clams, being sure that all bits of shell are removed. Dip each clam in beaten egg, then in finely sifted bread crumbs. Fry in deep fat at 390° F. for one minute. Drain on soft paper and serve at once.

VIII. SCALLOPS

SCALLOPS AND MUSHROOMS

1 pint scallops	2 egg-yolks
½ pound mushrooms, sliced	1 teaspoonful salt
1 cupful thin cream	¼ teaspoonful nutmeg
1 teaspoonful lemon-juice	Pinch cayenne
4 tablespoonfuls butter, fat, or	2 tablespoonfuls flour
oil	Buttered toast

Cut the scallops into medium sized pieces and simmer in their own liquor until they are tender; then drain. Melt two tablespoonfuls of the fat and sauté the mushrooms in it until light brown. Make a white sauce with two tablespoonfuls butter, flour, seasonings and cream. Combine the scallops and the mushrooms; add the egg-yolks well beaten and the lemon juice. Add this mixture to the white sauce and heat thoroughly. Serve on toast. Serves six.

BAKED SCALLOPS

1 quart scallops	2 eggs
¼ pound fat bacon	Cracker crumbs
2 tablespoonfuls vinegar	

Wash the scallops in salt water and drain. Pour boiling water over them, add the vinegar, let stand for two minutes, and then drain in a colander. Wipe dry. Season fine cracker crumbs. Roll the scallops in the crumbs, then dip them in the eggs beaten slightly, and then again in crumbs. Lay the scallops close together in a shallow pan. Cut the sliced bacon in narrow strips and scatter over the scallops. Bake about twelve minutes in a 450° F. oven, or under the broiler. Serves six.

SCALLOPS AND SWEETBREADS, CREAMED

1 pint medium sized scallops	1 teaspoonful salt
1 pair sweetbreads	4 good-sized mushrooms,
4 tablespoonfuls butter, fat, or	sliced
oil	Buttered toast
3 tablespoonfuls flour	1 cupful dried bread-crumbs
2 cupfuls milk	¼ teaspoonful paprika

Wash the scallops in very cold water. Cover with cold water, bring to a boil, and simmer very gently for fifteen minutes, but do not allow them to shrink or become tough. Prepare and cook the sweetbreads (P. 60.) Cut the sweetbreads into cubes, and if the scallops are very large cut them in halves or in quarters. Melt two tablespoonfuls of the fat and sauté the sliced mushrooms until golden brown. Combine with the scallops and sweetbreads. Make a white sauce with remaining ingredients, except bread-crumbs, then add the scallops, sweetbreads and mushrooms. Put the mixture into a greased casserole, sprinkle with the bread-crumbs, and bake for ten minutes in a 450° F. oven. Serve on toast. Serves six to eight.

IX. SHRIMP

SHRIMPS, CREAMED WITH CELERY

1 can shrimps	3 tablespoonfuls flour
½ cupful diced celery	3 tablespoonfuls butter. fat, or
1½ cupfuls milk	oil
½ cupful celery liquor	½ teaspoonful salt
⅛ teaspoonful pepper	

Cook the celery until tender in water to cover, drain the shrimps, and freshen in cold water. Make a white sauce of the fat, flour, seasonings, milk, and celery liquor. Add the celery-cubes and shrimps and serve on buttered toast with a garnish of celery-hearts. This makes four large or six small portions.

SHRIMPS AND OLIVES IN ASPIC

¼ cupful cold water
1½ tablespoonfuls granulated
  gelatine

½ cupful stuffed olives
1 pint highly seasoned clear
  consommé or chicken broth

2 cupfuls shrimps

Prepare the shrimps, either canned or fresh-cooked, removing the viscera and cutting into large pieces. Soften the gelatine in the cold water. Prepare the consommé or chicken broth and bring to the boiling point. Add the softened gelatine and stir until dissolved. Strain through a cloth and chill almost to the point of congealing. Wet a mold and arrange the jellied consommé in layers with the shrimp and sliced stuffed olives. Have a layer of jellied consommé on top. Chill, unmold, and garnish with water-cress. Serves six.

SHRIMPS, CONCORDIA CREAMED

2 hard-cooked eggs
1 can shrimps
Buttered toast

2 cupfuls white sauce
⅛ teaspoonful paprika
⅛ teaspoonful mace

Shell the hard-cooked eggs. Wash the canned shrimps, remove the viscera and chop them rather coarsely. Meanwhile prepare the white sauce, seasoning it highly, adding the paprika and mace. To the white sauce add the hard-cooked eggs sliced thinly and the chopped shrimps. Combine and serve on rounds of buttered toast. Serves six.

SHRIMP NEWBURG

Prepare as for lobster Newburg (P. 94) substituting shrimp for lobsters.

SHRIMP À LA KING

Prepare as for Chicken à la King (P. 72), substituting the shrimp for chicken.

X. FISH COCKTAILS

Shrimps, scallops, and other fish are cooked before serving in a cocktail. Oysters and clams are served raw. Large fish should be flaked and all thoroughly chilled. Arrange in cocktail glasses and pour over it a cocktail sauce.

COCKTAIL SAUCE

1 teaspoonful salt
¼ teaspoonful chopped parsley
1 teaspoonful chopped chives
1 teaspoonful melted butter
2 tablespoonfuls vinegar

¼ teaspoonful tabasco sauce
1 teaspoonful Worcestershire
  sauce
1 teaspoonful horseradish
½ cupful catsup

Mix well together and chill thoroughly.

Vegetables

I. FOOD VALUE

Practically all vegetables, particularly the non-starchy, are most valuable not only for the bulk they supply, but also for the mineral salts, vitamins and water so necessary in our diet.

II. GENERAL PREPARATION OF VEGETABLES

Asparagus: Cut off lower part of stalks as far down as they will snap. Remove all scales and wash. **Beans** (string): Remove strings, wash and snap or cut into one-inch pieces with scissors. **Beans** (lima): Shell and wash. **Beets:** Scrub thoroughly, being careful not to break the skin. Cut off the tops two inches above the roots. **Brussels Sprouts:** Pick over carefully, removing all wilted leaves. Wash in cold water and then let stand in salted water (1 teaspoonful to 1 quart) for thirty minutes to draw out insects. **Cabbage:** Pick off all wilted leaves. Cut in halves or quarters, remove the core and shred if desired. Let stand in cold salted water (1 teaspoonful to 1 quart) for thirty minutes to draw out insects. **Carrots** (young): Cut off tops and wash. If served whole, scrape skin off after cooking. If served sliced or diced, scrape skin before cooking. **Carrots** (old): Cut off tops if there are any. Wash and then scrape or thinly peel. **Cauliflower:** Cut off all leaves and stalk. Soak head down in cold, salted water (1 teaspoonful to 1 quart) for at least thirty minutes to remove all insects. **Celery:** Cut off roots and leaves. Scrub each stalk. Stand in cold water or wrap in cheesecloth wrung from cold water. Keep in refrigerator. **Corn:** Remove the husks, break off stem end and remove all silk.

103

Onions: Cut off stem end. Peel off all the outer skin, while holding the onion under water, to avoid eye irritation from the onion juice. **Peas:** Remove peas from pod. Wash thoroughly. Let over-matured peas stand in cold water for one-half hour before cooking. **Parsnips:** Cut off all leaves and stem. Scrub well. Scrape thoroughly. If young, cook whole, but if necessary cut in halves and quarters lengthwise. **Potatoes (white):** Scrub. For steaming or boiling, pare potatoes thinly, taking out all the eyes. If the potatoes are new, scrape off the skin or cook and then peel off the skin. For baking, scrub well, but do not remove the skins. **Potatoes (sweet):** Scrub and remove all bruised spots. Steam, boil or bake with skins on. **Spinach and All Greens:** Remove roots and carefully pick over, discarding wilted leaves. Wash in several waters to free it from all sand. In doing this, lift the spinach from one pan of water into another and repeat until it is clean. Merely pouring off the water each time does not remove the sand. **Squash (summer):** Choose young squash, so tender that a sharp edge pierces the skin easily. Wash and cut off stem end. If young and tender, cut in pieces, and remove the seeds. If the skin is tough, peel, remove the seeds and cut into pieces. **Squash (winter):** Wash, cut in pieces, remove the seeds and stringy portion and pare. **Tomatoes:** Wipe and cover with boiling water. Let stand one minute, and then skin, or hold the tomatoes over the heat by piercing with a fork, and when the skin bursts, remove and peel it off. **Turnips:** Scrub and slice crosswise in ¼-inch slices. Pare each slice.

III.   GENERAL DIRECTIONS FOR COOKING VEGETABLES

1. **Steaming.** a. Unless care is taken the valuable mineral constituents, as well as much soluble protein and sugar are lost in the cooking water. Particularly is this true of the boiling methods. For this reason, steaming is far better than boiling.

b. Simple, compact and inexpensive steamers can be purchased in either enamel ware or aluminum ware.

c. In using a steamer, place boiling water in the bottom and arrange the vegetables in the inset. Steam, following the time table for Boiling and Steaming on P. 105, and sprinkle with salt the last five minutes.

2. **Boiling.** a. To conserve the valuable constituents cook vegetables in only enough boiling water to cover the bottom of the kettle. Follow the time table for Boiling and Steaming on P. 105.

b. If you must boil the vegetables in more water, be sure that the water is boiling when poured over the vegetables. Save this cooking water and use it for cream soups, creamed vegetables, gravies and the like.

c. Sprinkle with salt last five minutes.

TIME TABLE FOR COOKING VEGETABLES

	Boil	Steam
Asparagus	15 to 30 min.	15 to 30 min.
Beans, string (young)	30 to 45 min.	30 to 45 min.
Beans, string (old)	60 to 90 min.	60 to 90 min.
Beets (young)	35 to 60 min.	35 to 60 min.
Beets (old)	2 to 4 hours	2 to 4 hours
Brussels Sprouts	15 to 30 min.	15 to 30 min.
Cabbage	13 to 20 min.	20 to 30 min.
Carrots	20 to 40 min.	20 to 40 min.
Cauliflower	20 min.	20 min.
Celery	20 to 30 min.	20 to 30 min.
Dandelion Greens	20 to 35 min.	20 to 35 min.
Green Corn	7 to 12 min.	7 to 12 min.
Onions	30 to 45 min.	30 to 45 min.
Peas	17 to 25 min.	17 to 25 min.
Potatoes (white)	35 to 45 min.	35 to 45 min.
Potatoes (sweet)	30 to 35 min.	30 to 35 min.
Spinach	30 to 35 min.	30 to 35 min.
Squash (summer)	15 to 40 min.	15 to 40 min.
Squash (winter)	50 to 60 min.	50 to 60 min.
Tomatoes	15 to 20 min.	15 to 20 min.
Turnips	35 to 45 min.	35 to 45 min.

3. For Steam Pressure Cooking see P. 219; Electric Fireless Cooking, P. 216; Baking, P. 107.

IV. GENERAL DIRECTIONS FOR SERVING VEGETABLES

1. Drain all cooked vegetables, add necessary seasonings, butter or sauces and serve *at once*. For sauces see chart P. 184: medium white sauce, cheese, mock hollandaise, drawn butter and vegetable sauce.

2. In the case of beets, drain and cover with cold water. Slip off the skins, slice and serve hot or cold.

V. SAUTÉD VEGETABLES

1. Sautéing is cooking any food in a frying-pan in a small amount of hot fat, such as bacon fat. Bananas, onions, tomatoes, green peppers, mushrooms and eggplant are cut in slices or other suitable pieces, first peeling all but the tomatoes, and green peppers. Then they are dredged with seasoned flour, browned slowly on one side in the hot fat, then turned and browned on the other side. Use butter for the mushrooms and cook gently to prevent burning. Add to them a little boiling water or cream and reheat before serving. Cooked and sliced white and sweet potatoes, as well as parsnips, are sautéd as above.

SAUTÉD CELERY

1 bunch celery	Butter
Salt	Pepper

Wash and dice the celery. Season with salt and pepper, and sauté in melted butter until tender. Allow one tablespoonful of butter for each cupful of diced celery. Serves six.

SAUTÉD CORN

12 ears corn	About ½ cupful hot water
½ teaspoonful salt	Speck pepper
2 tablespoonfuls bacon fat	

Cut off the tops of the kernels of corn, then using the back of a paring-knife scrape out the rest of the pulp, leaving the husks on the cobs. Add the salt, pepper and hot water, the amount of water depending upon the amount of milk in the corn. Melt the bacon fat in a frying-pan and when hot, add the corn mixture. Cover, simmer five minutes, then uncover and continue cooking about five minutes longer or until the corn is tender. Serves six to eight.

VI. SCALLOPED VEGETABLES—Almost any cooked vegetable may be scalloped.

1. Prepare a medium thick white or cheese sauce (see Schedule for Sauces, P. 184).

2. Arrange alternate layers of cooked vegetables and sauce in a greased baking-dish or casserole leaving sauce as the top layer.

3. Sprinkle with buttered crumbs and brown in a hot oven of 450° F.

VII. VEGETABLE SOUFFLES—(See Chart, P. 188).

VIII. VEGETABLE SOUPS

1. Cream Vegetable Soups (See Chart for Cream Soups, P. 186).

2. Vegetable Soups, Beef Stock Basis (See Meat Stocks, P. 47).

3. Vegetable Soups, Bouillon Cubes Basis (See Meat Stocks, P. 47).

VEGETABLE SOUP WITHOUT MEAT

⅔ cupful diced carrot	2 quarts water
⅔ cupful diced turnip	5 tablespoonfuls fat
¾ cupful celery	3 tablespoonfuls chopped parsley
1½ cupful diced potato	Salt
1 small onion, sliced	Pepper

Prepare the diced and sliced vegetables, cooking in the melted fat for five minutes, while stirring constantly.   Add the cold water and simmer gently for an hour or until the vegetables are tender.   Season with salt and pepper and add the chopped parsley.   Serves six to eight.

IX. BAKED VEGETABLES

Vegetables, prepared as usual, may be baked in the oven very satisfactorily.   Place them in a covered dish with a small amount of water and cook at the same time you are baking or roasting.

TIME TABLE FOR BAKING VEGETABLES

Vegetable	Temperature	Time
Lima Beans	450° F.	45 min.
Lima Beans	250° F.	75 min.
Green String-Beans	450° F.	75 min.
Beets (dry in skins)	450° F.	70 min.
Brussels Sprouts	450° F.	60 min.
Cabbage (covered with water)	450° F.	45 min.
Carrots	450° F.	30 min.
Cauliflower (covered with water)	450° F.	45 min.
Celery	450° F.	60 min.
Corn (cut from cob)	450° F.	30 min.
Mushrooms	400° F.	45 min.
Onions	400° F.	40 min.
Parsnips (sliced)	450° F.	30 min.
Green Peas	450° F.	45 min.
Green Peas	250° F.	65 min.
Stuffed Peppers	400° F.	35 min.
Small Potatoes (in skin)	500° F.	25 min.
Medium Potatoes	500° F.	40 min.
Large Potatoes	500° F.	60 min.
Squash (3-inch squares)	450° F.	60 min.
Stuffed Tomatoes	400° F.	35 min.
Whole Turnips (dry)	450° F.	60 min.
Cut Turnips	450° F.	35 min.
Casserole of Vegetables	350° F.	120 min.

Note—Vegetables were baked with an entire meal and the temperature based on that best suited for a roast.

X. POTATOES AND POTATO DISHES

1. Baked Potatoes. a. Select potatoes of uniform size, free of blemishes.   Wash and scrub them thoroughly.

b. If a crisp skin is desired, rub the surface over lightly with any unsalted fat or cooking oil before baking.

c. Bake small white potatoes in a very hot oven of 500° F. for 25 minutes, medium potatoes 40 minutes, large white potatoes 60 minutes, medium sweet potatoes 35 minutes.

d. When baked, remove from oven at once, slit the skin on top at right angles one inch, to let the steam escape.

e. Hold in a clean towel and with the fingers push the potato gently from the bottom softening it until it breaks snowy white and fluffy through the cuts in the top.

f. Place a piece of butter on top, sprinkle with paprika or finely chopped parsley and serve at once.

2. Boiled Potatoes. a. Wash and pare potatoes thinly, removing all eyes or leave in their jackets.

b. Cover with boiling water and boil gently until tender when pierced with a fine skewer or a fork.

c. Drain off the water at once, uncover the pot, dredge potatoes with a little salt, and shake the pot over the heat to dry them and make them mealy. Let the pot stand five minutes in a warm place. Serve potatoes at once in a hot dish.

CREAMED POTATOES
(See IV., P. 105)

CREAMED POTATOES, WITH EGGS

4 cold, cooked potatoes	6 hard cooked eggs
Salt	Pepper
2 cupfuls thin white sauce	Buttered cracker-crumbs

(See Schedule for Sauces on Page 184)

Cut the potatoes and eggs in one-quarter inch slices. Put layer of potatoes in greased baking dish. Sprinkle with salt and pepper, and cover with a layer of eggs. Repeat and pour over white sauce. Sprinkle with buttered cracker-crumbs and brown in a hot oven of 450° F. Serves six to eight.

FRENCH FRIED POTATOES

Wash, pare and cut potatoes in lengthwise strips one-quarter inch thick and one-quarter inch wide. Place in cold water while heating the fat to 395° F. Dry the potatoes thoroughly between clean towels and fry, a few at a time, for about 4½ minutes or until golden brown, crisp and well cooked.

MASHED POTATOES

5 hot cooked or baked potatoes   6 tablespoonfuls milk
1 teaspoonful salt   3 tablespoonfuls butter
Few grains pepper

Mash or rice the potatoes until free from lumps.   Add the salt, milk, butter and pepper.   Beat with a fork until light and creamy.   Reheat and serve in a hot dish.   Serves six.

PAN ROASTED POTATOES

Peel the potatoes, boil or steam 10 minutes.   Then put around the meat in roasting pan.   Bake 40 to 50 minutes, turning frequently, basting occasionally with the fat in the roasting pan

POTATO CAKES

To cold or hot well-seasoned mashed potatoes add sufficient beaten egg to make of proper consistency to form into cakes.   Roll cakes in flour and sauté a golden brown.   Or pack potato in small greased pans as soon as it comes from the table and set aside until ready for use. Turn from pan on to meat board.

POTATO CROQUETTES

(See Deep Fat Frying, P. 133)

POTATO AND ONION PIE

Pare and cut into thin slices six large potatoes and three onions. Butter a casserole and arrange a layer of the potatoes in it.   Dot with butter, cover with the sliced onions, and season highly.   Arrange a second layer of the potatoes in the dish, and continue in this manner until the dish is full, making the top layer of the onions.   Sprinkle with grated cheese, add one-half cupful of hot water, and cover.   Bake for two hours in a 350° F. oven.   If the pie seems too dry, add a very little more hot water to it during the baking process.   Remove the cover half an hour before taking it from the oven, permitting it to brown nicely.   Serves six.

RICED POTATOES

Press hot cooked potatoes through a potato ricer into a hot serving dish.

SAUTÉD POTATOES

(See P. 105)

SAVORY POTATO BALLS

6 medium sized potatoes	⅛ teaspoonful paprika
1½ teaspoonfuls salt	1 teaspoonful finely minced
4 teaspoonfuls butter	green pepper
1 egg	¼ teaspoonful celery salt
¼ cupful cheese	

Cook the potatoes until tender. Drain, dice and add the salt, butter, celery salt, paprika, green pepper and beaten egg. Beat well, make into balls the size of croquettes. Arrange in greased pans, brush with beaten egg, sprinkle with cheese and bake in a hot oven of 450° F. until brown. Serves six.

SCALLOPED POTATOES

4 medium potatoes	1½ cupfuls thin white sauce
Salt	(See schedule for sauces on
Pepper	P. 184)
2 tablespoonfuls butter	

Wash, pare and slice the potatoes thin. Cover with cold water and let stand three-quarters of an hour. Meanwhile prepare the thin white sauce. Drain the potatoes, and arrange in a greased baking dish, sprinkling each layer with salt, pepper and butter. Cover with the white sauce and bake at 350° F. for forty minutes. By thickening the milk in scalloped potatoes, the curdled appearance is avoided. Serves six.

XI. DRIED VEGETABLES

1. Dried Beans

BAKED BEANS WITH CORN

1 pint kidney beans	2 teaspoonfuls salt
1 teaspoonful baking soda	¼ teaspoonful pepper
¼ pound bacon	1 cupful boiling water
2 tablespoonfuls molasses	2 cupfuls fresh corn

Pick over the kidney beans, wash, cover with cold water, and soak overnight. Drain, add soda, cover with cold water, and simmer until tender. Drain and blanch with cold water. Cut bacon into cubes and add to the beans together with molasses, salt, pepper, and boiling water. Put in the bean-pot and cover with boiling water. Bake for six hours in a slow oven of 350° F., adding boiling water as needed. One hour before removing the beans from the oven add corn seasoned to taste. If canned corn is used, season and add one-half hour before serving. Serves six to eight.

BAKED KIDNEY BEANS, SAUSAGE STYLE

1 pint of kidney beans	½ teaspoonful mustard
½ teaspoonful baking soda	2 teaspoonfuls salt
1 onion minced fine	¼ teaspoonful pepper
½ pound sausages	1 cupful of hot water

Pick over the kidney beans, wash carefully, and soak in plenty of cold water overnight. In the morning, drain in a colander, cover with cold water, add baking soda and onion and parboil until tender. Drain again and blanch with cold water. Place a two-inch layer of beans in the bottom of the bean-pot. Cut sausages into one-inch pieces and arrange a layer of these over the beans. Repeat the layers until all are used up, having a layer of sausage on top. Mix together mustard, salt, pepper and hot water. Pour over the beans and add more boiling water, enough to cover. Cover the bean-pot and bake in the oven at 350° F. for six hours, uncovering the last half-hour. Add water as needed. This dish is particularly good served with a fresh tomato salad. If tomatoes are not in season, tomato jelly salad, pickled beets, or beet salad may be served. Serves six to eight.

BEANS WITH TOMATO SAUCE

1 pint beans	3 tablespoonfuls molasses
¼ pound fat salt pork	¼ teaspoonful pepper
2 teaspoonfuls salt	1 cupful boiling water
1 cupful tomato sauce	

Prepare the beans in the usual manner, soaking, parboiling, and blanching them. Pour boiling water over fat salt pork and scrape the rind until white. Then cut into narrow strips just through the rind. Put the beans in the bean-pot and bury the pork in them so that only the rind is exposed. Mix together salt, molasses, pepper and boiling water. Add sufficient more boiling water to cover the beans, and bake as previously directed, for six hours, adding boiling water as needed. One hour before serving add one cupful of tomato sauce. (See P. 184.) If you prefer the flavor of unstrained tomatoes in baked beans, soak, parboil and blanch the beans as above. Place two small onions in the bottom of the bean-pot, then add the beans, salt pork, and seasonings. After the beans have baked three hours at 350° F. add one and one-half cupfuls of canned tomatoes, well seasoned. Continue baking three hours longer, uncovering the pot the last half-hour.

BOSTON BAKED BEANS

2 cupfuls pea beans
¼ pound mixed salt pork
2 teaspoonfuls salt
½ teaspoonful baking-soda

¼ teaspoonful mustard
¼ cupful molasses
⅛ teaspoonful pepper
Boiling water

Pick over the beans carefully, wash, and soak in plenty of cold water overnight. In the morning, drain in a colander, cover with fresh cold water, add the baking soda, and parboil until tender; when easily pierced with a fork, the beans are sufficiently cooked. Drain again in colander and blanch with cold water. Pour boiling water over the pork and scrape the rind until white; then cut the rind in narrow strips. Put the beans in a beanpot. Bury the pork in these, so that only the rind is exposed. Put in a measuring cup the salt, mustard, pepper, and molasses and fill with boiling water. Stir and mix well, then pour over the beans; add sufficient boiling water to cover. Bake for six to seven hours in a slow oven of 350° F., removing the cover during the last hour to allow the pork to become crisp. Serves six to eight.

CREAMED LIMA BEANS

1 cupful dried beans
¾ cupful cream

Salt
Pepper

Soak dried beans overnight in cold water to cover. Drain, and cook in boiling salted water until soft. Drain, add cream and season with salt and pepper. Heat well and serve. Serves six.

KIDNEY BEAN CASSEROLE

1 pint of kidney beans
2 pared carrots
2 peeled onions
1 cupful canned tomatoes
2 tablespoonfuls butter

1½ teaspoonfuls salt
⅛ teaspoonful pepper
1 tablespoonful sugar
1 cupful diced left-over beef
  or lamb

Combine kidney beans soaked and cooked in salted water until tender, with carrots finely chopped and onions thinly sliced. Heat with tomatoes for about ten minutes and season with salt, and pepper, and sugar. Lay in the bottom of a greased casserole the left-over beef or lamb, sprinkle it with salt and pepper, and pour over it the combined vegetables. Dot with butter, cover, and cook at 400° F. until he vegetables are tender. Serves six to eight.

LIMA BEANS EN CASSEROLE

1½ cupfuls dried lima beans   2 medium-sized onions
¼ pound sliced bacon   Salt
1 cupful milk   Pepper
                    1 green pepper

Soak the beans overnight in water to cover. In the morning boil until soft and drain. Sear the bacon in a hot frying-pan; remove from pan and add the onions and seeded green pepper sliced. Cook these until soft. In a greased casserole place a layer of beans sprinkled with onions, small pieces of the bacon, and sparingly with salt and pepper; repeat until all is used. Over this pour the milk and bake at 400° F. from fifteen minutes to one-half hour. Serves six to eight.

SOY-BEAN LOAF WITH TOMATO SAUCE

½ pound soy beans   ¼ teaspoonful pepper
3 teaspoonfuls salt   2 cupfuls dry bread-crumbs
1 small onion, chopped fine   2 eggs, well beaten
2 cupfuls milk   Tomato sauce

Pick over and wash beans and soak them overnight. Drain and cook with the salt until tender. When done, drain, mash, and cool. Add all the other ingredients. Bake in a well-greased loaf pan for half an hour in a moderate oven of 400° F. Serve with plenty of well seasoned tomato sauce. (See P. 184.)

SOY-BEAN SOUP

1 cupful soy beans   1 half-inch cube salt pork or
1 onion   bacon
2 small carrots   1 cupful canned tomatoes
1 stalk celery   Salt
                    Pepper

Pick over and wash beans and soak overnight; drain and cook until soft (about three hours) in water with the pork, cut in small pieces. Mash and force them through a sieve together with the tomatoes. Add the carrots cut in shreds and the celery cut fine. Add one quart of water and cook until the vegetables are soft. Add salt and pepper to taste. If too thick add more water. Serves six.

SPAGHETTI AND KIDNEY BEANS

1 cupful spaghetti	3 tablespoonfuls flour
2 cupfuls dried kidney beans	2 teaspoonfuls salt
3 tablespoonfuls fat	¼ teaspoonful pepper
2 cupfuls stewed tomatoes	

Wash and soak the beans overnight, add one teaspoonful of salt, and cook them until tender. Break the spaghetti into pieces about an inch long and cook in boiling, salted water until soft. Drain. Make a tomato sauce. Melt the fat, add the flour, and cook till bubbling. Add the tomatoes and cook all until thickened. Mix together the spaghetti and beans, add seasonings, and sauce, and serve hot. Serves six to eight.

2. **Dried Lentils**

LENTILS AND RICE

1 cupful lentils	1 blade mace
1 cupful rice	1 teaspoonful salt
1 can tomatoes—No. 3	⅛ teaspoonful pepper
1 large onion	½ teaspoonful curry-powder
1 bay-leaf	2 tablespoonfuls fat

Wash lentils, cover with cold water, and soak overnight. Drain, cover with fresh boiling water, and cook slowly one hour. While lentils are cooking, boil in salted water, drain and dry the rice. While lentils and rice are boiling add to the tomatoes, the onion chopped fine, the bay-leaf and the mace; cook until reduced one-half; strain. Mix cooked lentils and rice; turn into a heated serving dish. Season the tomato with the salt, pepper, and curry-powder; stir in quickly the fat; pour over the lentils and rice and serve. Serves six.

3. **Dried Peas**

HOPPING JOHN

2 cupfuls dried whole peas	Ham bone and fat
1 cupful rice	Salt and pepper

Wash and soak peas overnight. In the morning drain and cover well with water. Add a ham bone or the roots of a boiled smoked tongue, or boil the peas in the water in which corned beef, smoked tongue, or ham has been cooked. Add also a few pieces of fat from any of these meats if at hand. Cook until the peas are nearly tender; take special care that they do not burn. When the peas are nearly tender, add the rice. Cook rapidly for twenty minutes, then set back to steam for one-half hour. Season, if needed, with salt and pepper. This makes a large quantity. Serves eight to ten.

PEA BISQUE

1 pint of peas	Ham bone
2 sliced onions	1 pint milk
1 chopped pepper	1 tablespoonful flour
1 bay-leaf	1 tablespoonful fat

The dried green peas, split peas, or the lima bean or marrow pea may each be employed in making this delicious soup.   Lentils also are very nice prepared this way.   Soak the peas overnight, and in the morning add sufficient water to make four quarts.   Place over the fire with two sliced onions, one chopped pepper, a bay leaf, and a ham-bone or any pieces of left-over meat that may be at hand, or the bisque may be made without meat or meat flavoring of any kind.   Cook the vegetable till very soft, which will require about three hours.   Mash the peas well, and press through a sieve, then return to the fire and season to taste. Add the milk and continue cooking for ten minutes.   Then blend together the flour and fat and add to the hot soup, stirring constantly to prevent it from becoming lumpy.   Serve hot with croûtons of bread, or pour the soup over hard Boston crackers which have been split, buttered, and placed in the bottom of the tureen.   Serves six.

SPLIT PEA SOUP

1 cupful dried split peas	4 tablespoonfuls fat
2 quarts cold water	3 tablespoonfuls flour
2 inch cube fat salt pork	1¼ teaspoonfuls salt
½ small onion	⅛ teaspoonful pepper
	1 pint milk

Pick over the peas, cover with cold water and let soak overnight. Drain, add the cold water indicated above, and the pork and onion. Simmer three and one-half or four hours or until soft.   Then press through a sieve or potato ricer.   Meanwhile in another saucepan, melt the fat, add the flour and stir until smooth.   Then add the pea pulp, salt, pepper and milk.   If too thick, add more milk.   Serves six.

XII. USING CANNED VEGETABLES

1. Canned vegetables and fruits suggest many delightful possibilities in cookery.

2. Never use a can which shows a bulge at top or bottom.   Wash the top of the can carefully before using the can opener.

3. If in opening a can, there is an outrush of air, or if liquid spouts out, the material in the can is very apt to be spoiled.

4. If on the other hand, the air is sucked in, it is a good sign, indicating that the vacuum has not been destroyed.

5. In removing from can, note color and texture and make sure there is no undesirable odor. It is well to boil all canned vegetables for five minutes before using or tasting them. Then, if you are going to make salad with them, cool before using.

6. Canned goods have a better flavor if they are opened and allowed to stand half an hour or so before using.

XIII.   SPECIAL VEGETABLE DISHES

BEETS WITH CREAM SAUCE

5 or 6 medium-sized beets	¼ teaspoonful salt
2 tablespoonfuls vinegar	⅛ teaspoonful pepper
2 tablespoonfuls butter, fat, or oil	1 cupful beet water
3 tablespoonfuls flour	½ cupful cream
1 teaspoonful sugar	2 tablespoonfuls chopped cress or parsley

Wash the beets thoroughly, being careful not to break the skin. Cook them in boiling, salted water until tender, and drain, saving the water. Rub off the skins and cut the beets in slices. Pour over them the vinegar. Make a sauce in the following manner: Melt the butter, add the flour, sugar, salt and pepper. Stir until well blended, then add the beet water. Cook until it thickens. Then stir in one-half cupful of cream and cook until smooth and thickened. Pour this sauce over the beets and sprinkle with cress or parsley. Serves six.

BEET GREENS WITH RING GARNISH

This is the most delicious and the very prettiest way of serving beet greens. Cook and chop beet greens, first removing the small beets. Season highly with salt, pepper, lemon juice, and oil or butter, and pack closely in a small, greased melon mold or a bowl, which should be set in boiling water to keep hot. Meanwhile boil or steam the beets which are cut from the greens—the beets should be about the size of walnuts—and skin. Put in a hot bowl and add salt, pepper, and a little butter. Tip out the greens from the mold on a hot, shallow dish, and surround with a close ring of the small beets. Serve all very hot.

PIQUANTE BEETS

4 medium-sized beets	½ teaspoonful salt
1 teaspoonful sugar	1 teaspoonful grated onion
1 tablespoonful vinegar	2 tablespoonfuls butter
Dash nutmeg	

Cook the beets until tender, allowing plenty of time. Slip off the skins, and chop in small bits. Place in a hot serving dish and pour over them the following sauce: Cook together for five minutes the butter, sugar, salt, vinegar, onion, and nutmeg. Serves six.

BRUSSELS SPROUTS IN SAVORY SAUCE

1 quart cleaned Brussels sprouts	¼ cup mild vinegar
1 teaspoonful mustard	2 tablespoonfuls salad oil
¾ teaspoonful salt	1 tablespoonful melted butter
1 teaspoonful sugar	½ teaspoonful curry powder
¼ teaspoonful paprika	1 teaspoonful minced parsley
1 beaten egg	½ teaspoonful grated onion

Cook the Brussels sprouts until tender in boiling, salted water. Drain well, place in a hot serving-dish, and pour over them this sauce: Mix the mustard, salt, sugar, paprika, egg, vinegar and salad oil. Cook in a double-boiler until thickened, then add the melted butter, curry powder, minced parsley, and grated onion. Whip well and use while hot. Serves six.

BRUSSELS SPROUTS WITH CHEESE

Cook the prepared sprouts, first letting them soak in slightly salted water one-half hour, until tender, but not broken, salting them the last part of the time. Drain thoroughly, place in a shallow baking-dish greased, and pour over them one pint of rather thick, highly seasoned white sauce. Combine carefully and cover the top with a thick layer of grated yellow cheese. Set in a medium oven of 400° F. until the cheese is melted and of a rich golden brown. For the white sauce, see P. 184.

SCALLOPED CABBAGE AND CELERY

3 cupfuls cooked cabbage	2 pimientoes
1 cupful cooked celery	1 egg
¾ cupful cracker crumbs	1 cupful milk
Salt	⅓ cupful cream
Pepper	2 tablespoonfuls butter

In a greased casserole place a layer of cooked cabbage chopped fine, and a layer of cooked celery also chopped fine. Over this layer sprinkle cracker crumbs, one-fourth teaspoonful of salt, a sprinkling of pepper, and pimiento cut in thin strips. Repeat, using three cupfuls of cooked cabbage and one cupful of cooked celery in all. Repeat the crumbs and seasonings. Beat the egg and add to it the milk and cream. Pour this mixture over the cabbage and celery. Sprinkle the top with crumbs, using three-fourths cupful in all. Garnish with strips of pimiento using two pimientoes in and on the dish. Dot with bits of butter, using two tablespoonfuls. Bake for twelve minutes in a 450° F. oven. Serves six.

RED CABBAGE WITH SAUSAGE

1 hard red cabbage	Salt, if necessary
1 pint stock or water	2 tablespoonfuls sharp vinegar
⅛ teaspoonful mace	1 tablespoonful butter or fat
⅛ teaspoonful pepper	1 tablespoonful flour

½ pound frankfurter sausages

Select a good, hard red cabbage, trim it nicely, and shave in thin slices. Place it in a saucepan, add stock or water, season with mace, pepper and salt, if necessary, cover and let simmer gently until the cabbage is tender. Fifteen minutes before removing from the fire, add vinegar to the liquid and thicken it with the butter or fat, and flour rubbed to a paste. While the cabbage is cooking, boil the frankfurter sausages until tender. Serve the cabbage with the sausages arranged about it in a decorative manner. Serves six.

BUTTERED CARROTS WITH GREEN PEA SAUCE

4 cupfuls diced carrots	1½ cupful medium white sauce
1 cupful canned or fresh cooked peas	(See Chart for Sauces, P. 184)

Prepare, cook and then dice carrots. Drain. Add peas to white sauce and pour over the seasoned carrots. Serves six.

CARROTS AND ONIONS, GIVERNY STYLE

Heap the middle of a hot chop dish with tiny, buttered carrots, allowing three carrots for each serving. Toast six rounds of bread, butter well, and sprinkle grated cheese over the surface. Arrange around the buttered carrots, and on each round lay three or four small, tender, cooked onions, which have been well seasoned with salt, pepper, and butter. Pour one tablespoonful of hot cream over each round and serve at once. Serves six.

CAULIFLOWER WITH MUSHROOMS

1 medium cauliflower	2 tablespoonfuls butter
1 cupful fresh or canned mushrooms	2 tablespoonfuls flour
1 cupful juice	1 teaspoonful salt
2 tablespoonfuls butter	¼ teaspoonful pepper
½ cupful cream or top milk	Parsley
	Rounds hot buttered toast

Break the cauliflower into rather large flowerets and cook until tender. Prepare rounds of hot, buttered toast, place on a hot serving-dish, and heap the pieces of cauliflower on them. Pour over these the following sauce and serve at once with parsley garnish: Chop the fresh or canned mushrooms and put them in a saucepan with a cupful of the juice and two tablespoonfuls butter. If fresh mushrooms are used, add part of the water in which the cauliflower was cooked. Simmer until the mushrooms are tender. Then add one-half cupful of cream or top milk, let come to a boil, thicken with the remaining two tablespoonfuls of butter and the flour blended together, and add the salt and pepper. Serves six.

CAULIFLOWER DUCHESSE

1 medium cauliflower	¼ teaspoonful salt
2 tablespoonfuls butter	2 tablespoonfuls chopped
3 tablespoonfuls vinegar	green pepper
2 tablespoonfuls chopped pimiento	

Cook the cauliflower until tender, drain, and leave whole or separate into flowerets, as preferred. Pour over a sauce made by melting the butter and adding to it the vinegar, salt and chopped green pepper and pimiento. Serves six.

SAVORY CAULIFLOWER

1 medium-sized cauliflower	1 cupful medium white sauce
¼ pound mushrooms	(See Chart, P. 184)
Toast	

Prepare the cauliflower, separating the flowerets. Cook until tender. Arrange in a shallow serving dish on rounds of hot, buttered toast and serve with the white sauce to which the mushrooms, which have been washed, skinned, sliced and sautéd in one tablespoonful of fat for three minutes, have been added. Serves six.

CELERY CUSTARD

2 cupfuls diced celery	4 eggs
2 small onions	1 teaspoonful salt
2 cupfuls milk	⅛ teaspoonful pepper

Cut the celery into very small dice and chop the onions fine. Cook both in the milk about five minutes or until partially tender. Add the salt and pepper and pour over the eggs beaten slightly. Bake in a greased dish which has been placed in a pan of water for about one hour, or until firm, in a 325° F. oven. Serves six.

CORN AND PEPPER SCALLOP

2 tablespoonfuls sugar	1 finely-chopped green pepper
1 teaspoonful salt	1 chopped red pimiento
1/8 teaspoonful pepper	2 cupfuls canned corn
1/2 cupful milk	1 cupful crumbs

Butter

Add sugar, salt, pepper, milk, green pepper and red pimiento to the canned corn. Fill greased ramekins one-third full, sprinkle with layers of fine bread-crumbs, then put in another layer of corn. Continue until the dishes are filled, having crumbs on top, about one cupful of crumbs being used altogether. Dot over each ramekin with butter, using one-half teaspoonful in each. Bake at 450° F. for twelve minutes. Serves six.

BACONIZED CORN AND MACARONI

2 cupfuls macaroni or spaghetti	1 cupful canned corn
1 1/2 cupfuls medium white sauce	1 teaspoonful salt
	1/4 teaspoonful pepper
	1/2 teaspoonful paprika

3 slices bacon

Cook the macaroni until tender in plenty of boiling, salted water. Drain. Add to the white sauce the seasonings, corn and cooked macaroni. Pour into a greased baking-dish and over the top lay the bacon cut in squares. Bake fifteen minutes, or until the bacon is crisp, in a 500° F. oven. Serves six.

SOUTHERN CORN PUDDING

1 can corn	1/8 teaspoonful pepper
2 eggs	2 tablespoonfuls melted fat
1 teaspoonful salt	2 tablespoonfuls sugar

1 pint scalded milk

Chop the corn. Beat eggs slightly and mix all ingredients together. Pour into a greased pudding dish and bake at 350° F. until firm. Serves six.

CREAMED CUCUMBERS

3 medium-sized cucumbers	2 cupfuls medium white
2 tablespoonfuls butter	sauce (See Chart, P. 184)

Dash mace

Wash and peel the cucumbers, cut them in halves lengthwise, gently scrape out all the seeds and spongy parts, and slice them. Then melt two tablespoonfuls of butter in a frying-pan, add the cucumbers, and sauté for five minutes, tossing the slices all the time. Add the white sauce and mace. Serve at once. Serves six.

CREAMED GREEN PEPPERS WITH CABBAGE

1 small cabbage	3 tablespoonfuls flour
6 green peppers	3 cupfuls milk
3 tablespoonfuls butter,	2 teaspoonfuls salt
fat or oil	¼ teaspoonful pepper

Select a small cabbage or one-half of a medium-sized cabbage; wash and shred it fine. Cook until tender, and then drain. Meanwhile, wash six green peppers and dry them. Place them directly over a low heat and toast them, turning frequently to prevent burning. Scrape off the blistered skin, holding the peppers beneath running water. Remove the seeds and cut with scissors in long, thin strips. Melt three tablespoonfuls of butter, fat or oil, in a deep frying-pan; add the pepper strips and flour. Stir well, and then gradually add the milk. Cover and simmer very slowly for fifteen minutes, or until the peppers are tender. Then add the cooked cabbage together with salt and pepper. Blend well, heat thoroughly, and serve at once. For Creamed Green Peppers, omit cabbage. Serves six.

STUFFED GREEN PEPPERS

2 eggs	1 cupful canned tomatoes
6 medium-sized green peppers	12 soda crackers
2 medium slices smoked ham	1 very small onion
Salt	Few sprigs parsley

Parboil the ham. Simmer five minutes. Drain, reserving the liquid. Put the ham and soda crackers through a meat-chopper; mix with the tomatoes and the eggs well beaten. Chop the onion and the parsley very fine and add to the mixture. Wash the peppers, cut them in half lengthwise, and remove the seeds. Fill the pepper shells with the mixture and place them in a shallow baking-dish, surrounded by the water in which the ham was cooked. Bake for twenty minutes in a 450° F. oven. Serves six.

GREEN PEPPER COMBINATION

6 medium-sized green peppers	2 tablespoonfuls flour
1 small onion	2 cupfuls milk
3 tablespoonfuls butter or	1½ dozen oysters
fat	18 thin slices bacon

Wash the green peppers and dry them well. Toast them over a low heat, turning frequently. Scrape off the blistered skin, holding them beneath running cold water. Remove the seeds and cut with scissors in long, thin strips. Mince the onion. Melt the butter or fat in a saucepan, add the minced onion and green peppers, and let them brown slightly. Stir in the flour and add the milk gradually. Cover and simmer very slowly for about one-half hour or until the green peppers are tender. Meanwhile, clean the oysters, wrap a thin slice of bacon around each, and fasten with small wooden skewers. Place under the broiler heat, or in a 500° F. oven, and bake until the bacon is crisp and brown. Arrange the green pepper mixture in the center of a deep platter and surround with the oysters. Serve at once. If desired, the oysters in bacon may be placed on slices of crisp toast and arranged around the green pepper mixture on the platter. Serves six.

ROASTED MUSHROOMS

1½ pounds mushrooms	Speck cayenne pepper
3 tablespoonfuls fat	¼ cupful boiling water
1 teaspoonful salt	½ cupful cream
¼ teaspoonful celery salt	1½ tablespoonfuls flour
2 tablespoonfuls cold water	

Wash, skin, and cut the mushrooms in halves. Place the fat in the bottom of a large shallow baking pan with a tight fitting cover. Lay in the mushrooms, sprinkle with the salt, celery salt and cayenne and then add the boiling water. Cover and bake at 400° F. for thirty minutes. Remove cover, add the cream and then thicken with flour stirred to a smooth paste in the cold water. Serve on hot buttered toast. Serves six.

BAKED PEAS

6 slices bacon	1 teaspoonful salt
1 pint fresh peas	⅛ teaspoonful pepper
1 cupful cream	½ cupful bread-crumbs

Cut the bacon in small pieces and brown, add the peas which have been cooked and drained, the cream, salt, and pepper. Put in a casserole and cover with the bread-crumbs and bake for twenty minutes at 400° F. Serves six.

CASSEROLE OF PEAS WITH CARROT SAUCE

¾ cupful soft bread-crumbs	1 tablespoonful chopped
1 cupful pea pulp	walnut meats
1 tablespoonful sugar	2 tablespoonfuls flour
1 egg	1½ teaspoonfuls salt
6 tablespoonfuls butter or	¼ teaspoonful pepper
fat	1 bunch new carrots
2¼ cupfuls milk	

Drain canned peas and force them through a purée sieve—enough to make one cupful. Mix together the bread-crumbs, pea pulp, sugar, egg, four tablespoonfuls butter or fat melted, walnut-meats, half the seasonings, and three-fourths cupful of milk. Turn into a well greased baking-dish, let stand fifteen minutes, cover, and bake forty minutes at 350° F. Serve with carrot sauce made as follows: Melt the rest of the butter in a saucepan, add the flour and the rest of the salt and pepper; cook until bubbling and add gradually the one and one-half cupfuls of milk. When well blended, stir in the carrots cooked until tender and then forced through a purée sieve. About one cupful of the carrot purée is about right. This recipe serves four to six persons.

SAVORY STRING BEANS

2 medium-sized onions	2 cloves
2 tablespoonfuls butter or fat	2 teaspoonfuls sugar
1 pint strained stewed tomato	1 quart canned or freshly
1 teaspoonful salt	cooked string beans
Dash of cayenne	¼ teaspoonful pepper

Shred the onions and sauté them in two tablespoonfuls butter or fat until tender and yellow; then add the strained stewed tomato. Season highly with the salt, pepper, cayenne, cloves and sugar. When boiling, add the canned or freshly cooked string beans and simmer from ten to fifteen minutes. Add a little more butter. Serve hot. Tomato sauce or any good canned tomato soup may be substituted for the stewed tomatoes, in which case the seasonings will be varied. In using tomato soup, dilute one-half. Serves six.

HUBBARD SQUASH WITH BACON

1 squash	⅛ teaspoonful nutmeg
1 teaspoonful salt	1 cupful cream
½ teaspoonful paprika	½ cupful bread-crumbs
5 or 6 slices bacon	

Cut a squash in quarters, removing the seeds. Cook until tender, and peel. Put through a sieve or potato-ricer enough squash to make three cupfuls. To this add the salt, paprika, nutmeg and cream. Mix all together, turn into a greased baking-dish, and sprinkle with one-half cupful of bread crumbs. Broil five or six slices of bacon until half done. Remove and place on the squash and bake in a 500° F. oven from twelve to fifteen minutes. Serves six.

SUMMER SQUASH AND ONION

2 summer squash, diced	4 tablespoonfuls butter, fat or
1 cupful minced white onion	oil
¼ teaspoonful pepper	2 teaspoonfuls salt
Paprika	

Wash the squash and remove the seeds. When diced, the squash should measure two quarts. Melt the fat in a stewing kettle, add the onion, and cook until the onion is a light brown color. Then add the squash, salt, and pepper. Cover the kettle and allow the mixture to cook over a low flame, without stirring, for ten minutes. Then continue cooking for thirty minutes, stirring frequently during this period to keep the squash from burning. Sprinkle the squash with paprika when ready to serve. Serves six.

TOMATO SLAW

1 small head cauliflower	1 teaspoonful mustard
2 tomatoes	1 teaspoonful sugar
1 green pepper	½ teaspoonful pepper
Yolk 1 egg	1 teaspoonful salad oil
½ cupful vinegar	1 tablespoonful cream
2 teaspoonfuls salt	

Cook the cauliflower, broken into small pieces, until tender. Slice the tomatoes thin and cut the pepper into shreds. Set in the refrigerator to cool. Combine the oil, vinegar, and seasonings, and place over fire until heated throughout. Then add the beaten egg-yolk, stirring constantly, and cook until thick. Allow to cool, and add the cream. Just before serving, arrange some of the cauliflower around each slice of tomato, placing the shredded pepper across the tomato in lattice-work fashion. Allow one tablespoonful of the dressing to each serving. Serves six.

BROILED TOMATOES

Tomatoes   Seasoned flour

Wash and slice the tomatoes one-half-inch thick. Dip in flour, which has been seasoned with salt and pepper. Place in a greased pan under the broiler heat and broil until brown on one side. Turn and brown on other side.

CREOLE TOMATOES

6 small or	1 tablespoonful flour
4 large ripe tomatoes	2½ tablespoonfuls butter
2 green peppers	½ cupful cream
1 small onion	Pepper
½ teaspoonful salt	

Peel the tomatoes and place them in a greased baking-dish. Chop the peppers (after removing all seeds) with the onion. Cover the tomatoes with the mixture, spread with bits of butter, using one and one-half tablespoonfuls, and sprinkle with salt and pepper. Bake in a moderate oven twenty to thirty minutes. Remove the tomatoes to rounds of buttered toast and keep warm. To the liquor in the dish add the flour and a tablespoonful of butter rubbed together, and then the cream. Cook till thick, season with salt and pepper, pour over the tomatoes, and serve at once. Serves six.

SCALLOPED TOMATOES

1 No. 3 can tomatoes	Salt
Few drops onion juice	Pepper
Buttered bread crumbs	

Season the canned tomatoes with salt, pepper, onion juice and sugar if desired. Arrange a layer of buttered bread crumbs on the bottom of a baking-dish. Cover with tomatoes and sprinkle top thickly with more buttered crumbs. Bake in a hot oven of 400° F. until the crumbs are brown. Serves six.

CREAMED TURNIPS AND ONIONS

12 small white onions	1¼ teaspoonfuls salt
6 medium-sized white turnips	⅛ teaspoonful pepper
3 tablespoonfuls fat	1¼ cupfuls milk
¼ cupful vegetable liquor	Minced parsley
3 tablespoonfuls flour	½ teaspoonful paprika

Skin the onions and pare and dice the turnips. Place both together in a saucepan and cover with cold water. Add one-half the amount of salt and boil for five minutes. Drain, cover with boiling water, and cook until tender. Drain, saving one-fourth cupful of the liquor. Melt the fat in a saucepan; add the flour, pepper, and the rest of the salt. Cook until bubbling, then add gradually the milk and the vegetable liquor, stirring constantly. Cook until thickened. Place the diced turnips in a serving dish; make a hollow in the center in which place the onions. Pour the white sauce over all and sprinkle the turnips with minced parsley and the onions with paprika or grated cheese. Green onions may be used in their season. Serves six.

PERFECTION TURNIPS

Pare and dice fine-grained, mild-flavored turnips, and cook until tender in boiling water, salted during the last part of the cooking. Drain carefully, and to each quart of diced turnips, add two tablespoonfuls of butter and let them stand on the back of the stove until the butter is absorbed. Just before serving, pour over them one and one-half cupfuls of medium white sauce (see Chart, P. 184), combine carefully, and serve very hot. These turnips will have an unusual flavor on account of stewing them in butter. Serves six.

SHOE-STRING TURNIPS IN CREAM

4 large yellow turnips	1½ cupfuls medium white
2 tablespoonfuls finely chopped pimientoes	sauce (see Chart, P. 184)

Pare the turnips and cut in one-fourth inch slices with a sharp knife. Cut each slice into strips one-fourth inch wide. Cook until tender. Then drain. Add the turnips and the red pimientoes chopped fine to the white sauce. Serve hot. Serves six.

STEWED YELLOW TURNIPS

Slice one yellow turnip, pare, and cut in dice. Boil until tender, salting the last half of the time with one and one-half teaspoonfuls of salt. Drain, put in a saucepan, and to each quart of diced turnips add one tablespoonful of butter, one-fourth teaspoonful each of salt, sugar, and paprika, and a dash of cayenne pepper. Shake over one table-spoonful of flour, stir carefully, and add one-fourth cupful of hot cream. Stir again and simmer for five minutes, shaking occasionally to prevent its adhering to the pan. Turn into a hot vegetable dish and serve at once. Serves six.

XIV. VEGETABLE COCKTAILS

Very good appetizers are made by serving one or more diced, cooked vegetables in French dressing. Cucumber and radishes or cauliflower and tomatoes are suggestive.

XV. VEGETABLE DINNER SUGGESTIONS

I
Cream of Celery Soup
Diced Carrots   Chopped Spinach
Steamed Rice
Apple and Green Pepper Salad
Coconut Custard   Caramel Sauce

II
Baked Potatoes
Baked Tomatoes   Buttered Cabbage
Lettuce Salad   French Dressing
Tapioca Cream

III
Poached or Scrambled Egg
Chopped Spinach   Buttered Carrots
Cole-Slaw
Chocolate Layer Cake

IV
Steamed Rice
Cauliflower with Mushroom Sauce
Buttered Beets   Spinach with Egg
Scalloped Apples   Cream

V
Fried Tomatoes with Egg Sauce
Mashed Potatoes, Buttered String-Beans
Celery and Cheese Salad
Chocolate Steamed Pudding Foamy Sauce

VI
Cream of Onion Soup
Croûtons   Parmesan Cheese
Spinach with Border of Stuffed Eggs
Scalloped Hominy and Tomatoes
Green Pepper Salad
Spanish Cream

Chowders

CELERY CHOWDER

4 cupfuls finely cut celery	2 tablespoonfuls fat
1 quart milk	1 tablespoonful flour
1 large potato grated	2 hard-cooked eggs
1 medium-sized onion	Salt and pepper to taste

Cook the celery in water to cover until tender, and force through a sieve, keeping the water as well as pulp. Add the milk and grated potato and cook five minutes. Chop the onion fine and sauté in one tablespoonful of the fat. When delicately browned, add to the first mixture. Chop the hard-cooked eggs and add. Thicken slightly with one tablespoonful of fat and the flour blended together. Season to taste with salt and pepper. Leaves and the tough outer stalks of celery may be used. Serves six to eight.

CLAM CHOWDER

1 quart clams	2 tablespoonfuls chopped celery
4 cupfuls potatoes cut in ¾-inch cubes	1 tablespoonful chopped green pepper
1½-inch cube fat salt pork	1 tablespoonful salt
1 sliced onion	⅛ teaspoonful pepper
8 common crackers	2 tablespoonfuls fat
4 cups scalded milk	
1 tablespoonful flour	

Clean and pick over clams. Heat to boiling point and chop. Strain the liquor. Cut pork into small pieces, try out and add the onion,

127

celery, and green pepper. Cook until a light brown. Parboil the potatoes, then brown in fat. Add chopped clams and two cups of boiling water, cook ten minutes. Add milk and crackers split in half. Cook three minutes. Melt the fat and blend with the flour. Use this to thicken the clam liquor; add just before serving as the clam broth tends to curdle the milk. Season. Serves six to eight.

CORN CHOWDER

6 ears corn or	¼ cupful sausage meat
2 cupfuls canned corn	1 sweet pepper
6 medium-sized potatoes	1 tablespoonful flour
1 onion or	1 teaspoonful salt
2 tomatoes	¼ teaspoonful pepper
1 cupful milk	Boiling water

Cut the corn from the cob and put it through the food chopper, together with the potatoes, onion, and chopped pepper—the latter may be skinned by first heating it in the oven. Brown the meat lightly in a saucepan, add the flour, then the vegetables chopped fine, and seasonings. Add boiling water barely to cover and simmer gently for one hour. Add the milk and more salt if needed. This is an excellent way to use old corn. The meat may be omitted and a ham-bone and two tablespoonfuls of fat substituted, or broth in which ham or corned beef has been cooked may be used in place of the water. Serves six to eight.

CANNED CORN AND CELERY CHOWDER

1 can corn	2 onions
1 head celery	¼ pound salt pork
1 quart milk	Salt and pepper to taste
2 cupfuls diced, cooked potatoes	

Dice the salt pork and put it in a frying-pan. When the fat begins to cook out, add the onions chopped fine and cook the two together until the latter are tender and the salt pork is browned. Cut the celery in inch-lengths and cook it till tender in salted water barely to cover. Add celery and the celery liquor to the milk with the potato, onions, and pork. Bring to the scalding point, turn in the corn, reheat, and serve with split and buttered brown crackers. Serves six to eight.

CORN CHOWDER BISQUE

2 slices salt pork	¼ teaspoonful pepper
4 small onions	6 ears corn
6 medium potatoes	¼ teaspoonful soda
4 medium tomatoes	1 quart hot milk
2 teaspoonfuls salt	1 tablespoonful flour
1 tablespoonful butter	

Cut the salt pork into one-quarter inch cubes, and fry until light brown and crisp in the kettle in which the chowder is to be made. Remove from the stove and add the onions finely minced, potatoes cubed or sliced, tomatoes peeled and diced, arranging them in layers. Sprinkle with salt and pepper over each layer, using two teaspoonfuls of salt and one-fourth teaspoonful of pepper in all. Cover with one pint boiling water and simmer until the vegetables are nearly tender. Then add the corn from the six ears which have been first scored down through the middle, the tips sliced off with a sharp knife, and the pulp pressed and scraped off. Cook ten minutes more, add the soda, and milk which has been thickened slightly with the butter and flour melted together. Stir rapidly while adding the milk, and serve hot with toasted crackers and a green salad. If canned corn is used, measure two cupfuls. Serves six to eight.

CORN AND TOMATO CHOWDER

2 cupfuls canned corn	1 cupful milk
1 cupful canned or ripe tomatoes	½ cupful grated cheese
2 cupfuls diced celery	½ cupful chopped pimientoes
2 tablespoonfuls fat	3 tablespoonfuls flour
1 quart cold water	1½ teaspoonfuls salt

¼ teaspoonful pepper

Place corn, tomatoes, diced celery, and one teaspoonful of salt in a kettle and cover with the cold water. Boil one-half hour. Melt fat, add flour gradually. Then add the cold milk, stirring constantly. Add the vegetable mixture to the white sauce, a little at a time, and seasonings. Add to the chowder the grated cheese and the pimientoes chopped fine. Stir until the cheese is melted. Serve piping hot. A cream soup may be made if desired, by straining out the vegetables before adding the white sauce. Serves six to eight.

LIMA BEAN CHOWDER

1 good slice pork	Salt
2 onions minced	Pepper
4 potatoes	1 pint hot milk
2 or 3 new carrots	1 tablespoonful flour
1 or 2 cupfuls fresh lima beans	1 tablespoonful fat

Dice the pork and fry in the kettle in which the chowder is to be made. Add the onions minced and cook in the fat until a very light brown, then add the potatoes cut in small cubes, the carrots sliced, the lima beans, and salt and pepper to taste. Cover with boiling water and simmer, covered, until all are tender. Then add the hot milk. Thicken slightly with the fat and flour blended together. Serves four or five.

CREOLE FISH CHOWDER

1 pound cod or haddock	Sprig parsley
½ medium-sized onion	Sprig basil
¾ cupful sliced potatoes	1 bay-leaf
1 tablespoonful bacon	Speck of pepper
¾ teaspoonful salt	1 pint boiling water
1 sprig thyme	½ cupful canned tomatoes

Cut the cod or haddock in chunks, mince the onion, and prepare the three-quarters cupful of sliced potatoes. Put the bacon cut in small pieces in the bottom of a kettle, and sauté until crisp. Then add the minced onion, salt, thyme, parsley, basil, bay-leaf, and speck of pepper. Then add the boiling water, the fish, the tomatoes, and the potatoes. Cover and let simmer gently for fifteen minutes or until the potatoes are tender and the fish is done. Serve hot. Serves six to eight.

LONGSHOREMAN'S FISH CHOWDER

½ pound fat salt pork	⅛ teaspoonful pepper
3 small onions	6 potatoes
3 pounds fresh haddock	3 cupfuls rich milk
1 tablespoonful salt	6 pilot biscuits

Dice the fat salt pork and sauté to a light straw color; remove the pork and sauté the onions in the fat. Strain out the onions and put the fat in the saucepan. Cut the fresh haddock in small pieces, rub with the salt, and dust with the pepper. Lay the haddock in the saucepan; add the potatoes pared and sliced, then the onions and the pork. Cover well with water and cook one-half hour or until the potatoes are tender. Add the milk and pilot biscuits broken in pieces. Bring all to a boil and serve. Serves six.

PARSNIP CHOWDER

¼ pound fat salt pork	2½ teaspoonfuls salt
1 onion	¼ teaspoonful celery salt
2 cupfuls raw, diced potatoes	¼ teaspoonful paprika
2 cupfuls raw, diced parsnips	⅛ teaspoonful pepper
1 quart scalded milk	3 cupfuls boiling water
	3 tablespoonfuls butter or fat

Dice the salt pork and place in the bottom of a chowder kettle. Add the onion, thinly sliced, and sauté both to a golden brown. Then add the diced potatoes and parsnips, the seasonings, and boiling water. Cover and simmer thirty minutes, or until the potatoes and parsnips are tender. Then add the scalding milk and bring all to the heating point. Add the fat and serve with toasted crackers. Serves six to eight.

VEGETABLE CLAM CHOWDER

4 tablespoonfuls fat	1½ teaspoonfuls salt
1 large onion chopped	¼ teaspoonful white pepper
3 small carrots, cut small dice	1½ quarts water
1 cupful stewed tomatoes	1 tablespoonful flour
3 cupfuls diced potatoes	25 round clams with liquor
1 teaspoonful thyme	1 tablespoonful butter

Cook onion in the fat until it is yellow. Add potatoes, carrots, one teaspoonful of salt, and water. In ten minutes add the tough part of the clams chopped. When potatoes are nearly done add the tomatoes. Five minutes before serving add the strained clam juice, and rest of clams, thyme, pepper, and one-half teaspoonful more salt. Bind with one tablespoonful butter and one tablespoonful of flour blended together. Serves six to eight.

Deep Fat Frying

The introduction of the fat thermometer which registers to 500° F. should solve the problem of deep fat frying for all housekeepers. The so called smoke test is often inaccurate, and the results are variable.

I. GENERAL METHOD

1. Select a deep pan, and fill about two-thirds full of any good fat or oil. Do not use butter.
2. Insert the fat thermometer and heat to desired temperature. (See Cooking Temperature Chart, P. 251.)
3. When hot enough, slip food into the fat and cook until golden brown on all sides and done. (See Cooking Temperature Chart, P. 251.) The food may be arranged in a frying basket and lowered into fat.
4. Remove food and drain on absorbent paper such as paper toweling or paper napkins.
5. When frying is completed, cool the fat, then strain through cheese-cloth into can.
6. If the fat is dark after using, clarify as follows: Add raw potato cut in one-quarter-inch slices to the fat and allow it to heat gradually. When the fat ceases to bubble and the potatoes are well browned, strain and store fat in cool place.

132

II. CROQUETTES

1. **Shaping**—Prepare croquette mixture, following specific recipes below. When cold, it is ready to shape. Allow about one rounding tablespoonful of the mixture to each croquette. Make into balls, cuddling rather than pressing the mixture between the palms till cylindrical. With the balls formed, the shape may be changed into rolls, ovals, cones or pear shape, as desired. Ice cream scoops are excellent for shaping conical croquettes.

2. **Crumbing**—Next coat the croquettes on all sides with finely sifted, dried bread crumbs. Then dip in beaten egg, adding one tablespoonful of water to each egg. Lift them out, and entirely coat again with bread crumbs. Let stand a while to dry before frying.

3. **Frying**—Fry the croquettes in deep fat, as directed above. (See Cooking Temperature Chart, P. 251)

4. **Croquettes in Variety**

MEAT OR FISH CROQUETTES

2 cupfuls cold chopped meat or fish
1 cupful thick white sauce
Salt, pepper
Minced parsley

1 teaspoonful lemon juice (if fish)
½ teaspoonful lemon juice (if meat)
Celery salt to taste

Prepare meat or fish. Have sauce very cold. Mix very carefully with fish or meat and season. Shape, crumb, egg, crumb again and fry as directed above. Makes about twelve croquettes.

RICE AND TOMATO CROQUETTES

½ cupful rice
1½ cupfuls canned tomatoes, or
¾ cupful brown soup stock and
¾ cupful canned tomatoes
1 slice onion
1 slice carrot
1 sprig parsley

2 cloves
3 peppercorns
1 teaspoonful sugar
1 egg
¼ cupful grated cheese
1 tablespoonful fat
½ teaspoonful salt

Cook three-fourths cupful tomatoes, the onion, carrot, parsley, cloves and peppercorns for five minutes. Strain. Add the stock and cook the rice in this liquid in a double boiler, as directed on P. 31. Remove from heat and add sugar, beaten egg, cheese, fat and salt. Spread on a plate to cool. Shape, egg and crumb, and fry. Makes from fifteen to twenty croquettes.

RICE CROQUETTES

½ cupful rice	½ teaspoonful salt
½ cupful boiling water	2 egg-yolks or 1 egg
1 cupful scalded milk	1 teaspoonful butter

Wash rice and cook in milk and water in top of double boiler until rice is tender, about forty-five minutes. Remove and add other ingredients. Spread on a shallow pan to cool. Shape, egg and crumb and fry in deep fat. Serve garnished with cubes of jelly. For sweet croquettes, add 2 tablespoonfuls powdered sugar and rind one-half lemon, to rice. Makes from fifteen to twenty croquettes.

FISH AND POTATO CROQUETTES

1 cupful cold flaked fish	1 egg or 2 egg-yolks
1 cupful mashed potatoes	2 tablespoonfuls fat
Salt and pepper to taste	Other seasonings as desired

If potatoes are cold, melt the fat and mix it with the fish, potatoes and other ingredients. Season carefully; minced parsley, celery salt and a little onion juice are desirable. Shape and crumb, egg and crumb again. Fry in deep fat. Serve on a hot platter, garnished with parsley and slices of lemon. Makes about ten croquettes.

Note—Cold, chopped, cooked meat, as chicken, beef, or veal may replace the fish. The whole egg may not be needed. It depends on moisture of fish or potatoes. Add part of egg at first. (See Page 133 for crumbing, etc.)

POTATO CROQUETTES

2 cupfuls riced potatoes	Pepper to taste
2 tablespoonfuls butter	2 egg-yolks or 1 egg
½ teaspoonful salt	Finely minced parsley

If potatoes are cold, melt butter and mix it with potatoes and other ingredients. Beat thoroughly. Cool, shape, crumb, egg, and crumb again and fry in deep fat. Serve at once on a hot platter garnished with parsley. Makes about ten croquettes.

Note—All the egg may not be needed. It depends upon the moisture in the potatoes. Add part of the egg at first. Croquette mixtures may be formed into round, flat cakes and sautéd.

SWEET POTATO CROQUETTES

To two cupfuls hot riced sweet potatoes add three tablespoonfuls butter, one-half teaspoonful salt, few grains pepper and one beaten egg.

Shape in small balls; roll in fine dry crumbs, then in egg solution and again in fine dry crumbs. Fry in deep fat. Makes about ten croquettes.

III. FRITTERS

1. Batter

1 cupful flour	¼ teaspoonful salt
1½ teaspoonfuls baking powder	⅓ cupful milk
3 tablespoonfuls powdered sugar	1 egg

Mix and sift dry ingredients. Combine milk and egg well beaten and add to dry ingredients, while beating constantly.

2. Fritters in Variety

APPLE FRITTERS

2 medium-sized sour apples   Batter mixture
Powdered sugar

Pare, core and cut apples in eighths. Cut in slices and add to batter mixture made as above. Drop by spoonfuls and fry in deep fat. (See P. 252.) Then roll in powdered sugar.

BANANA FRITTERS

4 bananas	2 teaspoonfuls lemon juice
Powdered sugar	Batter mixture

Peel, scrape and cut bananas in halves, lengthwise. Then cut in two pieces, crosswise. Sprinkle with powdered sugar and lemon juice. Let stand thirty minutes. Drain, dip in batter, and fry in deep fat. (See P. 252.)

CLAM FRITTERS
(See P. 99)

CORN FRITTERS

1 can corn	1½ teaspoonfuls salt
1¼ cupfuls flour	¼ teaspoonful paprika
1 teaspoonful baking-powder	2 eggs

Measure and sift flour, baking powder, salt and paprika together. Add corn and beaten egg yolks. Beat well, and fold in stiffly beaten egg whites. Fry in deep fat (see Cooking Temperature Chart, P. 252) or sauté in a frying-pan. Two cupfuls fresh cooked corn, cut from the cob, may be substituted for the canned corn, in which case a little milk may be added.

Sandwiches and Hors D'Oeuvres

I. GENERAL RULES FOR SANDWICHES

1. Choose bread at least twenty-four hours old.
2. Cut in thin even slices.
3. Cream the butter before using it for spreading on bread, and spread butter evenly and thinly on slice, and quite to the edge.
4. Afternoon tea sandwiches generally have the crusts removed while lunch box, picnic, or hot sandwiches may have the crusts left on.
5. Fancy shapes very often waste bread, circles especially, unless bread is baked in that shape.
6. Square loaves are best cut in strips, small squares, or triangles.
7. Care in seasoning the filling should be especially observed, also the filling must not be too moist, as the sandwich is thus made soggy.
8. Spread filling on evenly and not very thinly.
9. Lettuce sandwiches should be made as short a time as possible before using and kept in a cool place. Dressing used with these is inclined to soak into bread and make it soggy.
10. Preparation of meat. a. Remove all superfluous fat, gristle and dry edges and put through a food chopper. Season well and moisten with a little salad dressing, melted butter, or chilli sauce. b. Meat may be cut in thin slices, fat or gristle removed and fitted between the slices of buttered bread, with seasoning spread over meat.

II. CARE OF SANDWICHES

1. If sandwiches are to be kept, wrap in a damp cloth and place in the refrigerator.
2. When packing in lunch box or picnic basket, paraffin or wax paper will help to keep the sandwiches fresh.

III. SELECTED SANDWICH FILLINGS

ROLLED CELERY SANDWICHES

White bread	Butter
Celery	Thousand Island Dressing

Cut one-fourth inch slices of white bread from a rather fresh, moist loaf of bread. Remove the crusts and spread the bread slices with softened butter.   Meanwhile, cut stalks of cleaned celery into lengths equal to the width of the bread slices.   Fill these stalks with the Thousand Island Dressing.   Place a stalk on the edge of each slice of bread and roll into the bread like a jelly roll.   Roll all the sandwiches in a damp napkin and place in the refrigerator for a few hours.   The rolls should keep their shape.

CHICKEN ALMOND SANDWICHES

1 cupful chopped chicken
8 teaspoonfuls cream
¾ teaspoonful salt
White or graham bread

1 cupful chopped blanched
   almonds
¼ teaspoonful paprika
Dash pepper

Butter

Blend the chicken and almonds together with the cream and add the seasonings.   Spread between buttered slices of bread.   Either white or graham bread may be used.

CHICKEN KING SANDWICHES

1 cupful cold chicken
1 tablespoonful fat
About 6 tablespoonfuls
   thick white sauce
⅛ teaspoonful paprika
Bread
Butter

¼ cupful skinned
   mushrooms
1 tablespoonful sweet
   red peppers
½ teaspoonful parsley
Dash cayenne pepper
½ teaspoonful chopped onion

Wash and cut up the mushrooms and cook for five minutes in the tablespoonful of fat.   Mince the chicken, red pepper, parsley and onion.   Add to the mushrooms together with the highly seasoned thick white sauce.   Spread between buttered slices of bread.

CREAM CHEESE AND PINEAPPLE SANDWICHES

½ cupful cream cheese
½ cupful chopped pecan
   meats

Butter
½ cupful crushed pine-
   apple

Brown bread

Work the cream cheese with a fork until it is soft.   Then add the chopped pecan meats and shredded pineapple.   Mix thoroughly. Meanwhile cut thin slices of brown bread, and butter half the slices. Spread the remaining slices with the cream cheese mixture and form sandwiches.

CREAM CHEESE AND HORSERADISH SANDWICHES

Cream cheese	Horseradish
Boston brown bread	Butter

Mix equal parts of cream cheese and prepared horseradish. Spread on buttered slices of Boston brown bread and press another slice of bread on top of each.

CHILALY SANDWICHES

2 tablespoonfuls butter	¾ teaspoonful salt
2 tablespoonfuls chopped green peppers	2 tablespoonfuls cream Bread slices
2 tablespoonfuls chopped onion	½ cupful canned tomatoes ¾ pound soft mild cheese
1 egg	Speck cayenne pepper

Butter

Melt the two tablespoonfuls of butter, add the chopped green peppers and onions, and cook until tender. Then add the canned tomatoes which have been strained, and cook three minutes. Add the cheese cut fine and the salt and cayenne pepper. Stir constantly over a very slow heat until the cheese is melted and the mixture is smooth and creamy. Then add the cream and egg beaten slightly. Cook one minute longer while stirring. Remove, cool and use as a filling between buttered slices of graham, rye or white bread.

FAVORITE SANDWICHES

1 tablespoonful chopped pimiento	¼ cupful mayonnaise 1 tablespoonful chopped
½ cupful chopped celery	sweet green pepper
¼ cupful minced tuna fish	Bread ¼ teaspoonful salt

To the minced tuna fish add the celery and peppers; mix together well, moisten with mayonnaise and season with salt. Use as a filling for white bread sandwiches, making them thin and dainty.

DOMINO SANDWICHES

Brown bread	White bread
Butter	1 cupful chopped tongue
2 tablespoonfuls chopped dill pickes	3 tablespoonfuls mayonnaise Swiss cheese

Cut brown and white bread in one-eighth inch slices and spread with softened butter. Season the chopped tongue with the dill pickles and mayonnaise. Spread this mixture on slices of white bread. Over this put brown bread, then thinly sliced Swiss cheese. Repeat, having four layers. Trim off the crusts evenly, put under a weight and let stand several hours in a cool place. Cut crosswise in thin slices and serve.

MOCK DEVILED HAM SANDWICHES

3 frankfurters
¼ teaspoonful prepared mustard
3 tablespoonfuls mayonnaise
Butter
Bread

Boil the frankfurters, chill, remove skins, and put through the food chopper. Mix with mayonnaise and mustard and spread between slices of buttered bread. This recipe will make five large, full-sized sandwiches.

MOCK LOBSTER SANDWICHES

1 cupful cooked halibut
¼ teaspoonful salt
6 tablespoonfuls
  mayonnaise
1 bunch button radishes
Dash cayenne pepper
Bread
Butter

Flake cold cooked halibut and add to it a small bunch of red button radishes which have been finely slivered. Season with salt and cayenne and moisten with mayonnaise. Spread between slices of buttered bread and serve very cold.

PEPPER SANDWICHES

4 green peppers
½ teaspoonful onion
2 tablespoonfuls salad oil
¼ teaspoonful salt
4 walnuts
Bread
1 lemon
2 tablespoonfuls cooked
  salad dressing
1 large cream cheese
4 olives
Butter

Seed and chop the peppers fine. Cover with the juice of the lemon and let stand one hour. Add the finely chopped onion, salad dressing, oil, salt, cream cheese, chopped walnuts and olives. Mix together well. Spread between slices of buttered bread.

PIMIENTO SANDWICHES

White Bread
Graham bread
Canned pimientoes
Butter

Butter slices of white and graham bread. Arrange strips of pimiento over the surface of the bread and put a white and graham slice together for each sandwich. Cut in heart shapes.

PIQUANT SANDWICHES

Butter	2 tablespoonfuls peanut
1 cream cheese	butter
1 hard-cooked egg	1 tablespoonful green
1 sour pickle	pepper
⅛ teaspoonful salt	Dash pepper

Bread

Cream together the cream cheese and peanut butter. Chop very fine the egg, pepper and pickle and blend into the cream cheese. Add the salt and pepper. Spread between buttered slices of bread.

SAVORY SANDWICHES

½ cupful almonds	1 tablespoonful chopped
1 tablespoonful cooking	chutney
oil	1 large cream cheese or
2 tablespoonfuls chopped	an equal quantity of
pickles	cottage cheese
Salt	Paprika

Blanch the almonds and brown in oil in frying-pan. Chop fine. Season well with salt and paprika, and add pickles and chutney. Spread either bread or crackers with softened cream cheese and sprinkle with the almond mixture. This is sufficient filling to make up one small loaf of bread in sandwiches, if the slices are cut thin.

WATERCRESS SANDWICHES

Watercress	Brown bread

Butter

Cream the butter and spread liberally on the brown bread. Wash cress carefully and place on one slice of bread. Top with a second slice.

IV. GENERAL RULES FOR HORS D'OEUVRES

1. One must bear in mind that Hors d'Oeuvres are tidbits to sharpen the appetite rather than hearty dishes.
2. The Hors d'Oeuvres may be served on individual plates or arranged on one large platter.
3. The food must be arranged conveniently for eating, sliced thin or chopped fine if necessary.
4. Tempting Hors d'Oeuvres may be made from left-overs but they should blend with the balance of the meal.
5. A crisp green is almost invariably used which helps to make the desired color result.

V. SELECTED HORS D'OEUVRES RECIPES

BOSTON BOULETTES

½ cupful cold cooked chicken	¼ cupful chopped pecans
½ cupful diced, cooked celery	¼ teaspoonful salt
White sauce	Crumbs
Beaten egg	Deep fat
Watercress	Buttered Boston brown bread
	Pepper

Mix together the chicken, celery and pecans. Season with salt and pepper. Add enough white sauce so that the mixture may be easily handled and holds its shape. Spread on a plate to cool. When cool, form into tiny balls, roll in crumbs and egg and fry in deep fat at 390° F. until golden brown. Serve on a bed of watercress, accompanied by thin strips of buttered Boston brown bread.

FRUITY HORS D'OEUVRES

Watermelon balls	Pears
Peaches	Lemon juice
Chopped pistachio nuts	Maraschino cherries
Pineapple	Orange
Mint leaves	White grapes

For the summer luncheon the hors d'oeuvres dish may be filled with the above fruits. Marinate the watermelon balls in French dressing; slice the pears thin, cut in scalloped disks with a scalloped cutter, sprinkle with lemon juice and garnish in center with finely chopped maraschino cherries. Stone the peaches, cut in eighths, dip in lemon juice or orange juice and roll in finely chopped pistachio nuts. Dip the segments of sliced pineapple in powdered mint leaves. Bits of grapefruit or oranges or halves white grapes may be used to make a quintet of delicate, mouth watering appetizers.

PRUNES À LA BRUSSEL

Prunes	Lemon juice
Celery	Pecan meats
Cayenne	French dressing
Pimiento	

Soak and stew large California prunes till tender, but not soft. Chill and remove pits from a slit cut across one end, taking care not to break the prunes during this operation. Chop celery very fine and place in iced lemon water to blanch and chill. Dry the celery well, mix with chopped pecan meats and moisten with French dressing to which a few grains of cayenne have been added. Fill the prunes with this mixture. Serve standing upright with a fleck of pimiento on top for garnish.

DEVILED EGGS WITH ANCHOVY

Rounds bread	Butter
Hard-cooked eggs	1 tablespoonful minced
Dash cayenne pepper	chives
Mayonnaise	Tomato catsup
Anchovy paste	Parsley

Sauté rounds of bread in butter and spread with anchovy paste. Place on individual serving plates. On each round of toast place one-half of a deviled egg prepared in the following manner: Hard-cook the eggs, halve them lengthwise and remove the yolks. Add enough melted butter to the yolks to make a thick paste, then add a dash of cayenne and the chives. Moisten the mixture with equal parts of thick mayonnaise and tomato catsup, then fill the whites with it. Top with one tablespoonful of the mayonnaise and catsup mixture. Garnish with parsley.

Pies and Pastry

I. GENERAL RULES FOR MAKING PASTRY

1. The flour used should be a fine, soft, starchy flour.
2. Any good shortening may be used.
3. Everything must be at a low temperature.
4. Handle pastry as little and as lightly as possible.
5. Chill pastry when possible before shaping into pies.

II. PLAIN PASTRY

1. Sift together one and one-half cupfuls pastry flour, one-half teaspoonful baking powder and one-half teaspoonful salt.
2. Cut into the flour one-half cupful shortening. Use two knives and work until the whole resembles a coarse meal.
3. Gradually add cold water to make a stiff dough. Chill pastry for one hour if possible.
4. Turn on to a slightly floured molding surface and pat the pastry into a long narrow sheet one-quarter inch thick.
5. Roll up like a jelly roll and cut off as needed from the roll.

III. DOUBLE CRUST PIES

1. Cut off enough pastry for the under crust. Roll to about one-eighth inch in thickness and a little larger than the pie plate.
2. Fold the sheet of pastry in half and place on pie plate. Then unfold pastry.
3. Press lightly to fit pie plate and trim edges.
4. Fill lined plate with thinly sliced fruits as apples, rhubarb or peaches, fresh or canned berries as gooseberries, blueberries, cherries, etc. Sprinkle with sugar to sweeten. Watery fruits as cherries, blueberries and rhubarb should have about two tablespoonfuls of flour sprinkled over the surface before putting on top crust.
5. Roll out top crust one-eighth inch in thickness and one inch larger than plate.
6. Fold in half, make three slits one-half inch in length on center edge of folded side.
7. Moisten edge of lower crust with a little water and place upper crust in position and trim, leaving one inch on all sides.
8. Carefully fold and press down upper crust under lower crust all around the edge. Finish by making marks with tines of fork.
9. Bake pies according to the temperature chart. (P. 252.)

IV. ONE CRUST PIES

1. Roll out pastry, fold, and line pie plate as for double crust pie. leaving one inch over edge. Do not stretch the pastry.
2. Fold back the edge of the pastry all the way around and bring double fold to upright position.
3. Flute the double fold of pastry in the following manner: Place the index finger of the left hand against the fold on the inside so that it is between the tips of the thumb and index finger of the right hand, which are placed on the outside of the fold. Press firmly close to the pie plate with the thumb and index finger of the right hand. Remove the fingers and continue fluting around entire rim of pie. Pour in uncooked filling and bake. (P. 252.)

V. PASTRY SHELLS

1. For a pie in which the filling has been previously cooked as in the case of lemon pie, line a plate as directed for one crust pie. Flute edge.
2. Prick with a fork the entire bottom and side surface of the crust to prevent bubbles from forming during baking. Bake. (P. 252)

3. The paste may be placed over the back of a pie plate or for individual shells over the backs of muffin tins and baked. This kind of a shell holds the shape well but can not have the attractive fluted rim.

VI. FRUIT DEEP PIES

1. Any fruit may be used in a deep pie; peaches and apples are particularly good.
2. Prepare the fruit and put in deep baking dish, casserole or individual dishes. Season well with sugar and any spices desired. A little lemon juice and rind is good with apples. If fruit seems very juicy two tablespoonfuls flour may be added to each cupful of sugar used. If fruit seems dry add a small amount of water.
3. Cover the pie with pastry rolled one-fourth inch thick. Cut several gashes in crust and "flute" edge as directed above. Bake. (P. 252.)

VII. PIES WITH CUSTARD FILLINGS

CARAMEL CUSTARD PIE

4 tablespoonfuls sugar	1 tablespoonful cornstarch
1 cupful milk	¼ teaspoonful salt
2 eggs	½ teaspoonful vanilla
½ cupful sugar	Pastry

Line a medium-sized pie plate with pastry having a fluted edge. Place the four tablespoonfuls of sugar in a saucepan and stir over the heat until the sugar has been melted and turned a deep brown, but not burned. Add to the milk which has been scalded, and stir until thoroughly blended. Remove from the fire and pour gradually over the well-beaten eggs which have been mixed with the cornstarch and the one-half cupful of sugar. Add the salt and vanilla and pour into the pastry lined pie plate. Bake at 450° F. for ten minutes to set the rim, then reduce the heat to 325° F. for thirty minutes.

CUSTARD PIE

4 eggs	¾ cupful milk
6 tablespoonfuls sugar	1 teaspoonful vanilla
¼ teaspoonful salt	Few gratings nutmeg
	Pastry

Beat eggs slightly, add sugar, salt, vanilla and milk. Strain into pie plate lined with pastry. Sprinkle with nutmeg. Cocoanut may be sprinkled over the top of this pie before baking. Bake as Caramel Custard Pie.

CHOCOLATE PIE

1½ squares chocolate
1⅔ cupfuls scalded milk
⅔ cupful powdered sugar
½ tablespoonful cornstarch

½ teaspoonful vanilla
4 eggs
6 tablespoonfuls sugar
Pastry

Line a medium-sized pie plate with pastry having a fluted edge. Melt the chocolate over hot water, then add the hot milk and cook together until smooth. Add the sugar sifted with the cornstarch and stir until the boiling-point is again reached. Cool slightly, pour over one whole egg, the yolks of three eggs slightly beaten, and one-fourth teaspoonful of vanilla. Pour into the pastry-lined pie plate and bake as Caramel Custard Pie. Cover with a meringue made from the three egg-whites, granulated sugar and one-fourth teaspoonful of vanilla. Brown at 300° F. for fifteen minutes.

LEMON PIE

2 eggs
1 lemon
1 cupful sugar
2 tablespoonfuls flour

1 tablespoonful butter
¼ teaspoonful salt
1 cupful milk
Pastry

Line a medium-sized pie plate with pastry having a fluted edge. Beat the egg-yolks until thick. Add the juice and grated rind of the lemon and the sugar mixed thoroughly with the flour and salt. Blend together well and add the milk and the butter melted. Fold in the egg-whites beaten until they are stiff and dry. Pour into the pastry lined pie plate. Bake as Caramel Custard Pie.

ORANGE PIE

3 egg-yolks
¼ cupful sugar
Grated rind and juice 1 orange
1 tablespoonful melted butter

Grated rind and juice 1 lemon
3 egg-whites
6 tablespoonfuls sugar
1 tablespoonful orange juice
Pastry

Line a medium-sized pie plate with pastry having a fluted edge. Whip the egg-yolks with the one-fourth cupful of sugar, and add the orange rind and juice, melted butter, and lemon rind and juice. Mix thoroughly and place in the pastry lined pie plate. Bake as Caramel Custard Pie. Prepare a meringue from the egg-whites and six tablespoonfuls of sugar, adding the one tablespoonful of orange juice just before beating up for the last time. Arrange on the pie and brown at 300° F. for fifteen minutes.

OLD-FASHIONED MOLASSES CUSTARD PIE

1 cupful molasses	1 cupful milk
3 eggs	1½ tablespoonfuls flour
1 cupful sugar	2 tablespoonfuls melted butter
	Pastry

Line a large pie plate with pastry, having a fluted edge. Combine the molasses, egg-yolks slightly beaten, sugar, milk, flour, and melted butter and fold in the egg-whites last. Pour into the pastry lined pie plate and bake as Caramel Custard Pie. Two small pies may be made instead of one large, if desired.

PENNSYLVANIA PUMPKIN PIE

2 cupfuls pumpkin	½ teaspoonful ginger
3 egg-yolks	⅛ teaspoonful ground cloves
1 cupful brown sugar	⅛ teaspoonful allspice
¼ teaspoonful salt	¼ teaspoonful cinnamon
½ teaspoonful grated nutmeg	3 cupfuls scalded milk
	3 egg-whites

Peel and remove the seeds from a pumpkin of fine grain. Cut into pieces and steam until tender. Drain and mash through a sieve. You may use canned pumpkin.

To two cupfuls of pumpkin add the egg-yolks, brown sugar, salt, nutmeg, ginger, ground cloves and allspice and cinnamon. Mix well together, then add three cupfuls of scalded milk. Last of all, fold in the stiffly beaten egg-whites. Line a pie plate with pastry, coat with white of egg, and pour in the pumpkin mixture. Bake as Caramel Custard Pie. Squash may be used instead of pumpkin in this recipe. Makes two medium or one large and one small pie.

SQUASH PIE

1 cupful cooked squash	½ teaspoonful ginger
1 cupful cream	½ teaspoonful nutmeg
¾ cupful sugar, white or brown	½ teaspoonful salt
3 eggs	¼ teaspoonful mace
3 tablespoonfuls vanilla	White of egg
	Bread-crumbs

To one cupful of cooked squash which has been put through a sieve, or one cupful of canned squash, add the cream and sugar, either white or brown. Beat the eggs slightly and add to the squash and cream mixture with the vanilla, ginger, nutmeg and salt and mace. Line a pie plate with pastry. Brush the pastry with white of egg and sprinkle lightly with bread crumbs. Pour in the squash mixture and bake as Caramel Custard Pie. This pie is delicious spread with honey and topped with whipped cream.

VIII. PIES WITH CREAM FILLINGS

BUTTERSCOTCH PIE

6 tablespoonfuls butter	1½ cupfuls brown sugar
2½ cupfuls scalded milk	2 eggs
3 tablespoonfuls cornstarch	4 tablespoonfuls granulated
Pastry	sugar
	½ teaspoonful vanilla

Line a small pie plate with pastry having a fluted edge. Melt the butter and brown sugar together, and cook until a rich brown. Then add the scalded milk and let heat until the sugar is dissolved. Beat the egg-yolks slightly, add the cornstarch and pour the milk mixture over it gradually, stirring constantly. Add one-fourth teaspoonful of vanilla, pour into the pastry lined pie plate and bake at 450° F. for ten minutes to set the rim and then at 325° for thirty minutes, or until the custard is firm. Then cover with a meringue made from the beaten egg-whites to which the granulated sugar and one-fourth teaspoonful of vanilla have been added and brown at 300° F. for fifteen minutes.

LEMON PIE

1½ cupfuls sugar	2¼ cupfuls boiling water
4 tablespoonfuls flour	3 egg-yolks
5 tablespoonfuls cornstarch	Grated rind 1 lemon
½ teaspoonful salt	½ cupful lemon juice
3 egg-whites	6 tablespoonfuls granulated
½ teaspoonful vanilla	sugar
Pastry	

Mix sugar, flour, cornstarch, and salt well together. Add boiling water, stirring constantly. Cook for fifteen minutes in a double boiler, stirring as it thickens. Beat egg-yolks and pour cornstarch mixture into the eggs slowly stirring constantly. Return filling to double boiler, cook two minutes longer. Remove from fire, add lemon juice and rind. When cold pour into a baked pastry shell. Make a meringue of the egg-whites, granulated sugar and vanilla. Heap on pie and bake at 300° F. for fifteen minutes.

IX. SPECIAL PIE RECIPES

MINCEMEAT AND MINCE PIE

2 cupfuls finely chopped lean beef
4 cupfuls finely chopped, tart apples
2 cupfuls chopped seeded raisins
2 cupfuls currants
1 cupful finely chopped citron
2 teaspoonfuls salt
1 cupful suet chopped, or other fat
2 cupfuls sugar
1 cupful strong coffee infusion
1 tablespoonful ground cloves
1 tablespoonful cinnamon
1 tablespoonful nutmeg
1 cupful meat stock

Purchase clear, lean meat and boil until tender, cool in the liquor, then put through the chopper.   Mix the materials together in the order named.   Simmer slowly for about one hour, bottle hot, and seal.   This makes about five pints.   When making the pie, line a deep plate with crust, fill with mince meat, using one quart, and then put over the top one tablespoonful of cream, one tablespoonful of sugar, a few whole, seeded raisins, and two teaspoonfuls of butter in bits.   Put on the top crust and bake at 450° F. for thirty minutes.

GREEN TOMATO MINCE MEAT

1½ quarts green tomatoes
Salt
2 cupfuls chopped tart apples
1 chopped orange
3 cupfuls medium brown sugar
1 pound raisins or mixed chopped fruit
2 tablespoonfuls mixed ground spices

Slice the green tomatoes very thin.   Sprinkle with salt and let stand overnight.   Then drain and chop very fine.   Add the chopped tart apples and chopped orange; simmer two hours.   Add the brown sugar, raisins or mixed chopped fruit, and mixed ground spices, and simmer one hour.   This amount is sufficient for two good-sized pies. Cool the filling before putting into the pie crust.

RAISIN PIE

Grated rind and juice
  of 2 lemons
Grated rind and juice
  of 1 orange
1 cupful light brown sugar
2 cupfuls seeded raisins
1¼ cupfuls water
1 scant cupful walnut-meats, coarsely chopped
3 tablespoonfuls corn-starch
Pastry

Cook together all the ingredients except the corn-starch.   When it comes to a boil, thicken the mixture with the corn-starch with a small quantity of cold water.   Bake between two crusts.   (See P. 252.)

RHUBARB MERINGUE PIE

2 cupfuls diced rhubarb	¼ cupful sugar
¾ cupful sugar	2 tablespoonfuls flour
1 cupful milk	¼ teaspoonful salt
2 eggs	1 teaspoonful lemon juice
2 egg-whites	Pastry
4 tablespoonfuls sugar	¼ teaspoonful vanilla

Line a medium pie plate with pastry, having a fluted edge.   Stew the rhubarb and three-quarter cupful sugar until soft. Cool, add milk and two eggs beaten with one-quarter cupful sugar, the flour and salt.   Add lemon juice.   Pour into pastry lined pie plate and bake at 450° F. for ten minutes, and at 325° F. for twenty-five minutes.   Make a meringue of two beaten egg-whites, four tablespoonfuls of sugar and vanilla. Heap on pie and brown at 300° F. for fifteen minutes.

RHUBARB GELATINE PIE

2½ cupfuls stewed rhubarb	1 cupful cream
1 cupful granulated sugar	Pastry
½ cupful cold water	2 tablespoonfuls granulated gelatin

Line a medium-sized pie plate with pastry, having a fluted edge, and bake at 500° F. for twelve minutes.   Heat the stewed rhubarb with the sugar and pour it over the gelatine which has soaked five minutes in the cold water.   Stir until dissolved.   Let cool, stirring at intervals. When beginning to stiffen, beat well and fold in the cream, whipped. Allow to cool until ready to set and pour into the baked pastry shell. Chill thoroughly.

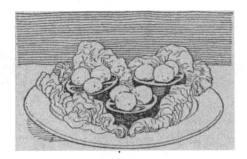

Salads and Salad Dressings

I. TREATMENT OF VEGETABLES, ETC., FOR SALADS

1. Lettuce, Parsley, Watercress, etc.
   a. Wash each sprig or leaf carefully, being sure to leave no small green insects, that so often infest lettuce.
   b. Let lettuce lie in very cold salted water for two or three minutes.
   c. Rinse again in cold water, looking carefully for insects.
   d. Drain in a sieve and let them lie between the folds of a clean towel for a few minutes.
   e. Set in a cool place. Look over the lettuce and parsley daily. Any water left on leaves drop to bottom of can and the leaves lying in this spoil quickly. The water also stagnates, developing odors. Take out the greens, wash can and dry thoroughly and return the greens.

2. Other Raw Vegetables or Fruit
   a. Wash well and cut into suitable pieces
   b. Let them lie in water a few minutes to crisp, then drain well in a strainer.
   c. Celery—use only inner tender stalks. Cut across stalk in ½ inch slices.
   d. Cabbage—cut in quarters and shred finely with a sharp knife, discarding tough heart.

150

e. Apples—pare, core and cut in dice (not small). Cut up apples just before mixing with dressing. Otherwise they will discolor. Serve at once.

f. Dates—wash, stone and cut in quarters. Do not put in water.

g. Oranges and grapefruit—Prepare as directed in the Preparation of Raw Fruit, Page 8.

h. Tomatoes—wash, peel and chill. Slice or dice as desired.

3. Cooked Fruit and Vegetables

a. Potatoes, beets, etc. Cut the peeled, cold, boiled vegetables in dice.

b. Asparagus, string beans, etc.—trim and arrange on lettuce leaves.

4. Meat for Salads—Veal, Chicken or Tongue

a. Cut in one half inch dice and season with salt, pepper and celery salt.

b. Mix with a vegetable or mix together two-thirds meat and one-third celery or cabbage. Mix with dressing and let stand an hour.

5. Fish

Leave in one large piece, in pieces large enough for individual service, or in flakes. Season with salt, pepper and lemon juice.

II. MIXING AND SERVING SALADS

1. Have everything cold and all ingredients chilled.

2. Mix vegetables or fruit, cut in pieces, very lightly, with two silver forks, to prevent any breaking or mashing.

3. Garnishes for Salads

a. Lettuce—Arrange a border of lettuce leaves in salad bowl, or one crisp lettuce leaf for individual service. A border of shredded lettuce may also be used.

b. Parsley—sprigs of parsley placed effectively.

c. Sliced cucumbers

d. Jelly Cubes—arranged inside border of lettuce, or one cube on individual plate.

e. Pimientoes—cut in pieces or fancy shapes (with vegetable cutter) may be molded in jellied salads or mixed with vegetable salads

f. Slices of firmly cooked egg—molded in bottom of jelly molds, or arranged inside border of lettuce or parsley sprigs.

g. Radishes.

4. When mixed, turn salad lightly from mixing bowl to serving dish or individual plates. Do not disturb again.

5. Some Special Directions for Serving
   a. **Eggs.** Hard cook the eggs (see P. 21). Serve halved or sliced.
   b. **Lettuce.** Shred lettuce and pile in a salad bowl or arrange small leaves in a bowl. Never mix lettuce with the dressing.
   c. **Fish.** Chill and arrange on a bed of lettuce or use a few parsley sprigs. Garnish with sliced cucumbers. Serve dressing separately.
   d. **Tomatoes.** Arrange on lettuce or use a few parsley sprigs. Use sliced cucumbers or little balls made of cream cheese. These balls may be rolled in chopped nuts. Serve dressing separately.
   e. **Tomato Jelly Salad.** See Gelatine Dishes (P. 196). Serve in individual molds or in one large mold. Slices of hard cooked egg molded in jelly are effective. A border mold of Tomato Jelly Salad and the center filled with meat or vegetable salad may be arranged. Serve dressing separately.
   f. **Potatoes, Beets, etc.** Prepare as directed. Season and mix with dressing. Allow salad to stand for an hour to blend flavors before piling in serving dish.
   g. **Asparagus, String Beans, Green Peas, etc.** Chill and serve on a bed of lettuce. Serve dressing separately.
   h. **Fruit.** A mixture of canned or fresh fruits is used in preparing a fruit salad, as oranges, bananas, pineapple or grapefruit, pineapple and strawberries. The fruits available for the season will determine the combinations used.

III. SALAD DRESSINGS

COOKED SALAD DRESSING

4 tablespoonfuls melted butter	1 teaspoonful salt
2 tablespoonfuls flour	1 teaspoonful mustard
1 cupful milk	Dash cayenne pepper
1 tablespoonful sugar	¼ cupful mild vinegar

2 eggs

Melt butter in top of double boiler. Add flour, stir until smooth, and then add milk. Cook until quite thick. Beat eggs slightly, add sugar, salt, mustard and cayenne pepper. Pour hot mixture over them slowly while beating constantly. Return to double boiler and cook until thick. Just before removing, add vinegar, and stir well.

FRENCH DRESSING

Salad oil	Pepper
Vinegar	Paprika
Salt	Mustard

Worcestershire sauce

Place a small lump of ice in a shallow bowl. Pour the salad oil slowly over ice, the amount depending upon the number to be served. Add vinegar sparingly, the exact proportion depending upon one's individual taste. Then add salt, pepper, enough paprika to make the dressing pink, and a dash of mustard or a few drops of Worcestershire sauce, here again letting the taste determine the proper amount. When all the ingredients are added, beat the mixture thoroughly with a fork until it is well blended, thick and smooth. Serve at once. Curry powder, horseradish, chopped sour pickles, capers or parsley, chilli sauce, tomato catchup, grated American or Roquefort cheese may be used in varying the dressing. Or the bowl may be rubbed with a clove of garlic.

MAYONNAISE DRESSING

1 egg	6 teaspoonfuls vinegar
1 teaspoonful salt	6 teaspoonfuls lemon juice
1 teaspoonful powdered	1½ cupfuls salad oil
sugar	Paprika
1 teaspoonful mustard	Few grains cayenne

Pepper

Into a conical-shaped bowl break the egg, and add the salt, powdered sugar, mustard, a dash of pepper and paprika, the cayenne, and one teaspoonful of vinegar. Beat thoroughly with a good Dover egg-beater, then add the oil, one tablespoonful at a time, beating thoroughly after each addition, until one-half cupful is added and the dressing is thick. Add lemon-juice and remaining vinegar.

SOUR CREAM SALAD DRESSING

1 teaspoonful mustard	½ cupful milk
1 teaspoonful sugar	1½ teaspoonfuls butter
½ teaspoonful salt	1 egg
Speck pepper	⅓ cupful hot vinegar
1 tablespoonful flour	½ cupful sour cream

Combine the dry ingredients in the top of the double boiler. Beat the egg, add the milk, and stir into the dry ingredients gradually. Cook, stirring constantly, until the mixture coats the spoon—do not let the water boil in the bottom of the double boiler. Add the hot vinegar and butter, and remove from the heat. Cool and add the sour cream. Pour over the salad and serve. This recipe serves six.

RUSSIAN DRESSING

12 tablespoonfuls mayonnaise	1 teaspoonful chopped capers
3 tablespoonfuls chopped pimientoes ·	1 tablespoonful tarragon vinegar
12 sprigs chives	3 tablespoonfuls whipped cream
6 tablespoonfuls chilli sauce	

Mix in order given, chill well and serve as desired.

THOUSAND ISLAND CREAM DRESSING

½ cupful mayonnaise made with tarragon vinegar	2 teaspoonfuls minced chives
	2 tablespoonfuls tomato catchup
2 tablespoonfuls finely chopped pimientoes	2 tablespoonfuls chilli sauce
½ cupful heavy cream	2 hard-cooked eggs

Mix in order given and chill.

FRUIT SALAD DRESSING

¼ cupful mayonnaise   ½ cupful cream

Whip the cream quite stiff and fold in the mayonnaise carefully. Serve with fruit salad.

IV. SELECTED SALAD RECIPES

1. Substantial Salads

CHICKEN SALAD

¼ cupful Roquefort cheese	½ cupful French dressing
Lettuce	1 hard cooked egg
Diced celery	Diced chicken
Cayenne pepper	Pimiento

Add the Roquefort cheese, or snappy, or grated mild American cheese to the French dressing. Add a dash of cayenne and the hard-cooked egg yolk, riced. Arrange the lettuce nests on individual serving plates. Place a spoonful of diced chicken and celery in the center of each and pour the dressing liberally over all. Garnish each with a ring or two of the hard-cooked egg-white and a strip of pimiento.

COUNTRY SALAD

2 cupfuls chopped cooked meat	3 hard-cooked eggs
2 cupfuls diced cooked potatoes	Cooked dressing
	Lettuce
1 cupful cooked, sliced carrots	3 small gherkins
	1 cupful diced celery

Combine the chopped, cooked meat, which may be corned beef, tongue or ham, with sufficient cooked dressing to mold. Pack in a cold mold and chill. Likewise, thoroughly chill the cooked potatoes and carrots. Let the diced celery stand in cold water to which a little lemon juice has been added. When ready to serve, line the salad dish with lettuce, unmold the meat in the center and arrange the potatoes tossed in cooked dressing around it. Place the border of carrots around the potatoes, then the celery drained and wiped dry. Chop the whites of the hard-cooked eggs and sprinkle over the salad. Press the yolks through a fine sieve and scatter over the meat. Garnish with halves of gherkins and pour cooked dressing over the vegetables. Potato balls or carrot slices cut in fancy shapes may be used. Serves six.

CUCUMBER SALAD WITH SALMON DRESSING

1 head lettuce	1 cupful cooked salmon
2 cucumbers	
1 onion	Pepper
Salt	Cooked dressing

Break apart, wash and dry the lettuce leaves, pare the cucumbers, and chill all. For each individual service, make a bed of lettuce leaves on the plate and upon it place thin slices of cucumber, some of the finely minced onion, and a sprinkle of salt and pepper. Put the salmon into a cold bowl, shred and remove bones; add to it, until right consistency to pour, a sour highly seasoned, cooked dressing. Beat thoroughly and pour over the lettuce and cucumbers. Serves six.

FRENCH CREAM POTATO SALAD

4 cupfuls cold boiled potatoes	3 tablespoonfuls chopped onion
3 stalks celery	2 teaspoonfuls salt
1/8 teaspoonful pepper	1/8 teaspoonful paprika
1/4 cupful vinegar	1/2 pint cream
2 tablespoonfuls butter	

Dice the potatoes and celery, mix with the minced onion, salt, pepper, and paprika, add the vinegar, and allow to stand fifteen minutes. Heat the cream and butter until the butter is melted. Pour over the potatoes, stirring with a fork, so that the potatoes will not be mashed. Serve cold. Serves six.

FAVORITE SALAD

2 cupfuls cooked diced potatoes	3 tablespoonfuls tarragon
2 cupfuls cooked diced beets	vinegar
½ cupful diced gherkins	¼ cupful French dressing
¼ cupful chopped chives	1 head lettuce
6 tablespoonfuls salad oil	1 cupful diced raw tomatoes
2 hard-cooked eggs	

Combine the diced potatoes, beets, gherkins and chopped chives. Marinate in the oil and vinegar in a cold place for one hour. Drain off the oil, then cover the vegetables with the French dressing. Arrange on a bed of crisp lettuce and garnish with the diced tomatoes and the eggs cut in eighths. Serves six.

HARLEQUIN SALAD

1½ cupfuls chopped tongue or ham	¼ cupful chopped gherkins
1 cupful cooked lima beans	⅓ cupful French dressing
3 hard-cooked eggs	1 head lettuce
1 sliced tomato	Sour cream salad dressing

Prepare and combine meat, lima beans, hard-cooked eggs, cut in eighths, and the chopped gherkins. Cover with the French dressing and marinate for at least one hour in a cold place. Pile on a bed of crisp lettuce and garnish with the sliced tomato. Serve with Sour Cream Salad Dressing, (P. 153.) Serves six to eight.

JELLIED SHRIMP SALAD

1 quart canned tomatoes	2 tablespoonfuls granulated gelatine
1¼ cupfuls water	1½ cupfuls shrimp
1½ teaspoonfuls salt	½ cupful finely diced celery
¼ teaspoonful pepper	¼ cupful diced green pepper
4 cloves	
1 bay-leaf	Cooked dressing
1 tablespoonful sugar	Lettuce
1 teaspoonful mustard	
1 small onion, minced	

Cook the tomatoes, one cupful of water, the salt, pepper, cloves, bay-leaf, sugar, mustard and minced onion together for fifteen minutes. Strain and pour the mixture over the gelatine which has been softened in one-fourth cupful of cold water. Cool until it begins to stiffen and add the shrimps, which have been cleaned, the viscera removed and cut in halves; then add the diced celery and the diced green pepper from which the skin has been removed by parboiling.   Pour into wet individual molds and chill until hardened.   When ready to serve, turn out on beds of lettuce, and garnish with cooked dressing, or mayonnaise, as preferred.   Serves six to eight.

ITALIAN EGG SALAD

4 hard-cooked eggs	½ teaspoonful salt
1 cupful cooked dandelion greens	⅛ teaspoonful pepper
1 small cream or Neufchatel cheese	¼ cupful well-seasoned French dressing
	½ cupful mayonnaise

Lettuce

Chop the eggs and greens very fine, separately.   Mix them together adding the cheese, salt, pepper and sufficient French dressing to make the right consistency to shape with the hands.   Chill, form into balls, and lay on a bed of lettuce.   Pour any remaining French dressing over them and garnish with mayonnaise.   Serves four to six.

MIXED VEGETABLE AND EGG SALAD

1 cupful shredded string beans	½ cupful sliced radishes
1 cupful peas	Lettuce-heart
1 cupful shredded cucumber	6 hard-cooked eggs
French dressing	Lemon jelly
Radish-roses	Parsley
	Mayonnaise

Mix together the peas and shredded string-beans, cooked, the shredded cucumber, and sliced radishes and let stand in a cold place for thirty minutes to marinate in French dressing.   Halve the hard-cooked eggs lengthwise, cut off the lower ends so that they will stand upright, and dip each one in a little tart lemon jelly, which is very cold, but not yet set; have the salad plates very cold and arrange these egg-halves in a circle.   They should stick at once if the jelly mixture contains enough gelatine.   Fill in with the vegetable mixture, top with a lettuce heart, and garnish with parsley and radish-roses.   Pass mayonnaise.   Serves six to eight.

MOCK LOBSTER SALAD

2 cupfuls cold cooked halibut	½ teaspoonful salt
1 cupful radishes shredded	⅛ teaspoonful paprika
⅓ cupful mayonnaise	

Flake the halibut.   Shred radishes with the skins on, measuring one cupful.   Mix with the halibut, add the salt and paprika.   Mix lightly with mayonnaise and serve on crisp white lettuce.   Serves six.

MOLDED CHICKEN AND CUCUMBER SALAD

3 cupfuls canned tomato	1 clove
6 celery sticks	2 tablespoonfuls gelatine
2 chopped onions	½ cupful cold water
3 teaspoonfuls salt	Lettuce
1 teaspoonful sugar	Mayonnaise
¼ teaspoonful pepper	Diced chicken

Sliced cucumbers

Combine the canned tomato, celery sticks cut in pieces, chopped onions, salt, sugar, pepper and clove. Simmer one-half hour. Then strain. While hot, add the gelatine which has been soaked in the cold water. Arrange alternate layers of diced chicken and sliced cucumbers in a cold, wet mold. Pour the tomato mixture over all and chill until firm. Serve on lettuce with mayonnaise. Serves eight to ten.

MOLDED EGG SALAD

6 eggs	Lettuce
½ teaspoonful salt	⅔ cupful mayonnaise
⅛ teaspoonful pepper	3 large tomatoes

Hard-cook the eggs. Cool them slightly, and while still warm, shell them and force through a potato-ricer. Add the salt and pepper and pack the riced egg down firmly into two glasses. Chill thoroughly and remove from the glasses by running a knife or spatula around the edge. It will then be possible to cut the egg into neat slices. Lay one of the tomato slices on each nest of lettuce and place a slice of egg on top. Pour a large spoonful of mayonnaise over all and serve. This amount will serve eight people.

NORWEGIAN SALAD

3 hard-cooked eggs	⅓ cupful French dressing
1 cupful red cabbage, shredded fine	Mayonnaise
	1 head lettuce
1 green pepper, chopped fine	¾ cupful stoned dates
½ cupful diced celery	1 small cream cheese

Separate the egg-whites from the egg-yolks. Chop the whites fine and stir lightly into the shredded cabbage which has been combined with the green pepper and celery. Add the mashed egg-yolks to the French dressing and pour over the cabbage mixture. Arrange on a bed of crisp lettuce and garnish with mayonnaise. Stuff the stoned dates with the cream cheese which has been softened with a little milk or cream. Arrange these stuffed dates as a border around the salad. Serves six.

PIQUANTE FISH SALAD

2 cupfuls flaked cooked halibut   ¼ cupful capers
½ cupful shredded radishes   ⅓ cupful French dressing
¾ cupful diced celery   1 head lettuce
Paprika   Mayonnaise

Shred the radishes with the skins on.   Then combine them with the
fish and celery, stirring lightly with a fork.   Pour the French dressing
over all.   Mix well and arrange on a bed of crisp lettuce.   Garnish
with mayonnaise and sprinkle generously with paprika and the capers.
Serves six.

POTATO SALAD

1 small onion, chopped.   2 slices bacon, diced
2½ teaspoonfuls salt   4 large sticks celery
½ cupful weak vinegar   ⅛ teaspoonful pepper
4 cupfuls sliced boiled   2 hard-cooked eggs
  potatoes   1 tablespoonful
3 tablespoonfuls salad   minced parsley
  oil   3 cooked beets

Put the chopped onion in a large bowl, add the salt, pepper and vinegar, and let stand ten minutes; then slice in the potatoes while still
warm, and mix thoroughly.   Add the oil, celery cut fine, bacon fried to
a crisp, and the bacon fat from frying the bacon; then add the parsley.
Arrange on a bed of chopped lettuce and garnish with the beets and
hard-cooked eggs that have been chopped.   Serves eight.

SHRIMP SALAD

1 pint can shrimps   2 tablespoonfuls
1 small bottle stuffed   pickled white pearl
  olives   onions
12 tiny sweet pickles   French dressing
6 green peppers   Mayonnaise
Lettuce   Whipped cream

Drain the shrimps, rinse with cold water and remove the viscera.
Break in good-sized pieces, and dress with French dressing.   Chill for
two hours, add the olives and sweet pickles sliced, and the onions.
Hollow out the green peppers to form cups, and stuff with this mixture.
Serve garnished with the lettuce and mayonnaise, the latter diluted
with a little whipped sweet or sour cream.   Serves six.

STUFFED TOMATO SALAD

6 medium-sized tomatoes	Salt
6 stuffed or hard- cooked eggs	Mayonnaise
	Pepper
French dressing	Lettuce

Peel the tomatoes. Hollow out to form cups. Dust with salt and pepper and marinate in French dressing for thirty minutes. Then slip a hard-cooked or stuffed egg into each tomato, and serve very cold with a garnish of lettuce and mayonnaise. Serves six.

TUNA AND APPLE SALAD

1 seven ounce can white tuna fish	1 cupful mayonnaise
4 small apples	2 green peppers
Juice one lemon	1 head lettuce
1¼ cupfuls diced celery	Paprika

Pare, core, and dice the apples. Sprinkle with the lemon juice to prevent discoloration. Then add the tuna fish which has been shredded and the diced celery. Combine with a fork and chill well. When ready to serve, add three-fourths cupful of mayonnaise. Arrange on individual beds of crisp lettuce and garnish with the remaining mayonnaise. Seed the green peppers. Slice in rings and arrange over the salad. Serves six.

VEAL SALAD

2 cupfuls cold veal,
   diced
	4 tablespoonfuls salad
	   oil

1 cupful diced string-
   beans or celery, or
   equal parts of each
	1½ tablespoonfuls
	   vinegar

	3 tomatoes
6 hard-cooked eggs	1 small cream cheese
½ teaspoonful salt	Mayonnaise
Paprika	Parsley
Few grains pepper	Lettuce

Chop the eggs rather coarsely, and combine them with the veal, string-beans, oil, vinegar, salt and pepper. Let stand thirty minutes to marinate. Then add mayonnaise to moisten. Arrange the salad in a mound on a large round platter, cover with mayonnaise, border with lettuce, and surround with the tomatoes sliced and overlapping. Garnish with the cream cheese formed into balls and dust with paprika, and a bit of parsley. Serves six.

2. Light Vegetable Salads

ASPARAGUS AND EGG SALAD

2 cupfuls cooked asparagus, diced	1 tablespoonful salad oil
	Lettuce or cress
2 cupfuls shredded lettuce	1 teaspoonful vinegar
2 hard-cooked eggs	Cooked dressing

Mix the asparagus and shredded lettuce with the salad oil and the vinegar. Add cooked dressing to moisten thoroughly, chill, arrange in nests of salad green, and garnish with the hard-cooked eggs and additional dressing. Serves six.

CARROT AND APPLE SALAD

1 cupful prepared apple	1 cupful prepared carrot
½ cupful mayonnaise	Lettuce

Cut the apple into very thin slices, arrange on lettuce, spread with mayonnaise, and sprinkle ground carrot on top. Place more dressing in center. Serves four.

CABBAGE SALAD

2 cupfuls shredded cabbage	2 tart, ripe apples
2 canned pimientoes, diced	¼ cupful nutmeats
	Mayonnaise
	Lettuce

Combine the shredded cabbage, apples which have been pared, cored and cut into matches, the diced pimientos, and the nut-meats coarsely chopped. Mix lightly with mayonnaise or cooked dressing, lay on a bed of white lettuce leaves, mask with a little more of the dressing, ornament with more diced pimientoes and a few quartered nut-meats and serve at once. Do not prepare this salad until needed. Either white cabbage or Chinese cabbage may be used. Serves six.

MARGUERITE SALAD

1 bunch watercress	1 tablespoonful vinegar
1 hard-cooked egg	⅓ teaspoonful salt
3 tablespoonfuls salad oil	Few grains pepper

Wash the watercress thoroughly and then crisp it. Pour the salad oil over a piece of ice in a bowl, add the vinegar, salt and pepper and beat until smooth and thick. Mix the dressing lightly with the watercress and arrange in a salad bowl, with the hard-cooked egg-white, cut into eighths lengthwise, placed in the center to simulate the petals of a flower. The egg-yolk should be sifted and piled in the center of the "flower." Serves six.

MOLDED BEET SALAD

2 cupfuls tiny beets	2 tablespoonfuls
2 tablespoonfuls	grated horseradish
vinegar	1½ tablespoonfuls
⅔ cupful hot water	granulated gelatine
1 teaspoonful salt	¼ cupful cold water
1 teaspoonful sugar	¾ cupful mayonnaise

1 head lettuce

Scrub the beets thoroughly and boil until tender; rub off the skin. Pour over them the vinegar, salt, sugar, horseradish, and hot water. Place over the heat and bring to the boiling point. Then add the gelatine, which has been softened in the cold water, and stir until dissolved. Pour into a shallow pan which has been previously wet with cold water. Set away to chill, cut in cubes, and serve on lettuce or cress with mayonnaise. This recipe will serve at least eight. Large beets may be used and cut into cubes about an inch in diameter after cooking.

NEAPOLITAN SALAD

About 2 cupfuls	3 canned pimientoes
celery strips	French dressing
2 green peppers	Lettuce

Cut the celery into short, thin strips. Cover the peppers with boiling water, let stand five minutes, remove at once, dry and chill; then cut into strips the same size as the celery; rinse the pimientoes in cold water, dry and cut in the same style as the celery. Mix with French dressing and serve in nests of lettuce. Serves six.

STUFFED GREEN PEPPER SALAD

3 medium-sized green peppers	¼ cupful chopped stuffed
1 small cream cheese	olives
¼ cupful grated American	Thin cream
cheese	Paprika
Salt	Lettuce

Mayonnaise

Remove the tops from the peppers, scoop out seeds, and boil five minutes in boiling salted water; then remove and chill. Mix together the cream cheese, American cheese, and olives, moisten with cream as needed, and season with salt and paprika to taste. Pack into the peppers, chill well, then slice and serve on lettuce leaves with a garnish of mayonnaise. The cheese mixture can be used as a spread for graham sandwiches. Serves six to eight.

STUFFED CELERY SALAD

1 small bunch celery	1 small cream cheese
1 head lettuce	French dressing

Mash the cream cheese with a fork until soft and creamy, adding a little cream or top milk if necessary. Fill the celery stalks with the cheese. Cut into one-inch pieces and serve on lettuce with French dressing. Serves six.

SWEET GREEN PEPPER JELLY SALAD

1 tablespoonful granulated gelatine	¼ teaspoonful salt
	1 bay leaf
¼ cupful cold water	1 piece parsley
1¼ cupfuls asparagus stock	¾ cupful mayonnaise
	Lettuce
3 or 4 stalks cold boiled asparagus	Radishes
	½ teaspoonful celery salt
3 small green peppers	

Soak the gelatine in the cold water. Cover the green peppers with boiling water and let stand five minutes; drain, remove stems and seeds, and put with the asparagus through the meat-chopper, using a coarse knife. Combine the asparagus stock, bay leaf and parsley and boil five minutes. Strain. There should be one cupful of liquid left. Pour this boiling liquid over the gelatine and stir until thoroughly dissolved. Add the chopped peppers, asparagus, salt, and celery salt. Mold in cold, wet custard cups. Serve with mayonnaise on crisp lettuce, garnished with slices of radish or finely diced cold, boiled carrots to give a touch of color. If canned asparagus and peppers are used, cut them in small pieces and use the liquid in the can. Serves six to eight.

TOMATO AND CABBAGE SALAD

1 small, firm head cabbage	1 finely chopped onion
	1 medium-sized cucumber
3 medium-sized tomatoes	1 small green pepper
	Salad dressing
Lettuce	

Shred the cabbage finely and add to it the chopped onion, one-half the green pepper chopped, and one-half of the cucumber, pared and diced. Mix well with either French dressing or cooked dressing, as preferred. Whichever is used, be sure that it is well seasoned. Peel the tomatoes and cut them in eighths. Pile the cabbage mixture in a salad bowl on leaves of lettuce and garnish with the tomatoes, the rest of the cucumber sliced, and the rest of the green pepper cut in strips. Serves eight.

CUCUMBER JELLY SALAD

3 medium-sized cucumbers	3 cupfuls boiling water
2 small onions	1½ tablespoonfuls granulated gelatine
Speck pepper	½ teaspoonful salt

Peel and chop the onions fine. Pare and slice the cucumbers. Combine. Add the salt, cover with the boiling water, and cook until the cucumbers are tender, replenishing the water. Meanwhile, soften the gelatine in two tablespoonfuls of cold water. When the cucumbers and onions are tender, press them through a potato-ricer. To the strained pulp and juice, of which there should be three cupfuls, add the pepper and salt if necessary. Reheat, add the gelatine, and stir until dissolved. Pour into cold, wet, individual molds. Serve on lettuce with mayonnaise and sliced tomatoes. Serves six to eight.

TOMATO AND CUCUMBER SALAD

1 large head lettuce	1 cucumber
4 medium-sized tomatoes	2 tablespoonfuls minced green pepper
French dressing	

Select a large, firm head of lettuce, and wash it without tearing the leaves apart. Set in a cool place to drain and crisp; then place on a large plate, stem-end down. Arrange inside the leaves the tomatoes, skinned and sliced and the cucumber, pared and sliced. Scatter the minced green pepper over all. Serve with French dressing or mayonnaise. In serving, the hostess separates a leaf or two of the lettuce and then places on them a few slices of tomato and cucumber. Serves eight.

3. Fruit Salads

APPLE AND WATERCRESS SALAD

3 large red apples	Bar-le-Duc or currant jelly
1 small cream cheese	French dressing
Watercress	

Wash and core apples, leaving the skin on, and cut crosswise into inch thick slices. Mix the Bar-le-Duc with cream cheese until a smooth paste is formed; spread this mixture on the slices of apple, allowing one slice to each portion. Mix French dressing with the watercress, lay it on one side of the salad plate and place the apple slices on the other. Serves eight.

BANANA AND CELERY SALAD

6 small bananas	6 large sticks celery
6 tablespoonfuls peanut	Lettuce
butter	¾ cupful mayonnaise

Stuff the cleaned celery sticks with the peanut butter and then cut into small pieces. Arrange on beds of lettuce with the bananas either sliced or diced. Serve with mayonnaise. Whipped cream may be added to the dressing, if desired. Serves six.

CANDLESTICK SALAD, INDIVIDUAL

1 slice canned pine-	Shredded coconut
apple	Strip green pepper
½ banana, cut cross-	Maraschino cherry
wise	Fruit salad dressing
	Lettuce

For the base of the candlestick, place the slice of pineapple on a leaf of lettuce and surround with fruit salad dressing piped through a pastry tube. For the candlestick, point the cut end of the banana half and place it in an upright position in the cavity of the pineapple slice. In the side of the banana stick the strip of green pepper to simulate the handle. On the top of the banana place the maraschino cherry or a strawberry, keeping it in position with a toothpick. Stick a piece of shredded coconut in the cherry for a wick. Serve additional salad dressing in tiny bonbon dishes at each plate. Serves one.

CHERRY AND CHEESE SALAD

Large, black canned	½ cupful finely
cherries	chopped walnuts
1 small cream cheese	⅛ teaspoonful salt
¼ cupful thin cream	Dash paprika
Lettuce	Mayonnaise

Remove the stones from the cherries, allowing six to eight for each serving. Combine the cream cheese, cream, chopped walnuts, salt and paprika and form into tiny balls. Chill the stoned cherries thoroughly and fill with the cheese balls. Serve on white lettuce leaves garnished with mayonnaise. Serve with buttered, hot, unsalted whole wheat crackers.

CUCUMBER AND PINEAPPLE SALAD

½ cupful vinegar
Juice ½ lemon
¼ cupful sugar
½ teaspoonful salt
2 tablespoonfuls
  granulated gelatine
¼ cupful cold water
1 cupful boiling water

Lettuce
⅓ cupful mayonnaise
¾ cupful cream,
  whipped
1 cupful diced
  cucumber
1 cupful shredded
  pineapple

Paprika

Soak the gelatine in the cold water five minutes, add boiling water, and stir until dissolved. Add the sugar, salt, vinegar, and lemon juice. When the mixture has begun to set, stir in the diced cucumber and shredded pineapple, preferably canned, and pour into wet, individual molds. Serve when stiffened, on crisp lettuce garnished with the mayonnaise to which the whipped cream has been added; sprinkle with paprika. This jelly may be colored with green vegetable coloring, if desired. Serves six to eight.

ENDIVE GRAPEFRUIT SALAD

12 stalks French endive
Scooped out pulp 1½ grapefruit

2 ounces crumpled Roquefort
  cheese

French dressing

Wash and dry the endive, chill thoroughly, and arrange on individual plates. Heap the grapefruit at the end of the stalks, and sprinkle it with the cheese crumbs. Pour French dressing over all. If necessary, romaine may be substituted for the endive. Serves six.

GINGER ALE SALAD

¾ cupful diced,
  canned pineapple
¾ cupful chopped
  grapefruit pulp
⅓ cupful blanched,
  shredded almonds
¼ cupful seeded
  malaga grapes

2 tablespoonfuls granulated
  gelatine
½ cupful cold water
Few grains salt
Few grains paprika
Mayonnaise
Lettuce
1 cupful ginger ale

Soak the gelatine in the cold water for five minutes, then dissolve it over hot water. Add one-fourth cupful of the ginger ale. Combine the diced pineapple, grapefruit pulp, malaga grapes, shredded almonds, salt and pepper and then add the remaining three-fourths cupful of ginger ale. Add the gelatine mixture, stir thoroughly and pour into individual molds which have been dipped in and out of cold water.

Chill thoroughly, unmold and serve on lettuce leaves, garnished with mayonnaise. Serves six to eight.

ORANGE-PECAN SALAD

1 banana	½ cupful pecan-meats
2 oranges	Lettuce
French dressing	

Remove skin from banana, cut in quarters lengthwise and again crosswise and roll in pecan-meats, finely chopped. Peel oranges, cut in slices crosswise, and remove the center core. Insert a cube of banana in center of each slice. Arrange on a bed of lettuce, sprinkle over remainder of pecans and French dressing. This will make eight portions.

SALAD MOUSSE

1 cupful stiff mayonnaise	2 tablespoonfuls
3 cupfuls cream	boiling water
1 teaspoonful gran-	1½ cupfuls mixed
ulated gelatine	fruit
Lettuce	Mayonnaise

Whip the cream stiff and combine lightly with the mayonnaise. Dissolve the gelatine in the boiling water and stir carefully. Add this to the mayonnaise a little at a time, while stirring. Then fold in the mixed fruit, cut in dice, which may be pineapple, oranges, pitted cherries, and strawberries. Pack the mixture solidly in a well-chilled mold and cover with greased paper, the greased side up. Adjust the cover of the mold and bury it in the cracked ice and salt, using one part of salt to four parts of ice. Allow to stand four hours, unmold on crisp lettuce leaves and serve with mayonnaise and browned crackers. Serves eight to ten.

SPOOK SALAD

Lettuce	Mayonnaise
Celery	Peaches
Apples	Cloves
Red grapes	Pimiento

Make a nest of lettuce leaves or shredded lettuce. On this place a salad made of celery, apples, and red grapes, allowing for each serving about two tablespoonfuls each of chopped celery and apples, and six grapes cut in half and blended together with mayonnaise. On this salad place a half peach with the rounded side up. Insert two whole cloves with the heads for the eyes, place another with the large end down for the nose, and a narrow strip of pimiento for the mouth. This strip may be placed at various angles.

RED CHERRY SALAD

1 can red cherries or	1 cupful sugar
1 pint stewed, fresh	Shelled pecans
cherries and juice	Whipped cream
1⅓ tablespoonfuls	Mayonnaise
granulated gelatine	1 tablespoonful
1 cupful orange-juice	lemon-juice

Lettuce

Strain the juice from the cherries (there should be one cupful), add the sugar and let come to a boil. In the meantime soak the gelatine in the orange and lemon juices combined for five minutes; pit the cherries, replacing the stones with halves of pecan-meats. Add the gelatine to the sirup, put the stuffed cherries into six individual molds, pour the sirup over while hot, and when stiff serve on lettuce with mayonnaise, combined with whipped cream in the desired proportions. Serves six to eight.

Frozen Dishes

I. GENERAL DIRECTIONS

1. Cream fresh from the separator or pasteurizer produces a coarse-grained ice-cream. To whip well and to remain whipped, a cream should be cold, should contain from eighteen to twenty-two per cent. fat, and should be twenty-four hours old.

2. A small amount of salt added to ice-cream brings out the flavor and improves the finished product.

3. In making ice-cream with a custard foundation, always mix the flour or corn-starch with the sugar and cook thoroughly with the milk before adding the egg.

4. A non-rich cream mixture can be improved by the addition of a small amount of gelatine or by the use of condensed or evaporated milk.

5. Ice-cream mixtures should never be put in the freezer when warm. Precooling cuts down the actual freezing period and gives a better product.

6. Never fill the can more than two-thirds full of the mixture to be frozen. Leave at least one-third the space for the swell.

7. Use only coarse freezing salt for freezing ices and ice-creams. Good results cannot be obtained with the use of table salt.

8. The ice should be fine and evenly crushed.

9. In freezing use the proportion of eight measures of ice to one

169

measure of salt.   You cannot be too careful in these measure-
ments.

10. Fill the freezer two-thirds full of ice before adding salt.   Then
add salt and ice in alternate layers.

11. Use two speeds in freezing ice-cream.   Turn very slowly until
the mixture begins to pull slightly or turn hard, then increase
the speed in order to whip the mixture.

12. Ice-cream may be frozen until of the consistency to serve immediately.   However, the Institute recommends that it be
frozen to the consistency of a very thick cream sauce, and then
packed and ripened.

13. If the ripening time is short, the packing mixture should be in
the proportion of four parts of ice to one of salt.   If longer,
use the eight-to-one mixture.

II. ICE CREAM   (See Chart, P. 191)

III. ICES & SHERBETS (See Chart, P. 193)

IV. MOLDING ICE CREAM MIXTURES

1. Have mold very cold.

2. Pack quickly with the frozen mixture, using a knife and spoon
to press it down.   Fill so that mixture will be forced down
sides of mold when cover is put on.

3. Smooth top of frozen mixture and cover with piece of greased
wax paper, with greased side up.

4. Adjust cover and seal with a two-inch wide strip of cotton
dipped in melted fat, wound tightly around.

5. Pack mold in mixture of three parts of ice to one part of salt;
so that it is completely buried.   Let stand two to three hours.

6. Two or more kinds of frozen mixtures may be arranged in
layers in the mold, or one kind used as a lining, the other
filling the center, thus making a Bombe.

V. FROZEN DESSERTS IN MECHANICAL REFRIGERATING UNITS

Excellent frozen desserts may be made in the ice pans of mechanical
refrigerating units if you carefully follow directions and are particular in
selecting recipes which are adaptable.   Due to the fact that mixtures
are stirred only occasionally when frozen in the ice pans, it follows that
those mixtures whose smoothness depends upon continuous stirring will
not prove as satisfactory as others.   On the other hand rich ice-cream
mixtures which contain a large proportion of cream, such as mousses,
and parfaits, are more easily adapted to this method of freezing.   To
obtain a satisfactory texture, ice-cream recipes must be modified to
suit the changed conditions of freezing.   A small amount of gelatine

should be added to give body and help prevent the formation of ice crystals, and as a further aid, the cream should be beaten stiff before it is added. Recipes for mousses, parfaits, Biscuit Tortoni, and all frozen mixtures which are usually packed in salt and ice and frozen without stirring, may be prepared with little or no change of method, and frozen in the mechanical refrigerator. The temperature in the trays is not constant but varies during the cycle of operation of the machine. Further, the maximum and minimum temperatures obtained in the trays depend on the adjustment of the temperature controlling device. Uniformly satisfactory results can be obtained only if the setting of your machine is such that the necessary freezing temperatures are maintained in the ice trays. If desserts are not obtainable in from five to seven hours, it may be that the setting for your particular box is too high for the freezing of these desserts, even though quite satisfactory for good refrigeration.

In that case it will be necessary to have the machine reset for a lower temperature if you wish very much to use it for freezing desserts. To have this done, means, of course, a higher operating cost, that is a greater consumption of current. From an economical standpoint this may not be desirable. In other words, it is for you to decide whether or not you wish to regularly pay a higher cost than necessary for good refrigeration in order that you may occasionally freeze desserts. After all, do not forget in making such a decision that the major function of the mechanical refrigerator is refrigeration. The freezing of desserts is a relatively minor function.

VANILLA ICE CREAM

2 cupfuls scalded milk	1 teaspoonful gelatine
1 cupful sugar	1 tablespoonful cold water
2 tablespoonfuls flour	1½ pints heavy cream
Yolks 2 eggs	2 teaspoonfuls vanilla

Scald the milk in the double boiler and add the sugar and flour which have been thoroughly mixed. Cook for fifteen or twenty minutes. Pour over the beaten egg yolks, return to the fire and cook for two minutes or until the mixture coats the spoon. Add to this while hot, the gelatine, which has soaked for five minutes in one tablespoonful of cold water, and chill the mixture. Whip the cream until stiff and fold into the cooked mixture. Add two teaspoonfuls of vanilla and one-eighth teaspoonful of salt. Pour into the tray of the refrigerator and freeze, stirring every thirty minutes until the mixture will hold its shape. The recipe serves six to eight.

CHOCOLATE ICE CREAM

Melt three squares (three ounces) of chocolate, add one-fourth cupful of hot water slowly and stir until smooth. Add to the Vanilla Ice Cream mixture.

COFFEE ICE CREAM

Add two tablespoonfuls of finely ground coffee to the milk. Scald and strain through several thicknesses of cheese cloth, then proceed as with the Vanilla Ice Cream.

CRUSHED FRUIT ICE CREAM

Any crushed fruit may be added. If the fruit is juicy as in the case of strawberries and crushed pineapple, drain well and increase the gelatine from one-quarter to one-half teaspoonful more than is given in the recipe for Vanilla Ice Cream. If the fruit lacks acid, as in the case of canned peaches or canned pineapple, add one to two tablespoonfuls of lemon juice. Add from one to two cupfuls of crushed fruit depending on individual taste. Proceed as with Vanilla Ice Cream.

WHITE PARFAIT

1 cupful sugar	½ teaspoonful gelatine
½ cupful water	1 tablespoonful cold water
Whites 3 eggs	1 tablespoonful vanilla

1 pint cream

Boil the sugar and water to 238° F. Pour slowly on to the egg whites which have been beaten stiff. Add gelatine which has been soaked for five minutes in one tablespoonful of cold water. Beat until cool and fold in the cream, which has been beaten stiff. Add the vanilla, pour into the refrigerator pans, and freeze without stirring. This recipe serves six to eight.

PINEAPPLE MOUSSE

2 cupfuls canned crushed pineapple and juice	2 tablespoonfuls cold water
¾ cupful sugar	2 tablespoonfuls lemon juice
	2 teaspoonfuls gelatine

2 cupfuls cream

Heat the pineapple to boiling and add the sugar, lemon juice, and gelatine, which has soaked for five minutes in two tablespoonfuls of cold water. Cool by putting in a container in a pan of water, to which the ice cubes have been added. When the mixture becomes thick and is beginning to congeal, fold in the stiffly beaten cream. Pour into the refrigerator pans and freeze without stirring. This recipe serves six to eight.

VI. ICE CREAMS IN VACUUM OR AUTOMATIC FREEZERS

Standard ice cream recipes suggested for use in a crank freezer may be prepared in a vacuum freezer with satisfactory results. It is our opinion that the resulting ice cream does not have quite the same velvety smoothness of that prepared in a crank freezer. However, we believe that the convenience of a vacuum freezer should appeal to many housekeepers and overbalance any slight difference in texture.

Icings

I. UNCOOKED ICINGS

Select confectioner's sugar, confectioner's powdered sugar, or frosting sugar. The fineness is designated by xxxx or xxxxxx, as the case may be. The latter makes the smoothest icing, but the former gives quite acceptable results. Never use powdered sugar, as it is too granular.

PLAIN ICING

1½ cupfuls confectioner's sugar   About 3 tablespoonfuls water
Few drops flavoring   or milk

Sift the confectioner's sugar into a bowl. Add the water or milk very gradually until thin enough to spread easily, but not run. Add flavoring and a bit of vegetable coloring, if desired. For Plain Chocolate Icing, add one-half ounce or one-half square of chocolate, melted, to the above recipe. For Plain Coffee Icing, use instead of water or milk, the same quantity of strong, clear, black coffee infusion, adding a few drops of vanilla. For Fruit Icing, use fresh or canned fruit juice instead of water or milk, omitting other flavoring.

SOFT ICING

2 egg whites   1 cupful confectioner's sugar
½ teaspoonful vanilla or almond extract

Beat egg whites until stiff. Add the confectioner's sugar gradually, continuing to beat with the egg beater until light and fluffy. Add the extract. This icing remains soft and is easy to spread.

BUTTER ICING

4 tablespoonfuls salt butter   2 cupfuls confectioner's sugar
½ teaspoonful milk   ¼ teaspoonful vanilla

Cream the butter in a bowl until soft. Then add the confectioner's sugar gradually, blending each addition of sugar thoroughly with the butter. When the mixture begins to get stiff, add milk, drop by drop, and the extract. Spread on cake when thoroughly cold.

This icing can be used with a pastry bag and tubes. To vary this icing, an egg yolk or strong coffee may be used in place of the liquid. For Chocolate Mocha Icing, sift two tablespoonfuls of cocoa with the sugar and add strong coffee infusion as the liquid. For Chocolate Butter Icings add ½ oz. or ½ square of melted chocolate to the above.

II. COOKED ICINGS (See Chart, P. 194)

Chart for Baking-Powder Biscuits and Shortcakes

Biscuits	Basic Ingredients	Additional Ingredients	Method
Baking-Powder Biscuits	2 c. flour ⅔ c. milk or water (about) 2 tbsps. shortening 4 tsps. baking-powder 1 tsp. salt		Cut shortening into sifted dry ingredients. Add liquid to make a soft dough. Roll lightly or pat into a sheet, cut into rounds. Place on greased pans. Bake at 450° F. 12-15 min. One beaten egg may be added, reducing the liquid to make soft dough.
Cheese Biscuits	Same as in Baking-Powder Biscuits	½ c. grated cheese	Add cheese with shortening or sprinkle on top of Baking-Powder Biscuits.
Fruit or Nut Biscuits	Same as in Baking Powder Biscuits	¾ c. currants, raisins, chopped figs, preserved ginger, or nuts. Candied cherries, brown sugar and cinnamon or nutmeg	Add fruit or nuts to Baking-Powder Biscuits before adding milk. Tops may be sprinkled with brown sugar and cinnamon or nutmeg. Candied cherries, raisins or nuts may be placed on top of thin rolled biscuits.
Orange Biscuits	Same as in Baking-Powder Biscuits	Cube sugar Orange juice Orange rind	Dip sugar cubes into orange juice, moistening thoroughly. Place one on each biscuit before baking. Sprinkle with grated orange rind.
Peanut Butter Biscuits	Same as in Baking-Powder Biscuits	¼ c. peanut butter	Use peanut butter as the shortening in Baking-Powder Biscuits.
Pinwheel Biscuits	Same as in Baking-Powder Biscuits	2 tsps. melted butter ¼ c. sugar ½—2 tsps. nutmeg or cinnamon	Roll Baking-Powder Biscuit dough into rectangle ¼ inch thick, brush with melted butter, sprinkle with sugar and cinnamon and roll up from long side as jelly roll. Brown or granulated sugar may be used. Cut in ¾-inch slices, lay with cut side down on greased pan. Bake 20 min. at 450° F.
Caramel or Butterscotch Biscuits	Same as in Baking-Powder Biscuits	1 c. brown sugar ¼ c. fat ½ c. raisins	Cream sugar and fat. Spread on rolled out dough. Proceed as in Pinwheel Biscuits. Raisins may be added before rolling up.
Pinwheel Fruit or Nut Biscuits	Same as in Baking-Powder Biscuits	1 c. raw chopped apples, cut stewed apricots, berries (floured), or ¾ c. dates, figs, raisins, currants, or nuts, or ½ c. peanut butter	Make and bake like Pinwheel Biscuits. Any fruits listed may be sprinkled on before rolling. Combinations may be made of dried fruits, nuts, candied orange, or grape-fruit peel or citron. Or spread with peanut butter before rolling.
Drop Biscuits	Same as in Baking-Powder Biscuits	Increase liquid from ⅔ c. to 1 c.	Make like Baking-Powder Biscuits. Drop from teaspoon or tablespoon into muffin tins or onto greased pan. Fruits and nuts may be added to drop biscuits, or make a depression in top of each biscuit, in which put 1 tsp. of orange marmalade, fruit or nuts.
Shortcake	Same as in Baking-Powder Biscuits	Increase shortening from 2 tbsps. to 2 cups of flour to ¼ c. or ⅓ c. to 2 cups of flour	Follow Baking-Powder Biscuit method. Bake in a thick layer and split, or make two thin layers, put together, bake and separate. Individual shortcakes may be made.
Crushed Fruit, Sliced Fresh or Sliced Canned Fruit Shortcake	Same as in Shortcake	1 qt. strawberries, raspberries, blackberries, loganberries, stewed blueberries, or huckleberries 1 qt. sliced or 1 can peaches, pineapple or apricots Sugar 1 c. cream, whipped	Crush berries or slice fruit, reserving choice berries or slices, for garnishing. Cut pineapple fine. Sweeten as needed; put between layers and on top of shortcake. Top with whipped cream and garnish with whole berries or slices of fruit.

All recipes in this chart serve six. **For detailed instructions, see P. 198.**

Chart for Quick Loaf Breads

Bread	Flour	Liquid	Other Ingredients	Special Directions
Nut Bread	3c. bread flour	1½ c. milk	¼—1 c. sugar 1 egg 1 tsp. salt 6 tsps. baking powder 1—3 tbsps. melted fat 1 c. chopped nuts	Sift together dry ingredients, add milk, beaten egg, nuts and fat. Beat well. Bake at 375° F.—1 hour. Either white or brown sugar may be used. Pecans, walnuts, almonds or peanuts may be used.
Whole Wheat Nut Bread	1½c. bread flour 1½ c. whole wheat flour	1½ c. milk	Sugar 6 tsps. baking powder 1 egg 1 tsp. salt 1—3 tbsps. melted fat 1 c. chopped nuts	Make and bake like Nut Bread. Allow to stand in pan 15 min. before baking. Any quantity of sugar up to ½ c. may be used.
Graham Nut Bread	1½ c. bread flour 1½ c. Graham flour	1½ c. milk	Sugar 1 egg 1 tsp. salt 6 tsps. baking powder 1—3 tbsps. melted fat 1 c. chopped nuts	Make and bake like Nut Bread. Any quantity of sugar up to ½ c. may be used, or ½ c. molasses may be used.
Bran Bread No. 1	1 c. bran 1 c. bread flour 1 c. Graham flour	1 c. sour milk	¼ c. molasses 1 tbsp. sugar 1 egg ¾ tsp. salt ½ tsp. soda 3 tsps. baking powder	Make like Nut Bread or mix sugar, salt, and egg. Add molasses and milk. Stir in dry ingredients. Bake at 350° F.—45 min.
Bran Bread No. 2	2 c. bran 1 c. whole wheat flour 1 c. Graham flour	1¾ c. sour milk	¼ c. brown sugar 1 egg 1 tsp. salt 1 tsp. soda 2 tsps. baking powder	Make like Nut Bread, or beat egg and add sugar, sour milk and soda, then dry ingredients mixed together. Let stand ½ hour. Bake at 375° F.—1 hour. Sweet milk and 4 tsps. baking powder may be substituted for sour milk and soda.
Oatmeal Bread	1½ c. whole wheat flour 1 c. cooked oatmeal	Milk	2 tbsps. molasses 1 egg 1 tsp. salt 5 tsps. baking powder 2 tbsps. melted fat	Mix fat and dry ingredients, add molasses, beaten egg and oatmeal. Add milk to make a rather stiff mixture—about ¾ c. depending on consistency of oatmeal. Let stand 15 min. Bake 45 min. at 375° F.
Date Bread				1 c. chopped dates may be substituted for nuts in any of the above breads. Raisins, currants, chopped prunes or figs may be used.
Nut and Fruit Bread				½ c each of nuts and fruit or other proportions desired may be used in above breads. Dates and walnuts, or figs and almonds are good combinations.
Peanut Butter Bread				Substitute ½ c. peanut butter for 1 c. nuts in Nut Bread. Cream peanut butter and sugar, or blend peanut butter with flour first.
Prune Bread	2½ c. whole wheat flour	Water Milk	8—10 large soft prunes ¼ c. brown sugar 1 tsp. salt 4 tsps. baking powder 2 tbsps. melted fat 2 tbsps. candied orange peel or preserved ginger	Wash prunes, put in cup and fill with water, soak overnight. Dry, stone, and cut prunes in small pieces. Add milk to water used for soaking prunes to make 1½ c. liquid. Make and bake like Nut Bread.
Boston Brown Bread	1 c. Graham flour 1 c. rye flour 1 c. corn-meal	2 c. sour milk	¾ c. molasses 1½ tsps. soda 1½ tsps. salt	Make like Nut Bread. Fill greased molds two-thirds full, cover closely and steam 3½ hrs. 1 c. floured raisins may be added, if desired

For detailed instructions see P. 199.

Chart for Quick Breads

Bread	Flour	Liquid	Other Ingredients	Special Directions
Plain Muffins	2 c. flour	1 c. milk	2 tbsps sugar 2—3 tbsp. melted fat 1 egg 4 tsps. baking powder ½ tsp. salt	Sift together dry ingredients. Add gradually milk, beaten egg and fat. Bake in hot greased muffin pans for 25 min. at 400° F. Sugar may be increased to 4 tsps. if desired. Two eggs may also be used. Makes 11 muffins.
Bran Muffins	1½ c. flour ¾ c. bran	1 c. milk	4 tbsps. molasses 3—4 tbsp. melted fat 1 egg ½ tsp. salt 5 tsps. baking powder	Mix together dry ingredients. Add molasses, milk, beaten egg and melted fat. Bake in hot greased muffin pans for 25 min. at 400° F. Makes 12 muffins.
Cereal Muffins	2 c. flour	1 c. milk	2 tbsps. sugar 2—3 tbsp. melted fat 1 egg 5 tsps. baking powder 1 tsp. salt 1 c. cooked cereal	Make same as plain muffins, mixing cereal with half of milk and adding to other ingredients. Makes 14 muffins.
Fruit Muffins	2 c. flour	1 c. milk	2—4 tbsps. sugar 2—3 tbsps. melted fat 1 egg 4 tsps. baking powder ½ tsp. salt ½—1 c. nuts or fruit	Make same as plain muffins, adding chopped nuts or chopped fruit. Dredge the fruit with 2 tbsps of the flour. Raisins, chopped dates, figs, apples, cooked prunes, apricots or blueberries may be used. Makes 13 muffins.
Whole Wheat Muffins	1 c. flour 1 c. whole wheat flour	1 c. milk	2 tbsps. sugar 3—4 tbsp. melted fat 1 egg 5 tsps. baking powder ½ tsp. salt	Make same as plain muffins. The sugar may be increased to 4 tbsps. if desired. Brown sugar may be used. 1 c. rye meal may be substituted for the whole wheat flour. This recipe makes 11 muffins
Popovers	2 c. bread flour	2 c. milk	2 tsps. melted fat 2 eggs ½ tsp. salt	Beat eggs slightly. Sift flour and salt and add alternately with milk. Add melted fat. Beat with egg-beater until smooth and full of bubbles. Fill hot greased pans two-thirds full. Bake 30 min. at 450° F. and 15 min. at 350° F. Makes 9 popovers.
Griddle Cakes	2½ c. flour	2 c. milk	1 tbsp. sugar 1 egg 4½ tsps. baking powder 1 tsp. salt	Sift together dry ingredients. Add milk, together with the egg beaten well. Beat all together until smooth. Bake on griddle heated to 350° F. For sour milk griddle cakes substitute a like quantity of sour milk for the sweet milk and 1 tsp. soda for the baking powder. 1 c Graham flour or corn-meal may be substituted for 1 c. white flour. Makes 15 cakes.
Bread Crumb Griddle Cakes	1 c. flour	2 c. hot milk	2 c. bread crumbs 1 tbsp. shortening 1 tbsp. sugar ½ tsp. salt 2 eggs 2 tsps. baking powder	Soak bread crumbs and milk together overnight, or until soft. Stir until smooth. Add fat, sugar, salt and egg-yolks beaten light. Add flour and baking powder sifted together. Fold in the stiffly beaten egg-whites. Bake on griddle heated to 350° F.
Waffles	2 c. pastry flour	1½ c. milk	5 tbsps. melted fat 2 eggs 4 tsps. baking powder ¼ tsp. salt	Sift together dry ingredients. Add gradually milk, beaten egg-yolks and fat. Fold in stiffly beaten egg-whites. Bake on hot waffle iron. Makes 6 to 8 waffles.
Corn-bread	2 c. corn-meal	2 c. sour milk	2 tbsps. melted fat 2 eggs 1 tsp. soda 1½ tsps. salt	Make same as plain muffins. Pour into hot greased baking pan or muffin pans and bake at 400° F. for 20-25 min. Makes 24 pieces.

For detailed instructions, see P. 200.

Chart for Raised Sweet Breads

Bread	Basic Ingredients	Additional Ingredients	Method
Sponge The amounts given will make 1 c. of sponge	½ c. scalded milk ¼ c. cold water ¼ yeast cake 2 tsps. sugar 1 c. flour		Add cold water to scalded milk. When lukewarm, add yeast cake, sugar, and flour. Beat with egg-beater until smooth. Set in warm place to rise until light and fluffy, about 3 hrs. or overnight in a cool place.
Swedish Bread 1 loaf	Basic Sponge	¼ c. melted fat 3 tbsps. sugar ½ tsp. salt ¼ tsp. almond extract 1 egg Reserve 1 tbsp. of white for glazing 2¼ c. flour	To light sponge, add fat, egg, sugar, and salt. Beat well. Add flour to make a stiff dough. Knead on a floured board until elastic. Stand in a warm place to rise, about 1 hr. When double in bulk, shape into loaves. Put in greased pans. Glaze top with white of egg, sprinkle with sugar. Let stand one hr. to rise. Bake at 375° F. for 60 min.
Swedish Tea-Ring	Same as Swedish Bread	2 tbsps. softened fat ¼ c. blanched almonds ¼ c. citron strips ¼ c. raisins (½ c. brown sugar mixed with ¼ tsp. cinnamon)	Roll dough into oblong sheet ¼ in. thick. Spread with fat. Sprinkle with brown sugar and cinnamon, chopped almonds, raisins and citron. Roll lightly to press in fruit. Roll up like a jelly roll. Join ends to form ring. Cut with scissors and shape. Glaze top with egg-white. Let rise, bake at 400° F. for 30 min.
Swedish Braid	Same as Swedish Bread	Reserve 1 tsp. egg-yolk for glazing instead of egg-white. Mix with 1 tsp. cold water ¼ c. chopped blanched almonds	Cut off three pieces of dough of equal size and roll. Then braid. Put on greased sheet, cover, let rise. Brush over with egg-yolk mixture and sprinkle with almonds. Bake at 400° F. for 30 min.
Philadelphia Cinnamon Bun	Same as Swedish Bread with almond flavoring omitted	2 tbsps. softened fat (¼ c. brown sugar mixed with ¼ tsp. cinnamon) 1 c. cleaned currants ¼ c. chopped raisins (1 c. sugar boiled to 310° F. with ¼ c. water)	Make like Swedish Tea-Ring. After rolling like a jelly roll, cut off in slices 2 in. wide. Place cut surface up in greased round pan. Cover and set to rise until double in bulk. Pour hot sirup over buns. Bake at 350° F. for one hour.
Dutch Apple Cake	Same as Swedish Bread with lemon extract instead of almond. Use 2 c. flour instead of 2¼ c.	1 tbsp. melted butter ¼ tsp. lemon extract (¼ tsp. cinnamon mixed with ⅓ c. brown sugar) ¼ c. cleaned currants 3 sour apples, pared, cut in eighths with cores removed Vary by using dried apricots, prunes or peaches soaked for 1 hr. and dried	Add currants to Swedish bread dough. Beat thoroughly and let rise. Spread in a greased dripping pan. Brush over with melted butter. Press sharp edges of apples into dough, in parallel rows lengthwise. Glaze with egg-white. Sprinkle with sugar and cinnamon. Let rise until double in bulk. Bake at 350° F. for 30 min.
Filled Bread	Same as Swedish Bread	Fig and Nut Filling ½ c. chopped figs or dates 1 tbsp. flour 2 tbsps. chopped candied ginger ¼ c. chopped walnut meats or cocoanut ¼ c. sugar ¼ c. water ¼ tsp. salt	Roll dough in oblong about ¼ in. thick. Make filling by mixing all ingredients together and cooking until thick. Cool and spread on dough. Roll up like jelly roll. Cut off in 1-in. pieces. Place on greased sheet to rise. When light, bake at 425° F. 20 min. May be baked in bread-pan one hour.

For detailed instructions, see P. 201.

Chart for Sponge Cake

Cake	Eggs	Flour	Other Ingredients	Special Directions
Angel Cake	1 c. egg-whites	1 c. pastry flour	1½ c. sugar ¼ tsp. salt 1 tsp. cream of tartar ½ tsp. flavoring	Beat egg-whites frothy with salt, add cream of tartar, beat until stiff. Gradually fold in sugar and flavoring. Last fold in pastry flour. Bake in ungreased tube pan at 320° F. for one hour.
Angel Cake Boiled Sirup				Cook sugar, cream of tartar and ¾ c. water to 238° F. or until it forms soft ball. Pour over stiffly-beaten egg-whites. Proceed as in Angel Cake.
Sponge Cake 6 Eggs	6 egg-yolks 6 egg-whites	1 c. pastry flour	1 c. sugar 1 tbsp. vinegar ¼ tsp. salt ½ tsp. flavoring	Beat yolks until thick; add sugar gradually. Add vinegar, flavoring, and flour sifted with salt. Fold in stiffly-beaten egg-whites and bake at 320° F. one hour.
Boiled Sponge Cake 6 Eggs	6 egg-whites 6 egg-yolks	1 c. pastry flour	1¼ c. sugar 1 c. water 1 tsp. cream of tartar ¼ tsp. salt ½ tsp. vanilla	Cook sugar and water to 238° F. or to soft-ball stage. Pour over beaten egg-whites; beat until cool; add beaten egg-yolks and vanilla. Fold in flour sifted with salt and cream of tartar. Bake as above.
Sponge Cake 4 Eggs	4 egg-yolks 4 egg-whites	1 c. pastry flour 1½ tbsps. corn-starch	1 c. sugar 4 tbsps. cold water 1½ tsps. baking powder, ¼ tsp. salt 1 tsp. lemon extract	Make and bake like 6-egg Sponge Cake, adding cold water after sugar has been beaten into egg-yolks. Coffee may be used in place of water, to make Coffee Sponge Cake.
Sponge Cake 2 Eggs	2 egg-yolks 2 egg-whites	1¼ c. pastry flour	1 c. sugar 1 tbsp. vinegar 5 tbsps. cold water 2 tsps. baking-powder ¼ tsp. salt ½ tsp. flavoring	Make and bake like 6-egg Sponge Cake, adding vinegar and water together.
Hot-Water Sponge Cake	2 egg-yolks 2 egg-whites	⅞ c. pastry flour	¾ c. sugar ⅓ c. hot water 1½ tsps. baking-powder ¼ tsp. salt ½ tsp. lemon extract	Make like 6-egg Sponge Cake, adding boiling water when half of sugar has been beaten into egg-yolks. Bake in 320° F. oven 25 to 40 min., depending on shape of pan.
Egg-Yolk Sponge Cake	6 egg-yolks	1⅓ c. pastry flour	1 c. sugar 2 tsps. baking-powder ¼ tsp. salt ½ c. hot water ½ tsp. flavoring	Beat egg-yolks until thick. Add sugar and continue beating. Sift together flour, baking-powder, and salt and add alternately with hot water, continue beating with egg-beater. Add flavoring. Bake at 320° F. one hour.
Caramel Sponge Cake				Make and bake like Boiled Sponge Cake, using brown sugar in place of white. Or caramelize ¼ c. sugar, add boiling water and when smooth add rest of sugar and cook to 238° F.
Chocolate Sponge or Angel Cake				Add 2 oz. melted chocolate to Angel or Sponge Cake, omitting 1 tbsp. flour, or use ¼ c. cocoa and reduce flour to ¾ c.
Jelly Roll			½ c. jelly	Bake Hot-Water Sponge Cake in a sheet, lining pan with greased paper. Turn out on towel, remove paper, trim off edges, spread with jelly. Roll and wrap in towel.
Orange Sponge Cake	6 egg-whites 6 egg-yolks	1 c. pastry flour	1 c. sugar 5 tbsps. water ½ c. orange juice Grated rind 1 orange	Make and bake like Boiled Sponge Cake, adding orange rind and juice just before egg-yolks

For detailed instructions, see P. 202.

Chart for Butter Cakes

Cake	Liquid	Flour	Other Ingredients	Special Directions
Two-Egg Cake	½ c. milk	1¾ c. pastry flour	⅓—½ c. butter or fat 1 c. sugar 2 eggs 2½ tsps. baking-powder ½ tsp. salt ½ tsp. vanilla	Cream fat and sugar. Add beaten egg. Sift dry ingredients together and add alternately with milk. Add flavoring. Eggs may be separated, beaten yolks added to butter and sugar mixture and stiffly beaten whites folded in last. ½ c. fat makes a richer cake.
One-Egg Cake	½ c. milk	1½ c. pastry flour	¼ c. fat or butter ¾ c. sugar 1 egg ½ tsp. salt 2½ tsps. baking-powder ½ tsp. vanilla	Make same as Two-Egg Cake. For a one-egg-yolk cake decrease sugar to ½ c. and increase baking-powder to 3 tsps. to make up for the smaller amount of egg.
White Cake	½ c. milk	2 c. pastry flour	½ c. butter or fat 1 c. sugar 3 egg-whites 2 tsps. baking-powder 1 tsp. vanilla ½ tsp. salt	Make same as Two-Egg Cake, folding in stiffly beaten whites last. One-fourth cupful of flour is added because of the three egg-whites.
Gold Cake	½ c. milk	2 c. pastry flour	⅓ c. butter or fat 1 c. sugar 4 egg-yolks 3 tsps. baking-powder ½ tsp. salt 1 tsp. vanilla	Make same as Two-Egg Cake, beating egg-yolks until thick and lemon colored and beating into the butter and sugar mixture. More baking-powder is used as there are no egg-whites to lighten the cake.
Apple Sauce Cake				Use ¾ c. unsweetened apple sauce in place of ½ c. milk. Add ¼ tsp. soda and decrease baking-powder to 1½ tsps.
Caramel Cake				Add 3 tablespoonfuls caramel sirup to any plain cake.
Chocolate Cake				Add 2-4 squares melted chocolate to any of the cakes. Add it to the fat and sugar mixture or at the last.
Coconut Cake				Use 1½-3 c. grated coconut saving half of it to sprinkle over top.
Coffee Cake				Use very strong cold black coffee as the liquid for any simple cake.
Fruit Cake				1 c. fruit may be added. Date and figs should be chopped, prunes cooked and chopped. A combination of fruits or fruits and nuts may be used. Strong coffee is good substituted for milk. Molasses may be used for ½ the sugar.
Maple Cake				Maple sugar may be used instead of granulated sugar. ½ c. maple sirup and ¼ c. corn sirup may be substituted for 1 c. sugar
Marble Cake				Part of batter may be colored with chocolate or vegetable coloring. The mixtures are put in pan alternately and in irregular amounts to obtain a variegated effect in the cake.
Nut Cake				1 c. nut-meats may be added to any of these cake recipes.
Orange Cake				Substitute orange juice for milk. Add 2 tbsps. grated orange rind.
Spanish Cake				Add 1 tbsp. cinnamon to Two-Egg Cake.
Spice Cake				Add ¾ tsp. to 1½ tsps. mixed spices to any simple cake.

All recipes in this chart serve six. For detailed instructions, see P. 203.

Chart for Cookies

Cookies	Basic Ingredients	Additional Ingredients	Method
Sugar Cookies	⅔—1 c. shortening 2 c. brown sugar 2 eggs, beaten 3 c. pastry flour 2 tsps. baking-powder ½ tsp. salt	1 tsp. vanilla or lemon extract, or 1 tsp. cloves, cinnamon, nutmeg or a mixture of spice 1 c. nuts, raisins, currants or combination, or 1 tbsp. caraway, anise or cardamon seeds 2 sq. chocolate, or ⅔ c. cocoa	Cream sugar and shortening, add eggs, then sifted dry ingredients, flavoring, nuts, or fruit. Form into roll, chill and slice; or chill dough, roll and cut. Roll very thin for wafers. Use ½ c. less flour for drop cookies. Bake on greased baking sheet at 450° F.—8 to 10 min.
Sour Milk Cookies	Use recipe for Sugar Cookies as foundation	½ c. sour milk 1 c. pastry flour ¼ tsp. soda ¼ tsp. salt	Make and bake like Sugar Cookies using larger proportion of shortening. Add milk and flour alternately. Sour cream may be used in place of sour milk, reducing shortening to ½ c. Same variations as in Sugar Cookies may be made.
Sweet Milk Cookies	Use recipe for Sugar Cookies as foundation	½ c. sweet milk 1 c. pastry flour ¼ tsp. salt ½ tsp. baking-powder	Make and bake like Sour Milk Cookies. Same variations as in Sugar Cookies may be made.
Hermit Cookies	Same as Sugar Cookies	2 eggs, beaten 1 c. nuts 1 c. raisins ½ tsp. cinnamon ½ tsp. nutmeg	Make same as Sugar Cookies. Drop by teaspoonfuls on greased baking sheet and bake at 450° F.—10 min.
Molasses Cookies	½ c. shortening ½ c. brown sugar ½ c. molasses 1 egg, beaten ¼ c. boiling water 3 c. pastry flour ¼ tsp. soda ½ tsp. salt 1 tsp. baking-powder	½ tsp. ginger ½ tsp. allspice, cloves, cinnamon, nutmeg or a mixture ½—1 c. raisins or currants	Make like Sugar Cookies. Mix molasses, and boiling water. For drop cookies use ½ c. less flour. Bake at 375° F.—15 min. For ginger snaps omit water, leavening, and ½ c. flour. Heat molasses, sugar, and shortening to boiling, add dry ingredients. Chill. Roll thin or drop by spoonfuls on baking sheet. 1 c. molasses may be used, omitting sugar and using 3 c. flour. Egg may be omitted.
Oatmeal Cookies No. 1	Same as Sugar Cookies	2 c. rolled oats 1 tsp. cinnamon 1 tbsp. vinegar ½ c. raisins ½ c. nuts	Make like Sugar Cookies, using the rolled oats in place of 1½ c. of the flour. Drop by spoonfuls on greased baking sheet and flatten with a spatula. Bake at 400° F.—10 min.
Oatmeal Cookies No. 2	1 c. shortening ½ c. sugar 1 c. molasses ¾ c. coffee 2 c. Graham flour 2 c. pastry flour 2 c. rolled oats ½ tsp. soda 1 tsp. baking-powder 1 tsp. salt	1 c. raisins ½ tsp. cloves 1 tsp. cinnamon	Make like Sugar Cookies, dropping from teaspoon on to greased baking sheet. Bake at 400° F.—10 min.
Peanut Butter Cookies	Same as Sugar Cookies, or Sour or Sweet Milk Cookies	⅔—1 c. peanut butter Chopped peanuts or halves of peanuts	Make and bake like Sugar Cookies, using peanut butter as shortening. If milk is used reduce slightly. Chopped peanuts may be added or sprinkled on top of cookies. Cookies may be decorated with peanut halves.
Filled Cookies	Same as Sugar Cookies, or Sour or Sweet Milk Cookies	For filling: 1 c. chopped raisins, figs or dates 1 c. sugar 2 tbsps. flour Juice ½ lemon ¼ c. boiling water	Cook together until thick, ingredients for filling. Cool. Roll cookies thin, cut in rounds. Put 1 tsp. filling on half of cookies, cover with remaining cookies, and press edges together. Bake at 450° F.—11 min.

For detailed instructions, see P. 205.

Chart for Baked Custards

Custard	Basic Ingredients	Additional Ingredients	Method
Baked Custard	4—6 eggs ¼—½ c. sugar ½ tsp. salt 1 qt. milk ½ tsp. vanilla	Brown sugar or maple sugar or honey Nutmeg or cinnamon Cream	Beat eggs; use 4 eggs for individual custards, 6 eggs for large custard. Add sugar, quantity depending on taste, and salt; mix; add milk and vanilla. Mix thoroughly. Strain into greased custard cups or baking dish; set in pan of warm water and bake at 325° F.—40 min. for small custards or 75 min. for large custard. Brown or maple sugar, or honey may be substituted for sugar; nutmeg or cinnamon may be sprinkled on top. ½ to 1 c. cream may be substituted for same amount of milk
Baked Apple Custard	Same as Baked Custard using 5 eggs and ½ c. sugar	6 medium-sized apples ¾ c. sugar 2½ c. boiling water ¾ tsp. nutmeg	Pare and core apples; boil ½ c. sugar and boiling water 10 min. Simmer apples in sirup till tender and drain, arrange in casserole and sprinkle with ¼ c. sugar. Prepare Baked Custard, add nutmeg; pour over apples; bake as Baked Custard.
Baked Apricot Custard	Same as Baked Custard	2 c. unsweetened apricot pulp Sugar ½ tsp. cinnamon	Make like Baked Custard, substituting apricot pulp for 2 c. of the milk and adding more sugar if necessary. Bake like Baked Custard. If canned apricot pulp is used omit sugar.
Baked Caramel Custard	Same as Baked Custard	Increase sugar to 1 c.	Scald milk; caramelize sugar and dissolve in hot milk; proceed as in Baked Custard. Or caramelize sugar, put 1 tbsp. in each cup, pour in custard mixture and bake.
Baked Chocolate Custard	Same as Baked Custard	2 sq. chocolate or ⅔ c. cocoa	Melt chocolate, mix with ½ c. of the milk scalded, or mix cocoa, sugar and ½ c. water, boil 1 min. Proceed as in Baked Custard.
Baked Coconut Custard	Same as Baked Custard	½—1 c. grated coconut	Add coconut to Baked Custard or its variations.
Baked Coffee Custard	Same as Baked Custard	1—2 c. strong black coffee or 3—4 tbsps. ground coffee	Substitute desired amount of coffee for an equal amount of the milk. Or scald the milk with the ground coffee and strain. Proceed as in Baked Custard.
Baked Marshmallow Custard	Same as Baked Custard	Marshmallows	Put a marshmallow in bottom of each cup and pour in custard mixture. Bake like Baked Custard.
Bread Pudding	1 qt. milk 2 c. bread, cake, or gingerbread crumbs 2 eggs ¾ c. sugar ½ tsp. salt ¼ c. melted butter	1 tsp. vanilla or ¼ tsp. nutmeg Jelly Same variations as in Baked Custard	Scald milk, add crumbs, soak ½ hr. Proceed as in Baked Custard adding butter last. Bake at 350° F.—1 hr. or until done. If desired spread with jelly, top with meringue made of whites of the eggs and 4 tbsps. sugar and brown at 300° F. Vary as Baked Custard.
Rice Pudding	3 eggs 2 c. milk 1 c. cooked rice ½ c. sugar ¼ tsp. salt	2 tbsps. grated lemon rind 3 tbsps. lemon juice Same variations as in Baked Custard	Beat eggs and combine with other basic ingredients, add lemon rind. Bake in greased baking dish at 325° F. 20 to 30 min. Lemon juice may be added. Whites of eggs may be used for meringue. Vary as Baked Custard.

All recipes in this chart serve six. For detailed instructions, see P. 206.

Chart for Starchy Desserts

Dessert	Liquid	Thickening	Other Ingredients	Special Directions
Blanc Mange or Corn-Starch Pudding	3 c. milk	5½ tbsps. corn-starch	4 tbsps. sugar 1 egg ¼ tsp. salt ½ tsp. vanilla	Use double boiler. Scald 2½ c. milk. Mix corn-starch, half of sugar and salt with ½ c. cold milk. Add to scalded milk and cook 25 min. Pour over egg beaten with remaining sugar. Return to double boiler and cook 1 min. longer. Add vanilla and pour in wet molds. The egg may be separated and the white used as a meringue folded in or piled on top. Use 6 tbsps. corn-starch if egg is omitted.
Brown or Maple Sugar Pudding	3 c. milk	5½ tbsps. corn-starch	4 tbsps. brown or maple sugar 1 egg ¼ tsp. salt ½ tsp. vanilla	Make same as Blanc Mange. Egg may be omitted.
Caramel Pudding	3 c. milk	5½ tbsps. corn-starch	6 tbsps. caramel sirup 1 egg ¼ tsp. salt ½ tsp. vanilla	Combine caramel sirup and 2½ c. scalded milk. Add dry ingredients mixed with ½ c. cold milk. Proceed as in Blanc Mange. Egg may be omitted.
Chocolate Pudding	3 c. milk	5½ tbsps. corn-starch	2 sq. chocolate or ⅔ c. cocoa 6 tbsps. sugar 1 egg ¼ tsp. salt ½ tsp. vanilla	Melt chocolate; add sugar, corn-starch, salt and ½ c. cold milk. Blend thoroughly and add 2½ c. scalded milk and proceed as in Blanc Mange. Egg may be omitted.
Fruit Pudding	1½ c. milk 1½ c. canned fruit juice or 3 c. fruit juice	6 tbsps. corn-starch	Sugar to taste ¼ tsp. salt	Make same as Blanc Mange. One egg-white may be used as a meringue folded in or used to top the pudding. It may be garnished with fruits.
Lemon Pudding	2 c. boiling water	6 tbsps. corn-starch	1¼ c. sugar ¼ tsp. salt 2 eggs Grated rind 1 lemon ⅓ c. lemon juice	Combine dry ingredients, add boiling water, stirring constantly. Cook in double boiler 25 min. Pour over beaten egg-yolks, return to double boiler and cook 1 min. Remove from fire and add lemon rind and juice. Use egg-whites as meringue.
Orange Pudding	1 c. boiling water 1 c. orange juice	5 tbsps. corn-starch	1¼ c. sugar 2 eggs 1½ tbsps. lemon juice ¼ tsp. salt	Make same as Blanc Mange, adding lemon juice last and reserving egg-whites for meringue.
Apple Tapioca	2½ c. boiling water	½ c. minute tapioca	7 sour apples pared, quartered and cored ½ c. sugar ½ tsp. salt ¼ tsp. nutmeg	Add boiling water, sugar and salt to tapioca. Cook in double boiler until transparent. Arrange apples in greased pudding dish. Sprinkle with nutmeg. Pour over tapioca mixture, bake at 350° F.—30 min. or until apples are soft.

All recipes in this chart serve six.   For detailed instructions, see P. 207.

Chart for Punches

Punch	Basic Ingredients	Variations	Method
Grape Punch	1 c. grape juice ½ c. orange juice 6 tbsps. lemon juice 6 tbsps. sirup 1 c. water or charged water	Lime juice ½ c. strong tea ½ c. coffee 1 c. ginger ale { ½ tsp. cinnamon { 36 whole cloves { ½ tsp. nutmeg Mint Sliced Fruit	Combine basic ingredients, add ice, chill and serve. Makes 5 c. Vary as follows: (1) use lime juice for part or all of lemon juice; (2) add tea, coffee or ginger ale; (3) add tea and ginger ale, or coffee and ginger ale; (4) add spices by boiling them together in the water 5 minutes. Strain. (5) Garnish with desired sliced fruit or sprigs of mint.
Grape Cider Punch	1 c. grape juice ½ c. cider ¼ c. lemon juice ¼ c. sirup 1 c. water or charged water	Same as in Grape Punch	Combine basic ingredients, add ice, chill and serve. Makes 4½ c. Vary and garnish as in Grape Punch.
Grape Orange Punch	1 c. grape juice 1 c. orange juice 6 tbsps. lemon juice ½ c. crushed pineapple ¼ c. sirup 1½ c. water or charged water	Same as in Grape Punch	Combine basic ingredients, add ice, chill and serve. Makes 5½ c. Vary and garnish as in Grape Punch.
Cherry Punch	1 c. cooked cherries and juice ¼ c. lemon juice ½ c. orange juice ¼ c. pineapple juice 6 tbsps. sirup 1 c. water or charged water	Same as in Grape Punch	Combine basic ingredients, add ice, chill and serve. Makes 4½ c. Vary and garnish as in Grape Punch.
Orange Punch	1 c. orange juice ½ c. lemon juice ¼ c. pineapple juice ¼ c. sirup 1 c. water or charged water	Same as in Grape Punch	Combine basic ingredients, add ice, chill and serve. Makes 4½ c. Vary and garnish as in Grape Punch.
Grapefruit Punch	1 c. grapefruit juice ¼ c. orange juice 2 tbsps. lemon juice ¼ c. cherry juice ¼ c. sirup 1 c. water or charged water	Lime juice ½ c. strong tea 1 c. ginger ale	Combine basic ingredients, add ice, chill and serve. Makes 4 c. Vary as follows: (1) use lime juice for part or all of lemon juice; (2) add tea or ginger ale; (3) add both tea and ginger ale; (4) Garnish as in Grape Punch.
Raspberry Punch	1 c. cooked raspberries, strawberries, blackberries or loganberries and juice ½ c. orange juice 6 tbsps. lemon juice ¼ c. sirup 1 c. water or charged water	Same as Grapefruit Punch	Combine basic ingredients, add ice, chill and serve. Makes 4½ c. If fresh berries are used crush and press through a sieve and use an additional 5 tbsps. sirup. Vary and garnish as in Grapefruit Punch.
Rhubarb Punch	1 c. rhubarb juice ½ c. orange juice 6 tbsps. lemon juice 3 tbsps. sirup 1 c. water or charged water	Same as Grapefruit Punch	Cook 3 c. cut rhubarb, 1 c. sugar and 1 c. water about 20 minutes; strain. Combine 1 c. strained juice with other basic ingredients, add ice, chill and serve. Makes 4 c. Vary and garnish as in Grapefruit Punch.

For detailed instructions, see P. 207.

Chart for Savory and Sweet Sauces

Sauces	Liquid	Thickening	Other Ingredients	Special Directions
Thin White Sauce	1 c. milk	1 tbsp. flour	1 tbsp. fat ¼ tsp. salt Dash of pepper	Use double boiler. Melt fat, add flour and seasonings. Add cold milk. Cook 25 min.
Medium White Sauce	1 c. milk	2 tbsps. flour	2 tbsps. fat ¼ tsp. salt Dash of pepper	Prepare like thin White Sauce.
Thick White Sauce	1 c. milk	4 tbsps. flour	3 tbsps. fat ¼ tsp. salt Dash of pepper	Prepare like thin White Sauce.
Cheese Sauce	1 c. milk	2 tbsps. flour	2 tbsps. fat ¼ tsp. salt Dash of pepper ½ c. grated cheese	Prepare like Medium White Sauce. Add cheese and stir until melted.
Mock Hollandaise Sauce	1 c. milk	1½ tbsps. flour	2 tbsps. fat ¼ tsp. salt 1 tsp. lemon juice 1 egg-yolk	Prepare like Medium White Sauce. Pour hot sauce on to beaten egg-yolk.
Tomato Sauce	1 c. stewed tomatoes	1½ tbsps. flour	2 tbsps. fat 1 slice onion ½ bay leaf 1 clove ¼ tsp. salt ¼ tsp. sugar	Cook tomatoes and seasonings 10 min. Rub through sieve. Blend fat and flour. Add tomato mixture and cook until smooth.
Drawn Butter Sauce	1 c. boiling water	2 tbsps. flour	4 tbsps. butter ¼ tsp. salt Dash of pepper	Prepare like Medium White Sauce. Add ¼ c. capers for Caper Sauce or 1 hard-cooked egg chopped for Egg Sauce.
Maitre d'Hotel Butter	3 tbsp. lemon juice		¼ c. butter ½ tsp. salt ¼ tsp. pepper ½ tbsp. finely chopped parsley	Cream butter and add other ingredients. Chill and cut in small circles. Serve on steak or fish.
Tartare Sauce	½ c. Medium Thick White Sauce ½ c. mayonnaise		½ tbsp. chopped chives ½ tbsp. chopped capers ½ tbsp. chopped olives ½ tbsp. chopped parsley	To White Sauce add remaining ingredients. Stir constantly until thoroughly heated. Serve with fish.
Brown Sauce	1 c. brown soup stock or 1 c. bouillon	2 tbsps. flour	2 tbsps. fat ¼ tsp. salt Pepper, slice onion, parsley, bay leaf, etc.	Prepare like Medium White Sauce. Add ½ c. sautéd mushrooms, if desired.
Clear Pudding Sauce	1 c. boiling water	2 tbsps. flour	4 tbsps. butter 3 tbsps. sugar ½ tsp. vanilla	Prepare like Medium White Sauce.
Caramel Sauce No. 1	1 c. boiling water ¼ c. cold water	1 tbsp. corn-starch	4 tbsps. caramel sirup ½ tsp. vanilla 1 tsp. butter	Combine boiling water and caramel sirup. Add corn-starch, blended with cold water. Cook 25 min. Add butter and vanilla.
Caramel Sauce No. 2	1 c. milk	1 tbsp. flour	1 egg-yolk 3 tbsps. caramel sirup 1 tsp. vanilla	Blend flour with some cold milk. Add to scalded milk and sirup in double boiler. Cook 25 min. Pour over beaten egg-yolk. Add vanilla.

All recipes in this chart serve six. For detailed instructions, see P. 208.

Chart for Savory and Sweet Sauces (Continued)

Sauces	Liquid	Thickening	Other Ingredients	Special Directions
Caramel Sirup for Custards, Ice-Cream Sauces, etc.	¼ c. water		1 c. sugar	Put sugar in a frying-pan over a low fire. Stir constantly until sugar is melted and straw colored. Remove from fire, add boiling water gradually, stirring as you add. Return to fire, cook until smooth and golden brown. This hardens on standing, but may be melted over hot water. If a thinner sirup is desired, add ½ cupful boiling water instead of ¼ cupful.
Chocolate Sauce	1 c. milk	1 tbsp. corn-starch or or 1 tbsp. flour and 1 egg-yolk	4 tbsps. sugar ½ sq. chocolate ½ tsp. vanilla	Melt chocolate in double boiler. Add sugar and corn-starch, then cold milk. Cook 25 min. If cocoa is preferred, use 2 tbsps. and ½ tbsp. fat.
Custard Sauce	1 c. milk	2 egg-yolks or 1 egg	2 tbsps. sugar ⅛ tsp. salt	Scald milk in double boiler. Pour over egg, sugar and salt mixed together. Return to double boiler and cook while stirring constantly, until mixture coats spoon. Remove at once. Do not let water boil in bottom of double boiler.
Foamy Sauce		2 egg-yolks 2 egg-whites	1 c. powdered sugar ½ tsp. vanilla 3 tbsp. butter ½ c. cream, whipped	Cream butter and sugar together. Add egg-yolks and beat over hot water. Fold in stiffly beaten egg-whites, vanilla and whipped cream if desired.
Fruit Sauce	1 c. canned fruit juice	1 tbsp. corn-starch	1 tsp. lemon juice	Blend corn-starch and 2 tbsps. fruit juice. Heat fruit juices and corn-starch. Cook 25 min. Add lemon juice.
Hard Sauce			1 c. powdered sugar ½ c. butter ½ tsp. vanilla	Cream butter, add sugar gradually and vanilla. Chill and form into a mold. Grate over it some nutmeg.
Lemon Sauce	1 c. boiling water	1½ tbsps. corn-starch	½ c. sugar 3 tbsps. lemon juice 1 tsp. butter	Pare lemon thinly and steep paring in the boiling water. Strain and stir in blended sugar and starch. Cook 15 min. Add lemon juice and butter.

All recipes in this chart serve six. For detailed instructions, see P. 208.

Chart for Cream Soups

Soup	Liquid	Thickening	Other Ingredients	Special Directions
Cream of Asparagus Soup	2 c. milk 2 c. asparagus water	4 tbsps. flour	4 tbsps. butter 1½ tsps. salt Speck pepper 1 tsp. grated onion Dash paprika 1 c. asparagus pulp or cooked asparagus tips	Use double boiler. Melt butter; add flour and seasonings while stirring. Add cold milk. When thickened, add asparagus water and asparagus pulp. Cook 35 min. Canned asparagus may be used.
Cream of Carrot Soup	2 c. milk 2 c. carrot water	4 tbsps. flour	4 tbsps. butter 1½ tsps. salt Speck pepper Dash paprika 1 tsp. grated onion 1 c. cooked carrot pulp or diced cooked carrots	Use double boiler. Melt butter, add flour and seasonings while stirring. Add cold milk. When thickened, add carrot water and carrot pulp. Cook 35 min.
Cream of Cauliflower Soup	2 c. milk 2 c. cauliflower water	4 tbsps. flour	4 tbsps. butter 1½ tsps. salt Dash paprika Speck pepper 1 tsp. grated onion 1 cup cooked cauliflower pulp	Use double boiler. Melt butter, add flour and seasonings while stirring. Add cold milk. When thickened, add cauliflower water and cauliflower pulp. Cook 35 min.
Cream of Celery Soup	2 c. milk 2 c. celery water	4 tbsps. flour	4 tbsps. butter 1½ tsps. salt Dash paprika Speck pepper 1 tsp. grated onion 1 c. cooked celery pulp or diced cooked celery	Use double boiler. Melt butter, add flour and seasonings while stirring. Add cold milk. When thickened, add celery water and celery pulp. Cook 35 min.
Cream of Corn Soup	2 c. milk 2 c. corn water	4 tbsps. flour	4 tbsps. butter 1½ tsps. salt Speck pepper Dash paprika 1 tsp. grated onion 1 c. scraped, cooked corn	Use double boiler. Melt butter, add flour and seasonings while stirring. Add cold milk. When thickened, add corn water and scraped corn. Cook 35 min. With canned corn, use 1 c. which has been strained and 4 c. milk.
Cream of Mushroom Soup	4 c. milk	4 tbsps. flour	4 tbsps. butter 1½ tsps. salt Speck pepper ½ tsp. grated onion ¾ lb. mushrooms	Melt butter in saucepan. Add mushrooms, washed, stemmed and sliced. Cook 3 min. Then add flour and the seasonings while stirring. When smooth, add milk and stir until smooth. Cook 35 min.
Cream of Pea Soup	2 c. milk 2 c. pea water	4 tbsps. flour	4 tbsps. butter 1½ tsps. salt Speck pepper 1 tsp. grated onion 1 c. sieved, cooked or canned peas	Use double boiler. Melt butter, add flour and seasonings while stirring. Add cold milk. When thickened, add pea water and pulp. Cook 35 min.
Cream of Potato Soup	2 c. milk 2 c. potato water	3 tbsps. flour	4 tbsps. butter 1½ tsps. salt Speck pepper 1 tsp. grated onion Dash paprika 1 c. cooked, riced potatoes	Use double boiler. Melt butter, add flour and seasonings while stirring. Add cold milk. When thickened, add potato water and pulp. Cook 35 min.
Cream of Tomato Soup	2 c. canned tomatoes 2 c. cold milk	4 tbsps. flour	4 tbsps. butter 1½ tsps. salt ⅛ tsp. pepper ½ bay leaf 1 tbsp. minced onion 1 clove ¼ tsp. celery seed ½ tsp. soda	Use double boiler. Melt 2 tbsps. butter. Add 2 tbsps. flour and 1 tsp. salt. Add cold milk. Combine tomatoes, ½ tsp. salt, pepper, bay leaf, onion, clove and celery seed; simmer 10 min. Thicken with 2 tbsps. of butter and 2 tbsps. flour, blended together. Strain, add the soda, and combine with white sauce.

All recipes in this chart serve six.   For detailed instructions, see P. 209.

Chart for Raised Rolls

Raised Rolls	Basic Ingredients	Additional Ingredients	Method
Sponge The amounts given will make 1 c. of basic sponge	½ c. scalded milk ¼ c. cold water ½ yeast cake 2 tsps. sugar 1 c. bread flour		Add cold water to scalded milk. When lukewarm, add yeast cake, sugar, and flour. Beat with egg beater until smooth. Set in a warm place to rise until light and fluffy, about 3 hours or overnight in a cool place.
Parker House Rolls	Basic Sponge	1 egg well beaten 2 tbsps. melted fat 1 tbsp. sugar ½ tsp. salt 2½ c. bread flour Melted butter	To light sponge, add additional ingredients except butter. Knead on a floured board until elastic. Let rise, about 1 hour. When double in bulk, roll out ¼ in. thick. Shape with a biscuit cutter. Make a crease through the middle of each with the dull side of the knife. Brush over half with melted butter, fold and press edges together. Place on a greased pan, cover and let rise. Bake at 400° F. 20 min.
Clover Leaf Rolls	Same as Parker House Rolls		Prepare dough as for Parker House Rolls. When double in bulk, shape into balls about 1 in. in diameter. Drop three into each section of a greased muffin pan. Brush with melted fat. Let rise and bake like Parker House Rolls.
Salad Rolls	Same as Parker House Rolls		Prepare dough as for Parker House Rolls. Roll out ½ in. thick. Shape with Biscuit Cutter. Let rise. When well puffed, make a deep crease in each biscuit with the handle of a wooden spoon, press edges together. Place closely in greased pan, brushing with fat between biscuit. Cover and let rise. Bake at 400° F. for 15 minutes.
Bread Sticks	Same as Parker House Rolls		Prepare dough as for Parker House Rolls. Roll out and shape with biscuit cutter. Roll each biscuit with the hand until about eight inches long, keeping a uniform size and rounded ends. Let rise. Bake like Parker House Rolls.
Luncheon Rolls	Same as Parker House Rolls	2 tbsps. fat 1 egg well beaten ¼ tsp. grated lemon rind	Prepare dough as for Parker House Rolls, using extra egg, fat and lemon rind. Let rise. Shape, using small cutter. Place in greased pan close together. Let rise. Bake at 400° F. for 15 min.
Potato Rolls	Basic Sponge	1 egg ¼ c. shortening ½ tsp. salt ¾ c. cold mashed potatoes 2½ c. bread flour	Prepare dough as for Parker House Rolls, adding additional ingredients to sponge. Let rise. Shape into small rolls, place in greased pan, brush tops with melted fat. Bake like Parker House Rolls.
Raised Muffins	1 c. scalded milk 1 c. cold water 2 tbsps. fat ¼ c. sugar ¾ tsp. salt ½ yeast cake 1 egg, well beaten 4 c. bread flour	For graham muffins substitute 2 c. graham flour for 2 c. of the bread flour.	Add fat, sugar, and salt to liquid when lukewarm. Add yeast cake, egg and flour. Beat five minutes with Dover egg-beater. Let rise overnight. Fill muffin pans two-thirds full. Let rise until rings are full. Bake at 425° F. 30 min.

All recipes in this chart serve six.

Chart for Soufflés

Souffles	Basic Ingredients	Special Ingredients	Method
Plain	2 c. medium white sauce 3 egg-yolks 3 egg-whites		Pour hot White Sauce into the beaten yolks, stirring constantly. Cool. Fold in stiffly beaten egg-whites. Pour into greased pudding dish or individual molds and place in pan of hot water. Bake at 375° F. until set. For variation use Thick White Sauce (P. 184).
Vegetable	Same as Plain. One c. water in which vegetables were cooked may be substituted for 1 c. milk in White Sauce	1 c. cooked vegetable rubbed through a sieve	Make and bake same as Plain Souffle. Add vegetable to egg-yolks with White Sauce.
Meat	Same as Plain	2 c. minced cooked meat Sage, celery salt, onion juice or other seasoning may be added with meat ½ c. bread crumbs may be substituted for ½ c. meat	Mix and bake same as Plain Souffle. Add meat to egg-yolks with White Sauce.
Fish	Same as Plain	2 c. finely flaked fish ½ c. bread crumbs	Mix and bake same as Plain Souffle. Add fish and bread crumbs to egg-yolks with White Sauce.
Cheese	Same as Plain	2 c. grated cheese ¼ tsp. each mustard, soda, paprika Speck of Cayenne	Mix and bake same as Plain Souffle. Add cheese and extra seasoning to White Sauce before adding to egg-yolks.
Custard	4 tbsps. butter 4 tbsps. flour 2 c. milk ¼ tsp. salt ½ c. sugar 1 tsp. vanilla 3 egg-yolks 3 egg-whites		Use a double boiler. Melt butter, add flour and stir until smooth, add milk and cook 15 min. Add sugar and salt. Pour on to beaten egg-yolks. Cool. Fold in stiffly beaten egg-white and vanilla. Bake same as Plain Souffle.
Chocolate	Same as Custard	2 oz. melted unsweetened chocolate	Mix and bake same as Custard, add chocolate to White Sauce before pouring into egg-yolks.
Caramel	Same as Custard		Make White Sauce as in Custard Souffle. Melt sugar directly over fire, stirring constantly. Add a small amount of White Sauce to melted sugar. Mix well. Pour back into double boiler and cook until perfectly smooth. Proceed as with Custard Souffle.
Coffee	Same as Custard Souffle except use 1 c. coffee instead of 1 c. of the milk		Mix and bake same as Custard Souffle.
Fruit	Same as Custard Souffle	1 c. cooked fruit drained and large fruit cut in small pieces	Mix same as Custard Souffle. Put fruit in bottom of greased baking-dish. Pour over it the souffle mixture. Bake at 375° F. until set. The fruit juice may be used for a sauce.

All recipes in this chart serve six.

Chart for Baked and Steamed Puddings

Steamed and Baked Puddings	Basic Ingredients	Additional Ingredients	Method
Cottage Pudding	¼ c. shortening ⅔ c. sugar 1 egg, well beaten 1 c. milk 2¼ c. flour 4 tsp. baking powder ½ tsp. salt 1 tsp. vanilla		Cream the shortening, add sugar and vanilla, then egg. Mix and sift flour, baking powder and salt. Add alternately with milk to first mixture. Turn into greased cake pan. Bake at 350° F. for 45 min. Or pour into greased molds and steam one hour. Serve with lemon, orange, or chocolate sauce.
Chocolate Pudding	Use recipe for Cottage Pudding as foundation	2½ squares melted chocolate	Make like Cottage Pudding. Add melted chocolate after the sugar Bake or steam like cottage pudding. Serve with vanilla or hard sauce.
Fruit Pudding	Use recipe for Cottage Pudding as foundation	1 c. of any one of the following fruits: Blueberries, huckleberries, red raspberries, stoned cherries, sliced pared apples, rhubarb, peaches, stoned dates, pressed figs, stoned prunes, dried peaches. Any canned fruit, drained well, the juice used for sauce	Mix and bake or steam like cottage pudding. Reserve 2 tbsp. of flour to mix with fruit. Wash fruit, dry, and chop large fruit fine. Dried fruits should be washed and steamed tender, then chopped. Mix with flour and stir in last. Serve with a fruit or hard sauce.
Ginger Pudding	¼ c. shortening ¼ c. brown sugar 1 egg well beaten ½ c. sour milk ½ c. molasses 1½ c. flour ½ tsp. soda 1 tsp. baking powder 1 tsp. ginger ½ tsp. cinnamon ½ tsp. salt	For variation, add any one of the following: 1 c. chopped apples, grated rind of ½ orange; or pour batter over 3 apples, pared, cored, sliced and placed in bottom of mold, with 2 tbsp. sugar and ¼ tsp. cinnamon sprinkled over them	Mix like cottage pudding. Sift the spices with the flour. Combine sour milk and molasses. Add alternately to egg mixture. Bake or steam like Cottage Pudding. Serve with fruit or hard sauce.
Suet Pudding	½ c. suet chopped fine ½ c. molasses ½ c. milk or water 1½ c. flour ½ tsp. salt ½ tsp. soda ½ tsp. cinnamon ½ tsp. nutmeg 2 tsps. baking powder ½ c. raisins	For variation add 1 c. of any one of the following in place of raisins: chopped figs, chopped dates, sliced citron, and currants mixed or stoned and chopped prunes	Mix together the suet, molasses and milk. Sift the flour and other dry ingredients together. Mix with fruit and add to first mixture. Pour into a well-greased mold and steam 2 hours. Or put into 6 individual molds and steam 35 minutes.
Plum Pudding	Use recipe for Suet Pudding as foundation	2 eggs well beaten ½ c. flour ¼ tsp. allspice ½ c. currants ¼ c. blanched chopped almonds ¼ c. citron thinly sliced in strips ¼ c. candied cherries cut in quarters 1 tbsp. chopped candied orange peel ¼ c. chopped figs	Make like suet pudding. Add eggs to suet mixture. Prepare fruit and mix well with extra flour. Add last. Pour into greased mold and steam three hours. Or pour into greased 1 lb. tin cans and steam two hours.
Steamed Dumplings	2 c. flour 4 tsp. baking powder ½ tsp. salt ⅓ c. shortening ½ to ¾ c. milk	2 c. of any one of the following fruits: Apples, blueberries, raspberries, stoned cherries, rhubarb, peaches; any canned fruit. 6 tsps. sugar 12 tbsps. cold water	Sift together flour, baking powder and salt. Cut in shortening. Add milk gradually to make a dough as stiff as for baking powder biscuit. Divide fruit in 6 greased molds, add 1 tsp. sugar and 1 tablespoon of water to each. Omit sugar and use juice of canned fruits. Place a piece of the dough on top of fruit. Steam 45 min.

All recipes in this chart serve six.

Chart for Doughnuts

Doughnuts	Basic Ingredients	Additional Ingredients	Method
Doughnuts I	1½ tbsp. shortening 1 c. sugar 1 egg	3 c. bread flour 4 tsp. baking powder ¼ tsp. cinnamon ¼ tsp. nutmeg 1 tsp. salt 1 c. milk Extra bread flour	Cream shortening and sugar until blended, then add beaten egg. Measure and sift together 3 c. flour and other dry ingredients. Add alternately with milk to sugar mixture. Beat well and add enough more flour to make a soft dough. Toss on floured board, roll to ¼ inch thickness and cut in desired shapes. Fry in deep fat at 360° F. Drain. When cool, roll in sugar.
Doughnuts II	Same as Doughnuts I	½ tsp. soda 3 c. bread flour 2 tsps. baking powder ¼ t p. cinnamon ¼ tsp. nutmeg 1 tsp. salt 1 c. sour milk Extra bread flour	Proceed as in Doughnuts I
Chocolate Doughnuts I	Same as Doughnuts I or II	Same as Doughnuts I or II with addition of 1½ sq. chocolate	Proceed as in Doughnuts I, adding melted chocolate to sugar mixture.
Chocolate Doughnuts II	3 eggs 2 sq. unsweetened chocolate 2 tbsps. shortening 1 c. cold mashed potatoes ¾ c. sour milk 1 c. sugar	4½ c. bread flour 4 tsps. baking powder 1 tsp. salt ½ tsp. soda ¼ tsp. nutmeg	Beat eggs until light. Add sugar and continue beating. Melt chocolate with shortening, add to eggs and sugar with potatoes and sour milk. Mix well, sift dry ingredients together and add, mixing to soft dough. Roll ¼ inch thick, shape and fry in deep fat at 365° F. Drain. The chocolate may be omitted for plain doughnuts.
Raised Doughnuts	1 compressed yeast cake 1 c. warm water 1 c. scalded milk 3½ c. bread flour	½ c. shortening 1 c. brown sugar 2 beaten eggs About 4 c. bread flour ½ tsp. salt	Soften yeast cake in the warm water. Cool the scalded milk and add yeast mixture and 3½ c. bread flour. Let stand about 3 hours in warm place. Cream fat, salt and brown sugar. Add beaten eggs and beat well. Add to yeast mixture with enough extra flour—about 4 c.—to make dough stiff enough to handle. Knead until elastic; let rise overnight. In morning, knead well, let rise until double in bulk. Then roll out part of dough to ⅓ inch thickness. Shape, lay on a floured board and let rise until double in bulk—about 45 min. Fry in deep fat at 350° F. until brown. When cool, roll in granulated sugar.
Jelly Doughnuts	Same as Raised Doughnuts	Same as Raised Doughnuts with addition of currant jelly, orange marmalade, or any sweet thick preserve	Proceed as in Raised Doughnuts. After dough has raised second time, turn it onto a floured board, roll to ¼ inch thickness, and cut in rounds. On each circle put 1 tsp. currant jelly or other preserve. Draw up the edges so that jelly is completely covered and press edges together firmly. Let stand on a floured board until light. Fry in deep fat at 350° F., turning frequently. Drain and when cool, roll in granulated sugar.

Chart for Ice Cream

Ice Cream	Basic Ingredients	Additional Ingredients	Special Directions
American Ice Cream—I	2 c. milk 1 tbsp. flour or corn-starch 1 c. sugar Few grains salt	1 egg 2 tsps. vanilla 1 qt. thin cream	Scald milk, reserving ½ c. Add flour or corn-starch mixed with sugar and salt. Cook 15 or 20 minutes. Beat egg, add reserved milk, combine with hot mixture, and cook 3 to 5 minutes longer. Remove, strain and cool. Add vanilla and cream. Freeze, using 8 parts of ice to 1 part coarse freezing salt. If preferred, omit flour and use 2 eggs, or use 2 egg-yolks instead of one egg. Makes 2 qts.
American Ice Cream—II	1 qt. milk ¾ c. sugar 3 tbsps. flour ¼ tsp. salt 3 tbsps. milk	1 egg 2 tsps. vanilla 1 c. heavy cream	Scald 1 qt. milk in double boiler. Combine ½ c. sugar, the flour, salt and 3 tbsps. milk. Add to scalded milk gradually while stirring constantly. Return to double boiler and cook 20 min., stirring often. Remove from heat, pour slowly over beaten egg, mixed with ½ c. sugar. Cool, add cream and vanilla and freeze as above. Makes 2 quarts.
Philadelphia Ice Cream	3 pts. thin cream 1 c. sugar Few grains salt	2 tbsps. vanilla	Scald cream in double boiler. Add sugar and salt. Cool, add vanilla. Freeze as above. Makes 2 quarts.
Banana Ice Cream	Use recipe for American I or II or Philadelphia Ice Cream	4 ripe bananas 2 tbsps. lemon juice	Peel, slice and mash bananas. Add lemon juice, combine with ice-cream mixture. Add sugar to taste.
Caramel Ice Cream	Use recipe for American I or II or Philadelphia Ice Cream	¼ c. boiling water	Caramelize sugar indicated in American or Philadelphia ice-cream, by melting with color of maple sirup in saucepan. Add boiling water and stir until smooth. Then proceed with recipe. Nuts may be added.
Chocolate Ice Cream	Use recipe for American I or II or Philadelphia Ice Cream	2 to 4 squares cooking chocolate ¼ to ½ c. hot water	Melt chocolate over hot water. Add hot water and stir until smooth. Add to ice-cream mixture.
Coffee Ice Cream	Use recipe for American I or II or Philadelphia Ice Cream	½ c. fresh ground coffee	Scald coffee with the milk or cream in ice-cream recipe. Strain through several layers of cheese-cloth. Proceed with recipe.
Grape Juice Ice Cream	Use recipe for American I or II or Philadelphia Ice Cream	1½ c. grape juice	Add grape juice to ice-cream mixture before freezing. Quantity of sugar will depend on sweetness of grape juice. If American Ice Cream is used, substitute heavy for thin cream.
Loganberry Ice Cream	Use recipe for American I or II or Philadelphia Ice Cream	1½ c. Loganberry juice Sugar to sweeten	Add loganberry juice to ice-cream mixture, just before freezing. Sweeten to taste. If American Ice Cream is used, substitute heavy for thin cream.
Maple Ice Cream	Use recipe for American I or II or Philadelphia Ice Cream	2 c. maple sirup	Substitute maple sirup for sugar in ice-cream recipe. Or use crushed maple sugar, dissolving it in the scalded milk or cream.
Nut Ice Cream	Use recipe for American I or II or Philadelphia Ice Cream	1 c. finely chopped nut-meats	Add nuts just before pouring ice-cream mixture into freezer.

All recipes in this chart serve twelve.

Chart for Ice Cream (Continued)

Ice Cream	Basic Ingredients	Additional Ingredients	Special Directions
Orange Juice Ice Cream	Use recipe for American I or II or Philadelphia Ice Cream	1½ c. strained orange juice	Add orange juice to ice-cream mixture. Amount of sugar depends on sweetness of fruit. With American Ice Cream use heavy cream.
Peach Ice Cream	Use recipe for American I or II or Philadelphia Ice Cream	2 c. washed and sieved, ripe or canned peaches Sugar to sweeten	Add sugar to sweeten fresh peaches and let stand 1 hour. Add to ice-cream mixture. If canned peaches are used add 4 tbsps. lemon juice.
Peppermint Ice Cream	Use recipe for American I or II or Philadelphia Ice Cream	1 lb. red and white striped peppermint candy	Crush peppermint candy and add to scalded milk or cream in ice-cream mixture. Omit the sugar.
Pineapple Ice Cream	Use recipe for American I or II or Philadelphia Ice Cream	1½ to 2 cups grated pineapple, fresh or canned. If the latter, drain. Sugar to sweeten	Add sugar to sweeten, fresh pineapple and let stand one hour. Add to ice-cream mixture. 2 tablespoonfuls lemon juice may be added to canned pineapple.
Pistachio Ice Cream	Use recipe for American I or II or Philadelphia Ice Cream	½ teaspoonful almond extract	Add almond extract and enough vegetable color to tint light green just before turning mixture into freezer.
Raspberry Ice Cream	Use recipe for American I or II or Philadelphia Ice Cream	1 qt. washed red or black raspberries Sugar to sweeten	Wash the fruit and put through a sieve. Add sugar to sweeten and combine with ice-cream mixture just before freezing. Raspberry juice may be substituted. If added to American Ice Cream, substitute heavy cream for the thin cream.
Strawberry Ice Cream	Use recipe for American I or II or Philadelphia Ice Cream	1—2 qts. strawberries washed and put through a coarse sieve	Add sugar to sweeten the washed strawberries. Let stand one hour. Add to ice-cream mixture just before freezing.

All recipes in this chart serve twelve.

Chart for Ices and Sherbets

	Basic Ingredients	Additional Ingredients	Special Directions
Apricot Ice	1 c. sugar ½ c. clear white corn sirup 2 c. water	4 tbsps. lemon juice 2 c. apricot pulp and juice	Cook sugar, corn sirup and 1 c. water to 240° F. Add lemon juice, rest of water and apricots. Cool, freeze, using 8 parts ice to 1 part salt. Makes 2 quarts.
Banana Ice	Same as Apricot Ice	2 bananas 1 c. orange juice 2 tbsps. lemon juice	Prepare and freeze as Apricot Ice, mashing bananas through coarse sieve. Makes 2 quarts.
Cider Ice	1 c. sugar 1 c. water 3 tbsps. lemon juice	1 qt. cider	Cook sugar, lemon juice and water to 240° F. Chill, add cider and freeze as above. Makes 2 quarts.
Grape Juice Ice	1½ c. sugar 3¼ c. water ¾ c. clear white corn sirup 3 tbsps. commercial pectin	6 tbsps. lemon juice 1½ c. grape juice	Cook sugar, 1 c. water, corn sirup and pectin to 230° F. Add lemon juice, grape juice and rest of water. Cool and freeze as above. Makes 2 quarts.
Orange Ice	1½ c. sugar ¾ c. clear white corn sirup 1¾ c. water	6 tbsps. lemon juice 3 c. orange juice	Cook sugar, corn sirup and 1 c. water to 240° F. Add lemon and orange juice and rest of water. Cool and freeze as above. Makes 2 quarts.
Strawberry Ice	1½ c. sugar ¾ c. clear white corn sirup 3 tbsps. commercial pectin	8 tbsps. lemon juice ¾ c. water 1½ c. fresh mashed strawberries	Cook sugar, corn sirup and pectin to 230° F. Add lemon juice, strawberries and water. Cool and freeze as above. Makes 2 quarts.
Banana Sherbet	1 c. water 1½ c. sugar	6 bananas mashed 2 c. orange juice 2 tbsps. lemon juice 1 egg white Diced orange	Combine water and sugar and cook until sugar is dissolved. Add orange juice, lemon juice and mashed bananas. Cool and freeze as above. When a soft mush in consistency, fold in the beaten egg white. Continue freezing until stiff enough, and serve, garnished with diced orange. Makes 2 quarts.
Cranberry Milk Sherbet	2 c. cranberries 2 c. sugar	3 tbsps. lemon juice 2 c. milk 1 c. cream	Wash and cook cranberries in water to cover until tender. Press through potato ricer. Add sugar and cook until sugar is dissolved. Chill, add lemon juice, milk and cream. Freeze as above. Makes 2 quarts.
Orange Cream Sherbet	3 c. water 2 c. sugar ¼ c. orange juice ½ c. lemon juice	1 c. cream	Boil sugar and water until sugar is dissolved. Cool; add lemon and orange juices. Freeze as above. When a soft mush, fold in cream, whipped. Continue freezing until stiff enough to serve. Makes 2 quarts.
Three Fruit Sherbet	Juice 3 lemons Juice 3 oranges 3 c. sugar	3 c. water 3 bananas 1 c. cream	Combine lemon and orange juices, sugar and water. Mash banana and add. Let stand one hour in cold place. Press through ricer. Add cream and freeze as above. Makes 2 quarts.

All recipes in this chart serve twelve.

Chart for Cooked Icings

Icings	Basic Ingredients	Additional Ingredients	Special Directions
All-Round Icing	2½ c. sugar ½ c. light corn sirup ½ c. water	2 egg whites 1½ tsps. vanilla	Combine sugar, corn sirup and water. Cook to 240°-242° F. or soft ball stage. Pour slowly over stiffly beaten egg whites, while beating constantly. Add vanilla and beat until almost cold, creamy to taste, and stiff enough to hold its shape. Can be kept in covered jar for week. If necessary soften with boiling water. This icing does not chip or crack even in 5 days.
Chocolate All-Round Icing	Use recipe for All-Round Icing	4 squares (4 oz.) unsweetened chocolate	Melt chocolate over hot water. Add to All-Round Icing any time after cooked sirup has been poured over beaten egg whites.
Coconut All-Round Icing	Use recipe for All-Round Icing	Coconut	Prepare All-Round Icing. Add coconut or sprinkle coconut over surface of cake after icing.
Coffee All-Round Icing	Subtitute ½ c. strong coffee infusion for ½ c. water in All-Round Icing recipe		Prepare as All-Round Icing.
Maple All-Round Icing	Substitute ¾ c. maple sirup for ½ c. water in All-Round Icing		Prepare as All-Round Icing. If sugar and maple mixture seem stiff, add ¼ c. water and then proceed.
Orange All-Round Icing	Use recipe for All-Round Icing	Grated rind 1 orange	Prepare All-Round Icing, adding orange rind to icing or sprinkling on top of cake.
Fluffy Icing	1⅔ c. sugar ½ c. water ⅛ tsp. cream of tartar	½ c. egg whites	Combine sugar, water and cream of tartar and stir until smooth. Cook without stirring to 260° F. or the hard ball stage, if the day is clear. Cook to 270° F. or the hard ball stage if the day is cloudy. If crystals appear on inside of pan, wipe down with damp cloth. When cooked, pour over egg whites beaten stiff. Beat until mixture leaves a spoon almost clean, or pulls away from side of bowl. Then ice cake.
Chocolate Fluffy Icing	Use recipe for Fluffy Icing	2 to 3 squares unsweetened chocolate	Melt chocolate over hot water. With a knife, fold in after the cooked sirup has been poured over egg whites.
Coffee Fluffy Icing	Substitute ½ cupful strong coffee infusion for ½ c. water in Fluffy Icing		Prepare as Fluffy Icing.
Maple Fluffy Icing	Substitute 1 c. maple sirup for ½ c. water in Fluffy Icing		Prepare as Fluffy Icing.
Orange Fluffy Icing	Use recipe for Fluffy Icing	Grated rind 1 orange	Prepare Fluffy Icing, adding orange rind after cooked sirup has been poured over egg whites. Yellow vegetable coloring may be added if desired.

Chart for Cooked Icings (Continued)

Icings	Basic Ingredients	Additional Ingredients	Special Directions
Creole Icing	1½ c. light brown sugar ½ c. water ⅛ tsp. cream of tartar	¼ c. egg whites ½ c. finely chopped nut meats	Combine brown sugar, water and cream of tartar and stir until smooth. Cook without stirring to 260° F., or the hard ball stage, if day is clear; to 270° F., or hard ball stage if day is cloudy. Wipe down with damp cloth crystals which form on inside of pan. When cooked, pour over stiffly beaten egg-whites. Beat until mixture leaves spoon almost clean or pulls away from side of bowl. Add nuts and spread. This icing is easy to work with.
Quick Cooked Icing	2 egg-whites 1¼ c. sugar 1 tbsp. light corn sirup 6 tbsps. water	1 tsp. vanilla	Combine unbeaten egg whites, sugar, corn sirup and water in top of double boiler. Beat constantly over the boiling water until the icing is fluffy and holds shape. Remove icing from hot water, add vanilla and mix well. Spread at once. This icing is desirable when the cake is to be served immediately, but it does not keep well.
Minute Fudge Icing	⅓ c. cocoa ¼ c. butter ¼ c. milk 1 c. sugar Pinch salt		Combine the ingredients listed. Boil one minute. Remove from fire and beat immediately until creamy enough to spread.
Fudge Icing	2 squares unsweetened chocolate 2 c. sugar ¾ c. milk 2 tbsp. light corn sirup	2 tbsp. butter 1 tsp. vanilla	Cut the chocolate in small pieces. Combine with sugar, milk and corn sirup, and cook slowly, stirring often, to 232° F. or a soft ball stage. Then remove from heat, add butter, and cool to 110° F. Add the vanilla and beat until creamy and thick enough to just hold its shape when dropped from a spoon.

Chart for Gelatine Dishes

Gelatine Dishes	Basic Ingredients	Additional Ingredients	Special Directions
Lemon Jelly	2 tbsps. gelatine ½ c. cold water 2½ c. boiling water	1 c. sugar ½ c. lemon juice	Soak gelatine in cold water 5 min. Pour boiling water over it, stirring until dissolved. Add sugar and fruit juice, stirring. Strain into cold wet molds. Chill until set. Makes about 1 qt. and serves six.
Orange Jelly	2 tbsps. gelatine ½ c. cold water 2 c. boiling water	1 c. sugar 1 c. orange juice 2 tbsps. lemon juice	Make same as Lemon Jelly. Makes about one qt. and serves six.
Coffee Jelly	2 tbsps. gelatine ½ c. cold water 3 c. hot clear, strong coffee	¾ c. sugar ⅔ tbsp. lemon juice	Soak gelatine in cold water 5 min. Dissolve in hot coffee. Add sugar and lemon juice, stirring until dissolved. Strain into cold wet mold, chill until set. Makes 1 qt. and serves 6.
Snow Pudding	Make ½ recipe for Lemon, Orange or Coffee Jelly	2 egg whites	Make same as Lemon, Orange or Coffee Jelly. Set aside to chill. When quite thick, beat with whisk or egg beater until frothy. Add egg whites beaten stiff and continue beating until stiff enough to hold shape. Mold again, serve with custard sauce (see P. 185). Serves 6.
Fruit Jelly	Use recipe for Lemon or Orange Jelly	Any one of the following: 1 c. diced bananas 1 c. diced orange 1 c. seeded Malaga grapes 1 c. fresh berries 1 c. diced canned pineapple	Make same as Lemon or Orange Jelly. Pour into cold wet mold and chill. When mixture begins to thicken, drop in prepared fruit.
Spanish Cream	1 tbsp. gelatine 3 c. milk ½ c. sugar	2 egg yolks 3 egg whites ⅛ tsp. salt 1 tsp. vanilla	Scald milk with gelatine in double boiler. When gelatine is dissolved, add sugar and pour slowly over beaten egg yolks, stirring. Return to double boiler, cook until thickened, stirring. Remove, add salt, vanilla and fold in egg whites beaten stiff. Pour into cold wet mold and chill. Serves 6.
Caramel Spanish Cream	Use recipe for Spanish Cream	¾ c. sugar	Make same as Spanish Cream, with this change: Melt one-half cup sugar until caramel in color. Add to scalded milk and gelatine. Stir until dissolved. Add remaining ¼ c. sugar to egg yolks and proceed. Dates, coconuts or nuts may be added. Serves 6.
Bavarian Cream (With Egg)	1½ tbsps. gelatine ½ c. cold water 2 egg yolks ¾ c. sugar 1½ c. scalded milk ⅛ tsp. salt	1 tsp. vanilla 2 egg whites 1 c. cream	Soak gelatine in water 5 min. Beat egg yolks. Add sugar and scalded milk slowly, stirring. Return to double boiler, add gelatine and salt. Cook until thickened. Remove and cool. Add beaten egg whites, cream whipped and vanilla. Pour into cold wet mold and chill. Serves 6.
Bavarian Cream (Without Egg)	½ tbsps. gelatine ¼ c. cold water 1 c. scalded milk ½ c. sugar ⅛ tsp. salt	1 pint cream 1 tsp. vanilla	Soak gelatine in cold water 5 min. Dissolve in scalded milk, add sugar and salt. Set bowl containing mixture in cold water. Stir occasionally until it begins to thicken. Add cream, beaten stiff, and vanilla. Pour into cold wet mold, chill. Serves 6.
Coffee Bavarian Cream	Use recipe for Bavarian Cream, substituting ½ c. strong clear coffee for ½ c. of the milk		

Chart for Gelatine Dishes (Continued)

Gelatine Dishes	Basic Ingredients	Additional Ingredients	Special Directions
Fruit Bavarian Cream	Use recipe for Bavarian Cream (without eggs) substituting 1 c. fruit juice and pulp for milk. Use sugar to sweeten		Make same as Bavarian Cream (without eggs) dissolving the soaked gelatine by standing the dish containing it in hot water.
Tomato Jelly	1½ tbsp. gelatine ½ c. cold water 2 c. stewed tomatoes ¼ small onion ½ bay-leaf	1 peppercorn 1 clove ½ tsp. celery salt Salt and pepper to taste	Soak gelatine in cold water 5 min. Meanwhile combine all other ingredients and cook 10 min. Strain, add gelatine and stir until dissolved. Pour into cold wet individual molds. Chill. Serves 6.
Jellied Waldorf Salad	1 tbsp. gelatine ¼ c. cold water ¼ c. boiling water ¼ c. lemon juice ½ c. orange juice ½ c. sugar 1 tsp. vinegar	1 c. diced celery 1 apple 1 c. chopped walnut meats	Soak gelatine in cold water 5 min. Add boiling water and stir until dissolved. Add all other ingredients. Pour into individual cold wet molds and chill. Makes 8 molds.
Charlotte Russe	1 tbsp. gelatine ¼ c. cold water 1¼ c. scalded milk 2 eggs 2 tbsps. sugar Few grains salt	½ pint heavy cream 3 tbsps. powdered sugar ¼ tsp. vanilla Sponge cake	Pour scalded milk slowly over beaten eggs, combined with sugar and salt. Cook in top of double boiler, stirring constantly until thick. Then add gelatine, soak in cold water for 5 minutes. Add beaten egg whites and chill until mixture begins to thicken. Then add cream, beaten stiff, powdered sugar and vanilla. Line round paper cases with strips of sponge cake. Fill with mixture and chill. Remove from cases and garnish tops with 4 narrow strips of sponge cake. Serves eight.

Cooking by Chart

The Hows and Whys

MAKING BAKING-POWDER BISCUITS AND SHORTCAKES
(See Chart, P. 174.)

Baking-powder biscuits masquerade under many names, but they are all biscuit dough made from a basic soft dough mixture in which the flour and liquid are in the approximate proportion of three to one. All kinds of shortcakes and biscuit mixtures may be evolved from simple variations in the proportion of shortening used, and from the addition of other ingredients.

It is not possible to give the exact amount of liquid in the basic dough mixture, as flours vary somewhat in the amount which they can absorb. About two-thirds cupful will be needed for two cupfuls of flour, although it may be as much as three-fourths cupful. The dough should be soft and handled lightly. It should not, however, be so soft and moist that the top of the rolled-out dough is rough. If the biscuits are to be dropped, the liquid is increased to one cupful, which makes a drop batter, the proportions being two to one. One cupful of Graham or whole wheat flour may be substituted for one cupful of the flour.

As in practically all flour mixtures, two teaspoonfuls of baking-powder are used for each cupful of flour. When using sour milk, use one-half teaspoonful of soda for every cupful of milk, as in other basic recipes for muffins and cake. Use thick sour milk. One-half teaspoonful of soda is equivalent to two teaspoonfuls of baking-powder and can therefore lighten only one cupful of flour. Use therefore two teaspoonfuls of baking-powder to every additional cup of flour.

One tablespoonful of shortening is allowed for each cupful of flour. Many prefer the shorter biscuit made by using two tablespoonfuls of shortening to each cupful of flour. This is particularly true of the Pinwheel Biscuits and their variations, which are not split and buttered. For very rich shortcakes this may even be increased to three tablespoonfuls of shortening for each cupful of flour.

Sift the dry ingredients together and then work in the shortening. Two knives will be found convenient and efficient for cutting in the shortening. Just as soon as the liquid is added to the biscuits, work quickly and with a light touch to turn out tender feathery biscuits. You may often find you can avoid last-minute preparation by mixing

198

the biscuits, all but adding the liquid, early in the day; then add the liquid, and bake just before they are needed. This will simplify the preparation of Sunday night suppers or tea. Some may prefer to prepare the biscuits for baking and then place them in the refrigerator until just before they are needed.

Dust the board and rolling pin lightly and evenly with flour. Turn the dough out on the board, sprinkle lightly with flour, and roll lightly or pat into a sheet. The biscuits may be made from one-fourth to one inch thick, depending on preference. Because the thinner biscuits are crisper, we chew them better and therefore digest them better than the thicker, softer biscuits. Flour the cutter slightly to prevent the biscuits from sticking. Place them on a greased pan, not touching each other but about one-half inch apart to keep the edges crusty. Bake at 450° F. for twelve to fifteen minutes.

MAKING QUICK LOAF BREADS (See Chart, P. 175)

The quick loaf breads are easy to make and will be a welcome change from the plain bread which is a staple in our diet. Bran breads will keep for several days, and it often proves convenient to have something like this on the emergency shelf. Besides serving them at meals you will find they are excellent sliced thin or made into sandwiches to serve with a cup of afternoon tea or at the bridge luncheon or after-theater party. The fruit breads are well liked by the children and are also good for them.

These loaf breads are made from the standard thick or drop batters, therefore the flour is in the proportion of two cupfuls to one cupful of liquid. This is the same proportion used in the basic recipe for muffins and for all flour mixtures of this consistency.

As in practically all flour mixtures, two teaspoonfuls of baking-powder are added for each cupful of flour, when sweet milk is the liquid. Whenever sour milk or molasses is used in all basic recipes, one-half teaspoonful of soda is required to neutralize the acid in one cupful of sour milk or molasses. As we have explained before, one-half teaspoonful of soda with one cupful of sour milk or molasses is approximately equivalent in lightening power to two teaspoonfuls of baking-powder. Therefore, the baking-powder should be decreased two teaspoonfuls for each half-teaspoonful of soda used.

The amount of sugar used may be varied according to taste, to the other ingredients, and to the use which you intend to make of the bread. Some people prefer a sweeter bread than others. If dates, raisins, prunes, or other sweet fruits are used, not so much sweetening will be required as for nut bread. If the bread is for children, you should make it less sweet than you might otherwise, as it is not wise to let the children acquire a taste for very sweet things. These breads are seldom made plain, but have nuts, fruit, or a mixture of these added to give them more flavor. The Bran Breads and Boston Brown Bread are sometimes made plain, as the molasses or brown sugar and whole grain flours give them a flavor, although most people prefer the addition of raisins to the Brown Bread, and fruit or nuts to the Bran Bread. One-pound baking-powder cans make excellent molds for steamed breads. Do not fill the molds more than two-thirds full, or the lid may be pushed off. Cover closely. The boiling water should come about half-way up on the molds.

MAKING QUICK BREADS (See Chart, P. 176)

Hot breads, or quick breads as they are often called, are made of various consistencies. They may be made from pour batters, that is, batters which are thin enough to pour; drop batters, or those which are thick enough to drop from the point of a spoon; or soft doughs, those which can be handled lightly.

In the first class of quick breads are popovers and griddle cakes, these using almost equal quantities of flour and liquid. By referring to the chart you will see that no leavening is included in the recipe for popovers. However, during baking the liquid in the batter is changed to steam very rapidly and expands to many times its volume, stretching the gluten walls of the flour which, with the help of the egg, form a hollow shell. It is for this reason that it is essential to bake popovers in a hot oven using a temperature of 450° F. for the first thirty minutes and lowered to 350° F. for fifteen minutes. Follow the procedure for popovers included in the chart, using iron or cast aluminum gem pans or glass or earthenware custard cups which hold the heat well. These should be heated and greased before filling.

You will note that all hot breads included in the chart, other than popovers, call for some added leavening agent as baking-powder or soda. Baking-powder contains soda and some acid such as cream of tartar. When liquid is added to the hot bread mixture, a chemical reaction takes place between the soda and the acid, forming a gas, carbon dioxide. This expands with the heat, thereby lightening the bread. Allow two teaspoonfuls of baking-powder to each cupful of white flour and two and one-half teaspoonfuls of baking-powder to each cupful of flour used in making whole wheat, rye, or bran muffins, as whole grain flours are apt to be heavier.

Soda is used for leavening when there is some acid present in one or more of the other ingredients, as in sour milk or molasses. The acid of this, acting with the soda, produces carbon dioxide which lightens the bread as we explained previously. As this reaction starts as soon as liquid is combined with the acid and soda, the soda should be sifted with the flour instead of adding it to the sour milk. One-half teaspoonful of soda will neutralize the acid in one cupful of thick sour milk or in one cupful of molasses. One-half teaspoonful of soda is approximately the amount present in two teaspoonfuls of baking powder and therefore can lighten one cupful of flour.   So in a recipe using one cupful of sour milk or molasses, one-half teaspoonful of soda, and two cupfuls of flour it will be necessary to add also two teaspoonfuls of baking-powder to lighten the batter sufficiently.   Only enough soda to neutralize the acid should be used as any soda left unacted upon has no lightening effect and will leave a bitter taste.

Muffins, in most instances, use two tablespoonfuls of sugar for two cupfuls of flour.   This may be increased to four tablespoonfuls if you desire a sweeter muffin.   Brown sugar may be used in the whole wheat muffins instead of white, increasing the quantity one-third, as brown sugar is not as sweet as white sugar.   In bran muffins molasses is generally preferred to sugar, and four tablespoonfuls are used, this being approximately equal to two tablespoonfuls of sugar.   In cornbread you may use no sugar or any amount up to four tablespoonfuls.

Only two teaspoonfuls of shortening are required for popovers. Waffles, however, which you wish quite crisp, require six tablespoonfuls of melted fat.   For most muffins from two to three tablespoonfuls of fat are used, depending on the tenderness which you desire.   However, for muffins using flour from the whole grain or bran, we found from three to four tablespoonfuls of melted fat more satisfactory.   In muffins you again have a choice of using one or two eggs to two cupfuls of flour. The two eggs, of course, will make a richer muffin than one egg will. If the eggs are quite small, we should recommend using two.

MAKING RAISED SWEET BREADS (See Chart, P. 177)

Raised sweet breads that may be served for breakfast, supper, or afternoon tea may be made from one basic sponge as given in chart. The recipes are merely suggestive, various flavors or spices may be used in the dough, brown sugar or maple sugar may be substituted for white and any combination of fruits may be used.

A sponge is made by thoroughly mixing the liquid with the yeast, part of the flour, and some of the sugar, and letting it rise in a warm place for three hours or in a cool place overnight.   We have found that a Dover egg-beater is an excellent utensil for making this mixture smooth.   Other materials such as eggs and spices, fat and salt, may then be beaten into the sponge just before the additional flour is added. It is possible in this way to make several kinds of breads and rolls from the same sponge, by adding varied ingredients to the sponge after it is ready to mix into a dough.   The recipe for sponge given in the chart makes one cupful of sponge, which is sufficient for one loaf of bread, or one ring.   This recipe may be doubled or tripled, if you wish to make several different kinds of sweet bread, using one cupful of the sponge for each type.   Bread flour, and not cake or pastry flour, must always be used when the leavening agent is yeast.

One factor to be watched carefully in bread making is the temperature. A high temperature will kill the yeast, while a low temperature will prevent it from growing. 65° F. to 70° F. is the best temperature for bread rising overnight, while for bread raised in the daytime 80° F. brings a quicker result. If raised at too high a temperature, the bread will be heavy and sour. The bread must double in bulk each time, which requires about sixty minutes. It may be difficult with some of the fancy shapes to determine when the dough has reached this stage, but after a little practise you can tell by the lightness to the touch. The large amount of sugar and fat in the sweet bread necessitates a longer period of rising.

Because a low temperature retards the growth of the yeast plant, the dough, or part of it, either plain or shaped ready for baking, may be placed in the refrigerator and baked fresh the next day. After removing from the ice-box, let the dough stand in a warm place to rise until double in bulk. This will require more time because the dough is chilled. The egg and sugar in these sweet breads make the dough difficult to handle. A little extra flour may be used on the board, but the dough should be handled as lightly and kept as soft as possible. Different millings of the same brand of flour will absorb varying amounts of liquid. For this reason it may be necessary to add more flour than is indicated in the chart. You must be careful, however, not to get the dough too stiff.

The bread will continue rising for the first ten minutes it is in the oven, and this must be considered in shaping the loaf or ring so that the bread will not go over the edge of the pan. If it should be desirable to bake the bread before it has doubled in bulk, you may put the bread in a cool oven and gradually bring the temperature up to the required degree. This gives the rolls or bread a chance to rise quickly at a comparatively high temperature, before the yeast is killed. The sweet breads brown rapidly, so it is wise to cover them with a paper the last fifteen minutes of baking.

MAKING SPONGE CAKE (See Chart, P. 178)

Probably the most popular cake to serve with afternoon and evening collations is sponge or angel cake. When it is well made and light, fluffy, and tender, it well deserves this popularity.

Sponge cakes are made with no shortening, which distinguishes them from the butter cakes. Also, a true sponge or angel cake contains no leavening, depending on eggs to lighten the cake. However, many sponge cakes decrease the number of eggs and add some baking-powder for leavening. These cakes also require no shortening, and the texture of the finished cake is very much like that of true sponge cakes. The methods of making and baking are practically the same.

The recipes for true sponge or angel cake all call for cream of tartar or vinegar, both of which are weak acids. These are used for the purpose of stiffening the albumen of the egg-whites, and help to keep the mixture firm.

Select eggs which are in good condition. They should be at least twenty-four hours old to beat well, and should also be very cold. The egg-whites should be beaten until quite stiff, that is, until a point will hold its shape, or the bowl can be inverted, but not until they are dry. This beating incorporates a quantity of air which lightens the cake by expanding with heat. Egg-yolks, when used, should be beaten until thick and lemon-colored. Due to the fact that they contain quite a large percentage of fat, they will not beat up so stiff as the whites, nor can much air be incorporated in them. Fine-grained granulated sugar should be used. Pastry flour should always be used. Sift it before measuring and then sift four or five times that it may be light and fluffy. The flour should be folded in lightly at the last. For the flavoring you may use vanilla, lemon or orange. For Angel Cake many like almond or a mixture of almond and vanilla.

Of great importance is the baking of sponge cakes. We have found that a temperature of 320° F., which is a slow oven, is the most satisfactory temperature for baking sponge cakes. The use of a heat-regulated oven or a portable oven thermometer makes the maintaining of this temperature simple and accurate. If too high a temperature is used, the cake will not rise sufficiently, due to the cooking of the batter before the air has expanded. Egg is also toughened by a high temperature; therefore the cake would not have the tender crumb desired.

After baking invert the cake in the pan on a cooling rack and allow to cool in the pan. It often comes from the pan by its own weight, but if it does not, it may be loosened around the sides with a spatula or fork when cool. If you attempt to remove the cake from the pan while it is still warm, it will frequently shrink. If the cake is baked in a tube pan, as angel and sponge cakes frequently are, the time required for the baking is one hour. Sponge cakes may be baked in layers, and put together with a filling. Whipped cream is often used for a sponge-cake filling. A layer sponge cake, or a loaf split in layers, may be used for shortcakes. Layers should be baked about twenty-five or thirty minutes.

For Jelly Roll, use the Hot-Water Sponge Cake recipe. The sponge-cake batter is baked in a thin sheet for twenty-five minutes, the pan first being lined with a greased paper. Remove the cake from the pan at once. You must work quickly, as the cake will crack if it is allowed to cool before rolling. The edges are trimmed off, because these are usually somewhat crusty and will break if one attempts to roll them.

MAKING BUTTER CAKES (See Chart, P. 179)

Every housekeeper delights in serving perfect cake to her family, but often she is proficient in making only one kind. Why not serve a variety of cakes and always be sure of the results? Let us turn the search-light on the mystery of cake-making, and simplify your problems.

In the Chart for Butter Cakes, we are giving you a foundational butter cake recipe which is a two-egg cake, and a number of variations which are easily obtained. By always observing certain rules in making this foundational cake and all other cakes, success will be insured. Always use ingredients of a good quality. All ingredients must be measured accurately to obtain invariably good results. Use pastry flour sifted before measuring, and fill the cup without shaking down the flour. If you can not obtain pastry flour, deduct two tablespoonfuls from each cupful of bread flour which you use instead of pastry flour. Blend the ingredients thoroughly, cream the butter and sugar until fluffy, and add the flour and liquid alternately so that the batter becomes neither too thick nor too thin. Butter cakes should be baked in pans which have been greased with an unsalted fat and lightly dredged with flour. These cakes may be baked as layer cakes, sheet cakes, loaf cakes, or cup cakes, but all should be baked by temperature. Bake layer cakes at 375° F. for twenty minutes, sheet or cup cakes at 375° F. for thirty minutes, and loaf cakes at 350° F. for forty-five minutes.

If the egg-whites are beaten separately and folded in last, the cake will be a little lighter than if the whole eggs are beaten and added to the shortening. You will see from the chart that when one egg is used the fat, sugar, and flour must all be decreased because of the decrease in liquid supplied by the egg. Egg-yolks contain some fat. As no egg-yolks are used in White Cake, one-half cupful of fat, the higher proportion for the two-egg cake is used. Three egg-whites, when beaten stiff and folded in last, lighten the cake considerably. Therefore use one-half teaspoonful less of baking-powder in the White Cake, but in Gold Cake, which has no egg-white, increase the baking-powder one-half teaspoonful.

The recipes in this chart all call for sweet milk. However, if you wish, you may substitute the same quantity of sour milk for sweet milk, allowing one-half teaspoonful of soda to neutralize the acid in one cupful of sour milk. One-half teaspoonful of soda is approximately the amount present in two teaspoonfuls of baking-powder. Therefore, when one-half cupful of sour milk and one-fourth teaspoonful of soda are used, deduct one teaspoonful of baking-powder from the recipe. Sour cream may also be substituted for sweet milk in the One or Two Egg Cake, using three-fourths cupful of cream, omitting the fat and adding soda in the same proportion as for sour milk.

Brown sugar may be used in place of granulated sugar, except when you wish to keep the cake perfectly white, or when the brown sugar might hide some other flavor which you wish to predominate. Use about one and one-third cupful of brown sugar for every cupful of granulated sugar. Any of the variations in the chart may be applied to the foundational two-egg cake or the other three cakes built from this foundational cake recipe. It is also possible to combine variations and have still more varied cakes. For instance, spices may be added to a number of the other cakes, as to the Apple Sauce Cake or Chocolate Cake, or nuts may be added to Maple or Spanish Cake.

MAKING COOKIES (See Chart, P. 180)

Do you keep the cooky jar filled, or do you find that you can not afford the time for rolling and cutting cookies? It does take time to roll out cookies, but there are shorter methods. You may shape the dough into a roll, chill it thoroughly, and slice it with a sharp knife. A still shorter method is to drop the mixture in the form of a very stiff batter from a teaspoon on to the baking sheets. The cookies made by these two methods will not be uniform in shape, but consider the time saved. It takes twice as long to roll and cut cookies as to slice them, and from two to five times as long as to drop them, depending on the dough and the skill of the individual. Do you have the time to roll and cut cookies except when you want fancifully shaped ones for special occasions?

You will be wise to keep the cooky jar subject to rules and regulations, especially for the children. They, of course, should understand that raids on the cooky jar between meals, and particularly just before meals, are taboo. All cookies, whether rolled, sliced, or dropped, are made from a basic stiff dough, with less flour used for the stiff batter for drop cookies. This stiff batter will spread a little in the oven. From the Chart for Cookies you will see that some cookies are made with beaten egg as both a leavening agent and as the only liquid used. In others, eggs are used chiefly as a leavening agent and either sweet or sour milk or water as the liquid.

Brown sugar brings additional flavor and a rich brown color to the cookies, but you may use white sugar if it is more convenient. In substituting brown sugar, use one and one-third cupfuls for every cupful of sugar called for. From two-thirds to one cupful of shortening are used with three cupfuls of flour depending on the richness desired. Use the less rich mixture when making the cookies for the children.

To lighten the cookies, use two teaspoonfuls of baking-powder with three cupfuls of flour. This is less than the amount used in the basic recipes for cakes, muffins, and biscuits, as cookies need not be so light as these mixtures.

You may need a little more of some blends of flour than is indicated in the schedule, but for the best rolled cookies keep the dough as soft as can be handled. To make the stiff batter for drop cookies from any of these basic rolled or sliced cookies, use one-third to one-half cupful less flour.

In rolling out cookies, it is easier if the dough is first chilled in the refrigerator. Otherwise more flour will be needed, and the cookies will not be so tender. Flour the board and roller slightly and roll out with a light touch as much prepared dough as can be handled quickly, keeping the rest in the refrigerator to prevent its softening. Save all pieces left between cookies until the last and roll together, as repeated working in of these pieces adds more flour and toughens the cookies.

BAKING CUSTARDS (See Chart, P. 181)

Baked custard with its variations has many points in its favor as a simple, nutritious dessert. It is quickly and easily made and can be prepared several hours before serving, a point which every housekeeper will appreciate. Mothers will find that children who do not like milk or eggs as such will usually accept them eagerly in the form of custard.

An ideal custard is of a firm, jelly-like consistency with a smooth texture. This consistency depends upon two factors: first, the correct proportion of eggs and milk; and second, the baking temperature. Experience has proved that one egg to one cupful of milk is the right proportion for individual custards, and six eggs to one quart of milk if it is baked as one large custard. The sweetening and flavoring are matters of taste and so may be varied to suit individual preference. Do not make the custard very sweet for the children. The occasional use of brown or maple sugar or honey in place of granulated sugar will give a flavorsome variation.

To make baked custard, beat the eggs only enough to mix well; next, blend in the sugar and salt. Last, stir in the milk and flavoring and strain. Grease the custard cups lightly so that the custards will unmold quite easily when cold. Place the filled cups in a shallow pan containing about half an inch of warm water, as a protection against the custards' reaching the boiling temperature. It is usually due to the wrong baking temperature that many a custard proves to be a disappointment. Egg and milk mixtures require a low temperature to prevent curdling. So bake the custards slowly at 325° F. about forty minutes if individual custards, or seventy-five minutes if a large custard. Remove them from the oven when cooked, as excess cooking will cause curdling. A good test is to dip a silver knife in water, then insert it in the center of the custard. If the knife comes out clean, the custard is cooked; if the knife is coated, longer cooking is necessary. The individual custards when unmolded may be served plain or with sliced fruit or berries.

Too often Bread Pudding has been a stiff and soggy mass made by merely adding milk and flavoring to a comparatively large quantity of bread and baking this. Such a dish is truly unpalatable. Good Bread Pudding and Rice Pudding should be made by using the correct proportions of rice or crumbs to eggs and milk. We have included two excellent recipes for these dishes in the chart.

MAKING STARCHY DESSERTS (See Chart, P. 182)

Corn-starch is generally used in thickening starchy desserts as well as the dessert sauces. It has almost twice the thickening power of flour. Allow two tablespoonfuls of corn-starch to each cup of milk. In using eggs in these desserts, remember that one egg is approximately equal in thickening power to one tablespoonful of flour or one-half tablespoonful of corn-starch. For this reason, you will note that in the chart one-half tablespoonful of corn-starch is deducted when one egg is used.

It is always important to separate the starch grains before the hot liquid is added to the starch. To accomplish this in the starchy desserts, the corn-starch and half of the sugar—or all the sugar in case no egg is used—are mixed and then blended with one-half cupful of cold milk. The liquid is heated, using a double boiler. The starch and sugar, mixed with the cold milk, are stirred into the hot milk. While the mixture is thickening, it is stirred constantly to prevent the separated starch grains from running together and forming lumps. It should be cooked for twenty-five minutes to insure a well-cooked mixture. If egg is used, it should not be added until the starch mixture is cooked, as that takes much longer to cook than the egg. The egg should be beaten with the remaining half of the sugar, and then part of the hot starch mixture poured into the beaten egg while stirring constantly. If the egg is poured into the starch mixture, there is danger of the egg cooking in small tough particles. Return all to the double boiler and cook one minute longer. Sometimes the yolk only may be used for thickening, and the white used as a meringue on top or beaten into the pudding. When beaten into the pudding, it makes it very light and delicate in texture.

Fruit juices, fresh or canned, may be used as part or all of the liquid in sauces and desserts. Lemon juice should not be added until after the liquid is thickened.

MAKING PUNCHES (See Chart, P. 183)

Punch, or any fruit juice beverage, has its own place in the diet, particularly in the summer. We all know the importance of eating fruit for its vitamins and minerals. Also we must not forget six glasses of water a day! Punch combines these in a pleasing way.

In the Chart for Punches, we are giving you a variety of basic punch recipes. We believe that every housekeeper would do well to keep an emergency shelf in her refrigerator stocked with punch possibilities. Needless to say, this shelf should include bottled fruit juices, ginger ale, and carbonated water if you like it. Then, too, it is a distinct saving of time, when you are in the kitchen in the morning, to squeeze as much orange and lemon juice as will be needed for the next two or three days.

Put it in jars and tuck it in your refrigerator—it will be cold and ready for immediate use. As for sugar sirup, prepare a quantity of it at a time. Boil sugar and water together gently for five minutes, using one cupful of sugar to every one-half cupful of water. Bottle the sirup and keep it in the refrigerator, too! With such an emergency shelf, who fears the unexpected guest?

You may use plain water to dilute the punch if you desire. However, at least part carbonated water will add a tang to the punch and give it more character. Strong tea, prepared as for drinking, may be added to any punch, adding from one-half cupful to one cupful to the basic recipe. This will give a slightly different flavor and will increase the quantity as it is used in addition to the water. Coffee may be used in the same way. Ginger ale adds zip and sparkle to a mild punch and may be added alone or with the tea or coffee. A little lemon or lime juice should always be used, if possible, as it gives the beverage life.

You can vary the quantity of sirup to suit your taste, but do not make it too sweet. A tart drink will quench the thirst and refresh you more than a sirupy one. Remember, too, that the sirup you add has calories or fuel value. Do not feel that you must always follow these basic recipes exactly. With them as a guide, venture new combinations. The sirup from any canned or fresh stewed fruit may always be added, but do this before adding your sugar sirup, to avoid over-sweetening. Play with the proportions given, and see what delightful surprises you can concoct.

If possible, it is well to make the punch early and let it ripen, that is, let the flavors blend. Ice is added to chill the punch thoroughly. This melting of the ice will dilute the punch still more. If there is not time to permit melting, add more ice water to the punch to make the quantity given in the chart. You may also vary the strength of the punch to suit your taste. If the punch is served in a punch bowl, pour it over a block of ice, which should come above the punch. For receptions, punch is generally served in small, handled cups, a ladle being used to fill them from the punch bowl. Otherwise it may be served in glasses over cracked ice.

Slices of fruit, such as peaches, oranges, lemons, or bananas, may be added to the punch. Cherries, strawberries, seeded grapes, diced or crushed pineapple, and maraschino cherries are also excellent garnishes. In serving the punch put a little of the fruit in each glass or cup. If the punch is served in tall glasses, you may place a slice of orange or lemon on the rim, the sliced fruit having been slit for this. Sprigs of mint may be added to each glass of some punches. But however it is garnished, be sure to serve the punch very cold.

MAKING SAVORY AND SWEET SAUCES (See Chart, P. 184)

White Sauce forms the basis of many other sauces. Once its preparation is mastered, the variations are simple indeed. Flour is usually the starch used in making White Sauce, while corn-starch is found in dessert sauces. When starch of any kind is mixed with liquid and heat is applied, the starch grains in cooking absorb the liquid, swell, burst, and form a gelatinous substance which thickens the liquid around it. If hot liquid is carelessly added to flour, it will collect in large or small masses throughout the liquid, and the outer grains in each mass will begin to cook, forming a gelatinous coating. This cooking prevents the penetration of the water to the inner grains, causing a lumpy mixture. Therefore, flour and corn-starch grains should be thoroughly separated, either by blending equal amounts of the starch with fat, as in White Sauce, or by combining equal parts of starch and sugar, or starch and a small amount of cold liquid, as in dessert sauces. Then the entire quantity of cold or hot liquid may be added. While the starch is cooking, the liquid should be constantly stirred to prevent the separated grains from running together again.

In using eggs in any dishes thickened with starch, they should not be added until the starch has first thickened the liquid, as starch takes longer to cook. Stirring separates the jelly-like particles finely and evenly, but if cooked too long, these particles of egg become tough, forming small lumps and giving the mixture a curdled appearance. Beaten egg will also thicken very quickly when poured directly into a hot liquid, so the safer method is to beat the eggs, stir part of the hot, thickened liquid into the beaten eggs, and return all to the double boiler, stirring only one minute longer without boiling.

MAKING CREAM SOUPS (See Chart, P. 186)

The importance of making good cream soups can hardly be over-estimated. Being served at or near the beginning of a meal, an appetizing soup will go far toward making a real success of dinner.

And yet, how many of us unconsciously discard one of the most valuable basis for cream soup making—the vegetable waters which have been used in cooking vegetables. Vegetables should be cooked by steam whenever possible. However, when boiling must be employed, the residue water which contains such valuable vitamins and mineral salts should be used in making soups and gravies. Save the vegetable waters. They will add much in the way of natural flavor and vitamins to your cream soups.

Although with careful watching one may make cream soup in a saucepan, it is easier to use a double boiler unless the quantity is too large, for a double boiler proves an excellent means of keeping the soup warm until serving time without fear of scorching.

A thin white sauce forms the basis of practically all cream soups, the vegetable water and pulp being added to the prepared white sauce. The general directions for making a cream soup are as follows: Melt the butter in the top of a double boiler. Add the flour while stirring constantly and cook until smooth and well blended. Then add the cold milk gradually and the seasonings and cook until the mixture is smooth and thickened. Then add the required amount of vegetable water and reheat. Plan to reserve the vegetable water and vegetable required for the next day's cream soup when cooking the dinner vegetable the day before.

Occasionally you may prefer a vegetable cream soup made with white sauce and vegetable water as a basis without the addition of any vegetable pulp or diced vegetable. Oftentimes it is a very pleasant variation to combine two vegetables as carrots and peas, potatoes and celery, or green beans and carrots, in the cream soup. If the soup seems to lack in color as in the case of potato or celery soup, the addition of chopped parsley, watercress, green pepper or pimiento, or a dash of paprika proves colorful. Left-over creamed vegetables pressed through a ricer may be used as pulp, with all milk as the liquid.

A beaten egg may also be added to any cream soup. In blending the egg and cream soup, add a small amount of the hot soup to the beaten egg, and then gradually pour this mixture into the entire quantity of cream soup, while stirring.

The Chart of Cream Soups will give you comprehensive procedures to follow. There are cream soups of other vegetable flavors which may suggest themselves to you. For such soups, use the same proportions of milk, vegetable water, and vegetable pulp as given in the chart, varying the seasonings to suit the taste.

Getting the Most Out of Your Kitchen Equipment

Good Housekeeping Institute lays great stress on the use of suitable equipment as an aid in housekeeping. Recent years have brought great improvements in kitchen equipment, as well as many new types of devices. Unless this modern equipment is used to the best advantage and given reasonable care, it can not be expected to return maximum service. A word about kitchens and their equipment is therefore in place here.

For many years the Institute has been investigating and testing household equipment. In addition to searching engineering tests each piece of equipment is used as it would be in the home. We know, then, just what every device can do for the housekeeper, how it will stand up under continued use, and what care it requires. We go still further. Long years of experience have kept us in close touch with what the market is offering the housekeeper. We separate the good from the poor and all equipment measuring up to our standards we place on our List of Tested and Approved Devices a valuable buying guide which may be secured from Good Housekeeping Bulletin Service for 15 cents.

I. KITCHENS PLANNED FOR CONVENIENCE—The kitchen should be easy to work in, step saving and restful with attention given to floors and wall finishes. The large equipment should follow the general order of work in preparing meals and the small equipment should be grouped conveniently around that working center at which each piece is used most. Housekeepers will find it to their advantage to give some thought to making their kitchen as efficient a workshop as possible. The Institute bulletin "Kitchens Planned for Convenience" considers the kitchen in great detail, its ventilation, floors and walls, storage spaces, lighting and service outlets for using electrical devices, the sink, garbage disposal and equipment for dishwashing, refrigerators, the different kinds of ranges and the selection of small equipment utensils. The proper care of equipment and utensils is given much attention. The bulletin is well illustrated and gives a number of kitchen plans, showing the most convenient arrangement of equipment large and small. It can be obtained from Good Housekeeping Bulletin Service, 119 W. 40th St., New York City, for 25 cents.

II.   THE KITCHEN RANGE

1.   Cooking by Temperature—Considering that cooking temperatures are so important in cookery, it is fortunate that the housewife has suitable instruments for measuring these.   When the oven is not equipped with a regulator, an oven thermometer may be used.   The mercury tube of the oven thermometer is mounted on a suitable frame or backing and provided with a base so that it will stand upright, or equipped with a hook so that it may be suspended.   Naturally the range of the thermometer and the calibrations, are suited to those temperatures used in oven cookery, namely, from about 200° F. to 600° F. For other than oven cookery, such as deep fat frying and candy making, there are thermometers of the mercury type with suitable mountings and with ranges and calibrations to meet the requirements.   Women who depend on their own judgment of oven heat must necessarily expect baking failures at times, for the human senses are poor in gaging temperatures.   Oven thermometers approved by the Institute are absolutely reliable, and will insure uniformity in baking results unknown to the housewife who has not used one.   These thermometers can be used with any fuel, or any type of range.

The oven regulator is a thermostatic device which can be set to automatically maintain the oven at any desired temperature.   It usually has a hand wheel or pointer together with a graduated scale by which the setting is made.

2.   Managing the Gas Range—A gas range will give the best service when managed with a view to getting the most from it for the least expenditure of time and fuel.   At the Institute, we have made a study of time and fuel-saving methods by actually preparing meals for a week at a time and carefully noting the results.   The gas meter was always read at the end of each meal, so that we were able to determine more closely the fuel-saving value of the methods used.

By conserving fuel we do not mean that only food requiring a short cooking period should be used.   We included many foods which needed long cooking, but used fuel and time-saving methods in preparing them.   In preparing a dish which necessitates long cooking in the oven plan your menus so that you may at the same time prepare other dishes which can be used for the same meal or a later meal.   The pressure cooker will cut down the time for long top-stove cooking.

We found the oven meal a great time and fuel saver, because, in cooking by temperature, (see page 252) the waste of gas through overheating the oven and the need for watching the food were eliminated. By consulting the Institute Cooking Temperature Chart, the exact time and temperature for each food were ascertained.   Of course, we found it necessary to select foods requiring the same temperature, but after they had been put in the oven no thought was given them until they were ready to be taken out.

3. **Oven Meals by Temperature**—As we found that oven meals saved fuel and also saved much time because the cooking food required no watching, the Institute planned a number of oven meals particularly adapted to the warm summer months, when a cool kitchen means so much.

Menu No. 1—400° F.
Roast Chicken
Buttered Potatoes and Onions
Creamed Carrots   Cornbread
Strawberries and Cream

Menu No. 2—350° F.
Scalloped Ham and Potatoes
Corn and Green Pepper Scallop
Cottage Pudding—
    Lemon Sauce

Menu No. 3—450° F.
Roast Beef
Pan Roasted Potatoes
Buttered Sliced Onions
Baking Powder Biscuits
Strawberry Short Cake

Menu No. 4—400° F.
Beef Loaf
Creole Tomatoes
Mashed Potatoes
Muffins
Apple Crisp

Menu No. 5—325° F.
Sliced Cold Meat
French Cream Potato Salad
Carrot Timbales
Gingerbread with Whipped
    Cream

Menu No. 6—500° F.
Broiled Chops
Baked Potatoes
Scalloped Asparagus
Buttered String-Beans
Lemon Meringue Pie

Most of the recipes for the above dishes will be found by consulting the index at the back of the book.

4. **Using the Electric Range**—Utensils used for cooking on the electric range will be much the same as those used on other ranges. The utensils for top stove cooking should have flat bottoms and be of a size which will entirely cover the heating unit. When more than one food is to be cooked on top of the stove, it is economical to use duplicate or triplicate saucepans. Use only enough current to keep them boiling gently. Acquire the habit of turning your current to medium or low when possible.

Because of the loss of heat by radiation, top stove cooking on the electric range is much more expensive than oven cooking. The ovens of all electric ranges are well insulated and so retain the heat. Then too, a number of dishes can be prepared at one time in the oven. So, in arranging your menus, plan to cook as many oven meals as possible. At the same time if there is room, include a dish for the following day. (See P. 212.)

If gas is available also, some use a one or two burner gas plate as a supplement to an electric oven as it usually means more economical top stove cooking. There is a type of electric range equipped with top stove gas burners in addition to top stove elements. Many electric ranges are now equipped with both a time and a temperature control which means that the meal can be put in the oven and |the clock set for both the time to start and shut off the current while the temperature control maintains the desired temperature. In planning meals to be cooked with the time control, it is better to select those dishes which can be prepared and left in the oven for a short time, before the heat is turned on, so that one can put the meal in the oven and leave the kitchen.

In setting the clock, there are two things to be taken into consideration, the time your oven takes to preheat to the required temperature and the time the food takes to cook. In estimating the cooking period remember that the oven is so well insulated the food will continue cooking for some time after the current is shut off. This should be considered as part of the cooking period. A little practise will tell you just what part of the cooking period this is, in your oven.

The following summer meals for a week which can be easily changed to suit any season were prepared in the electric range with a view to using the oven as much as possible. In preparing Monday's luncheon the individual custards were baked for dinner, and at dinner the peas, in a covered container were cooked in the oven for Tuesday's luncheon. For Tuesday's luncheon the bacon for the Baked Peas was broiled under the top element while the oven was heating. The Cream Puffs for dinner and potatoes (diced) sufficient for dinner and for Wednesday's luncheon were cooked while the peas were baking.

For dinner on Wednesday sufficient Braised Beef was cooked to serve at luncheon on Thursday. In preparing Thursday's luncheon a pie shell was baked for the pie served at dinner.

When Thursday's dinner was being prepared a loaf cake was baked for dinner on Friday. At Saturday's luncheon the Cherry Cobbler was baked, the sweet potatoes and string beans were partly cooked for dinner and the rhubarb was cooked for Sunday breakfast. The Turnovers for Sunday supper were also prepared then.

A Week of Menus Prepared in the Electric Range

MONDAY

BREAKFAST—Fuel Cost, $.063
Orange Juice
Rolled Wheat   Cream
Scrambled Eggs, Whole Wheat Muffins
Coffee   Milk

LUNCHEON—Fuel Cost, $.051
Cheese Fondue
Cabbage and Nut Salad   Rye Bread
Sliced Peaches   Cream

DINNER—Fuel Cost, $.067
Delmonico Roast   Brown Gravy
Baked Potatoes
Asparagus with Butter Sauce
Endive   French Dressing
Baked Custard   Coffee

TUESDAY

BREAKFAST—Fuel Cost, $.009
Raspberries   Cream
Waffles and Syrup
Coffee   Milk

LUNCHEON—Fuel Cost, $.087
Baked Peas
Carrot Salad   Corn Bread
Drop Cookies   Iced Coffee

DINNER—Fuel Cost, $.045
Fruit Cocktail
Sliced Meat Loaf (cold)
Creamed Potatoes   Spinach
Jellied Tomato Salad   Mayonnaise
Cream Puffs

WEDNESDAY

BREAKFAST—Fuel Cost, $.042
Grape Juice
Prepared Cereal   Cream
Poached Eggs   Toast
Coffee   Milk

LUNCHEON—Fuel Cost, $.033
Potato and Cheese Croquettes
Tomato Sauce
Ginger Ale Salad   Mayonnaise
Graham Bread

DINNER—Fuel Cost, $.132
Braised Beef
Roast Potatoes   Buttered Carrots
Cole Slaw   Rolls
Strawberry Ice   Coffee

THURSDAY

BREAKFAST—Fuel Cost, $.018
Sliced Oranges
Prepared Cereal   Cream
Bacon   Rolls
Coffee   Milk

LUNCHEON—Fuel Cost, $.048
Cold Sliced Beef with Dressing
Fruit Salad   Muffins
Iced Chocolate   Wafers

DINNER—Fuel Cost, $.063
Scalloped Potatoes
Buttered Beets   Spinach
Egg Salad   Fruit Gelatine Pie

FRIDAY

BREAKFAST—Fuel Cost, $.033
Fresh Sliced Peaches
Farina   Cream
Toast   Jam
Coffee   Milk

LUNCHEON—Fuel Cost, $.033
Asparagus and Egg Piquante
Cabbage Salad   Brown Bread
Watermelon

DINNER—Fuel Cost, $.078
Baked Haddock   Tartar Sauce
Buttered Potatoes and Onions
Cucumber and Tomato Salad
Cake   Punch

A Week of Menus Prepared in the Electric Range (Continued)

SATURDAY

BREAKFAST—Fuel Cost, $.024

Cantaloupe
Prepared Cereal   Cream
Omelet   Toast
Coffee   Milk

LUNCHEON—Fuel Cost, $.042

Tomato and Cheese Salad
Baking-Powder Biscuits
Raspberries   Cream
Iced Tea

DINNER—Fuel Cost, $.03

Candied Sweet Potatoes
Creamed String Beans
Stuffed Egg Salad   Russian Dressing
Deep Cherry Pie

SUNDAY

BREAKFAST—Fuel Cost, $.027

Baked Rhubarb
Bread Crumb Griddle Cakes   Syrup
Coffee   Milk

DINNER—Fuel Cost, $.087

Smothered Chicken   Cream Gravy
Buttered Peas   Mashed Potatoes
Watercress Salad   Biscuits
Peach Ice Cream   Iced Tea

SUPPER—Fuel Cost, $.012

Cucumber and Pineapple Salad
Mayonnaise
Peanut and Cream Cheese Sandwiches
Turnovers   Iced Coffee

5. **Top-of-the-Stove Ovens**—There are a number of small portable ovens on the market for use on a top burner. Those tested and approved by the Institute can be relied upon to give good results. As some top stove ovens are opened by removing the top, a thermometer can not well be used with them. Portable ovens are very useful when a regular oven is not available.

III. MEALS IN THE ELECTRIC FIRELESS COOKER

The electric fireless cooker is taking the place of the non-electric cookers. When the work which these cookers will do is thoroughly understood they can be used as valuable supplementary cooking devices.

Because a good cooker is well insulated there is not a great loss of heat through radiation. It is therefore possible to cook an entire meal without heating up the house. It is easily moved about and can be attached to any convenience outlet. It requires little attention after the food is put in.

In using the one-well cooker at the Institute we used with it a one-unit electric table stove, since there may be times when one has to use the cooker in place of a range as far as possible. Menus for as many as eight may be prepared in such a cooker. An electric toaster and percolator would of course add to the convenience of meal making.

It is possible to use the electric cooker in either of two ways. It may be used exactly as you use the oven of your range for baking breads, cakes, and pies, and for roasting meat; or it may be used for foods which can be cooked slowly for several hours at a lower temperature. When using the cooker as an oven, the heat is left on during most of the cooking process in order to maintain the higher temperature necessary, and the same attention must be given it as for oven cookery. For long cookery, the electricity is either turned off, or in some cookers is shut off automatically, as soon as the food reaches the desired temperature. The cooking is continued on the retained or stored heat, but at a much lower temperature than in the quick direct method.

Chicken and other meats, when cooked at the same time as vegetables, may be successfully browned, but we advise you not to expect what the Institute defines as "true roasts," unless these meats are cooked by themselves. When water is added to meats in cooking, we term it "braising," not roasting, and in the cooker the moisture from the cooking vegetables gives braised and not roast meat. We found that in preparing chicken, better results were obtained when the chicken was cooked for thirty minutes before the vegetables were put into the cooker.

IV. SUCCESSFUL COOKING ON OIL RANGES

In many homes the use of an oil range is an all-year round proposition, and there are few of us who have not, at some time or another, experienced the necessity of using an oil range for at least a few weeks, if only in a summer bungalow.

Oil ranges, in general, are divided into two classes, the wick and wickless type, each efficient in operation if correctly used. We have found by actual test that if the oil range is to be used for baking, roasting, broiling, and top-stove cookery, a three or four burner size is most efficient. This will permit you to use a one or two burner oven for baking and still have a burner available for top-stove cooking at the same time.

Before attempting any cookery whatever, see to it that the oil range is set absolutely level. This is particularly true of the wickless type of range. Adjusting devices on the legs and a spirit level mounted on the stove are sometimes provided to assist in keeping the stove level. If the range is not level, excess oil may get to the burner during operation, or the oil will creep over the collar when not in operation, both of which will cause undue smoke and odor.

In the wick type of range, although it is desirable, of course, for the range to set level, it is usually dirty burners and wicks which cause the trouble. The easiest way of keeping them always clean is to give them just a bit of care each day. With this type of range the important factor is to see that the wick itself is kept absolutely clean. Do not cut or trim the wick. It is better to wrap a piece of tissue-paper tightly around the first finger and clean off the charred wick by patting down the entire surface of it. Do not rub in a circular motion, as this will cause unevenness of the wick. One type of range has a patent device for doing this.

For the wickless type of range, remove the chimney and spreader, if there is one, and with a small whisk broom gently brush off the burners and asbestos collars. If this routine cleaning has not been properly done more strenuous cleaning will have to be done. For this cleaning we have found the following suggestions helpful:

Take out the collar and scrape off any charred carbon which may have collected on the burner bowl or collar. We do this with a small screw-driver or knife. Then wipe off with a cloth wound over the blade of the knife. This will get most of the carbon out of the burner bowl, but small particles of it may drop down into the main feed pipe. To get rid of these particles, a hatpin or small wire should be run down through the hole which supplies the oil to the burner bowl from the feed pipe; then unscrew the nut at the end of the range farthest from the supply tank and flush the oil through it, which will carry out any sediment that may have collected there.

V. TIME-SAVING METHODS IN THE PRESSURE COOKER

Too many think of their steam pressure cooker only in connection with canning and the occasional cooking of tough cuts of meat. It has however a distinct place in the everyday preparation of meals. Not only is it possible to prepare many individual foods in it, but with careful planning entire meals can be served from it. It is possible also to cook with less water than when the foods are boiled, and so none of the flavor is lost. Stews and boiled meats often have a richer flavor when cooked in the pressure cooker than when prepared in the ordinary way.

A glance at the time table on page 219, will show how much time and fuel are saved over the ordinary method of cooking. Steam pressure cookers may be used with equally successful results on a gas, coal, kerosene, or electric range, or even over a one-unit electric table stove. They may be purchased in more than one size according to the capacity desired. Inset pans and racks for holding the various foods are usually furnished.

Before using any pressure cooker, study carefully the directions accompanying it, particularly in reference to closing and opening the cooker at the beginning and end of the cooking period. The edges of the top and the upper rim should be wiped perfectly dry and fitted together according to the directions accompanying the cooker. This precaution is especially necessary in the type of cooker that is fastened by means of clamps, to prevent the steam from leaking out around the edges of the top.

TIME TABLE FOR COOKING
Steam Pressure 15 Lbs.

Meats and Fish: Minutes

Beef Stew.	40
Beef Loaf.	30
Beef Tongue	75
Chicken Fricassee	30-40
Corned Beef.	75
Halibut (1 inch thick)	20
Ham, Shoulder	65
Leg of Lamb	40
Leg of Mutton.	50
Loin of Pork	50
Pot Roast	50
Roast Fowl	45-55
Roast Veal	40
Salmon (1 inch thick)	20

Vegetables:

Beans (lima)	15
Beans (string).	12
Brussels Sprouts.	6
Beets	20-30
Cabbage	8-10
Carrots	8
Cauliflower (divided).	4-5
Celery	7
Greens, beet	10
Onion	8-10
Parsnips	8
Peas	8
Potatoes (white).	10
Potatoes (sweet).	8
Pumpkin	8
Rice	15
Spinach	8
Squash (winter).	18
Turnip.	10

Those Three Meals a Day

I. A GUIDE TO BALANCED MEALS

Good meals are not only interesting, attractive and well-cooked meals that suit the pocketbook, but those that do not keep the home-manager too long in the kitchen. They should also be well balanced as to food value, in order to keep the family fit.

It is by no means a simple matter to keep all these things in mind in preparing meals day in and day out, week in and week out. It is so easy to get into a rut and not always easy to pull out of it. We all tire of deciding just what to prepare three times a day.

In helping our readers with their meal planning for many years, the Institute has found that the best way out is to have a few simple guides to which one can constantly turn and see the problem as a whole.

The Institute Daily Diet for the Adult and for Children are guides to balanced meals and therefore the foundation for all types of meals. Instead of giving them in terms of calories and protein, vitamins and mineral matter, we have outlined a general plan for the day which allows for a wide variety in types of meals and in the dishes to be served but which very clearly shows what each day's meals should include. It considers meals for children as well as for grown-ups.

DAILY DIET FOR THE ADULT

1. Check up on your weight, according to age and height.

2. If you are the right weight, aim to keep this weight and weigh weekly.

3. Balance your meals for the day as follows:

a. One pint of milk a day either as beverage or partly in soups, sauces or desserts.

b. Two generous servings of non-starchy vegetables (such as carrots, lettuce, spinach, string beans, cabbage, beets), at least one of these raw whenever possible.

c. One serving of fresh fruit, raw if possible.

d. One moderate serving of meat, or a meat substitute such as cheese or egg dish.

e. One egg a day in addition to this.

220

f. To make up the energy requirement for the day add breads (including whole wheat), starchy vegetables (such as potatoes and baked beans), cereals (including whole grains), desserts, butter and cream.

4. Drink plenty of water, at least six glasses a day.

5. If you are overweight cut down on the foods in (f) above, sufficiently to lose weight steadily. If you are underweight increase the amounts of foods in (f) sufficiently to gain steadily. Also follow directions on page 223 for "Meals for Reducing." Keep a daily diet diary.

6. Take outdoor exercise daily.

DAILY DIET FOR CHILDREN FROM THE SECOND YEAR

1. Aim to have your child show a steady increase in height and weight. Check up on these frequently.

2. Regularity of meal times, simplicity of menu, and a happy atmosphere, together with fresh air and sunshine and plenty of sleep are keynotes to successful child feeding.

3. The child's diet should contain:

a. One quart of milk daily either as a beverage or partly in soups, sauces and desserts.

b. One egg each day either simply cooked or included in custards or similar dishes.

c.. Cereal once a day, usually hot and whole grain, with other hot or, ready-to-serve cereals occasionally substituted for variety.

d. For tooth exercise, stale crusts, toast or hard crackers should be furnished each day for chewing.

e. A green vegetable every day, with spinach, tomatoes and cabbage often represented.

f. Fruit juices or fresh fruit every day, with preference given to oranges.

g. No meat until the fourth year and then only one to three ounces, depending upon the age. Choose only tender, well-cooked chicken, lamb, lean beef, mutton or lean, easily flaked fish. Serve at the noon meal, never at night.

4. Encourage drinking of water up to six glasses a day.

The above guides indicate that a balanced diet is one including a variety of foods. It is the only safe one. In any one meal avoid

serving two foods that are of similar food value. For example, macaroni and potatoes, or rice and potatoes should not be served together.
They are all too rich in starch. Eggs or cheese as the main part of any
dish have little place in a meal in which meat or fish is served, as they
are all protein or body-building foods.

Fruits and vegetables are high in fiber or cellulose which is valuable
to us as ballast or roughage, a sort of broom to keep the digestive tract
clear. As our diet is so often lacking in roughage, making constipation
a very common complaint, we have advised generous servings of fruits
and vegetables daily and the plentiful use of whole grains. These
foods also supply the valuable mineral salts and vitamins, and vegetables should therefore not be cooked in much water, especially when
this is drained into the sink.

II. MEALS FOR THE CHILDREN

As a baby begins to have solid food it should be given in small
amounts and in proper form. At first only mild fruit juice, especially
orange juice and the cooked and strained pulp from mild fruits should
be given. An egg yolk mixed with a little baked potato should be included. The daily menus for children given here are typical of
what they should get at various ages. These are based on our Daily
Diet for Children from the Second Year. When children are ten years
old they should be eating what adults are, provided the adults are
eating only foods best suited to them. Eating between meals should
be avoided, especially candy, and other sweets.

TYPICAL DAILY MENUS FOR CHILDREN

During the Second Year			After the Third Year		
Food Stuff	Amount	Calories	Food Stuff	Amount	Calories
Warm Milk	1 cup	170	Hot Cereal	4 Tbsp.	80
Orange Juice	3 Tbsp.	20	Toast and		
Strained Oat-			Butter	1 piece	90
meal	2 Tbsp.	40	Milk	1 cup	170
Zwieback	1 piece	35	Orange Juice	4 Tbsp.	25
Warm Milk	1 cup	170	Milk	1 cup	170
Poached Egg			Cracker	one	25
Yolk	one	50	Asparagus Soup	½ cup milk	90
Baked Potato	2 Tbsp.	20	Whole Egg		
Stale Crust	3 pieces	50	Poached	one	75
Strained Spinach			Baked Potato	small one	50
Pulp	2 Tbsp.	15	Toast and		
Warm Milk	1 cup	170	Butter	1 piece	90
Strained Prune			Junket	½ cup milk	85
Pulp	2 Tbsp.	30	Rice	1 Tbsp.	55
Strained Farina	3 Tbsp.	50	Milk	1 cup	170
Warm Milk	1 cup	170	Zwieback	1 piece	35
Zwieback	1 piece	35	Apple Sauce	¼ cup	80
		1025			1290

Typical Daily Menus for Children (*Continued*)

When Six Years Old			For the Ten-Year-Old		
Food Stuff	Amount	Calories	Food Stuff	Amount	Calories
Sliced Orange	one	80	Baked Apple	one	100
Hot Cereal	4 Tbsp.	80	Ready-to-serve		
Milk	1 cup	170	Cereal		90
Toast and Butter	2 pieces	180	Milk	1 cup	170
Milk	1 cup	170	Toast and		
Zwieback	2 pieces	70	Butter	2 pieces	180
Roast Chicken-			Milk	1 cup	170
breast	1 ounce	50	Bread and Jelly	2 pieces	200
Baked Potato	small one	50	Round Steak	1½ oz.	75
Mashed Carrots	½ cup	25	Baked Potato	small one	50
Bread and Butter	2 slices	180	Tomato and		
Tapioca Custard	½ cup milk	100	Lettuce Salad		20
Plain Cooky	one	35	Ice Cream and		
Hot Milk with			Cooky	½ cup milk	200
little cocoa	¼ cup milk	100	Bread and		
Milk Toast	1 cup milk	170	Butter	2 pieces	180
	1 piece toast	50	Cream of Pea		
Stewed Prunes	6 small	100	Soup	¼ cup milk	95
			Macaroni	2 Tbsp.	55
			Saltines	three	50
			Stewed Figs	6 small	100
			Bread and		
			Butter	1 piece	90
			Milk	1 cup	170
		1610			1995

III. MEALS FOR REDUCING

We measure foods in terms of calories and should only take as many calories as we actually require for our work and exercise.   Control your calories and you can control your weight, if you are in normal health. That is why in our Daily Diet for the Adult we advise the overweight person to cut down on starchy vegetables, breads, cereals, desserts, butter and cream as these are all comparatively high in calories, and are considered concentrated foods.   •

Plan to banish that "empty feeling" by eating rather generously of the bulky foods such as the green and non-starchy vegetables and the fruits, for these give few calories as compared with the bulk they supply. A good selection is as follows: Asparagus, Brussels sprouts, cauliflower, celery, lettuce, spinach, tomatoes, cabbage, string beans, grapefruit, fresh peaches, pineapple, and strawberries.

Special meals need not be prepared for the person who wishes to reduce.   In fact it is much safer to keep to a regular diet and reduce slowly.   Eat the same meals as the rest of the family adapting these to your own needs.   At breakfast, for example, take milk instead of cream on the cereal and add no sugar to it; use butter sparingly and take a very small serving of bacon if it is on the menu.   You will find that you can cut down the calories well over one-half.   For the other meals avoid such foods as gravy, rich sauces, sweet desserts and mayonnaise dressing on the salad and do not eat much bread.   Eat generous servings of the vegetables except the starchy ones, and use fruit for dessert. The main point is to eat as little as possible of those foods high in calories, that is, those containing much fat, starch or sugar.

IV. COUNTING THE COST OF MEALS

The skill of the cook and the time she is willing to spend in turning the cheaper staple foods into attractive, well-cooked dishes, with a skillful combination of flavors and textures, play a large part in meal costs.

Protein foods such as eggs and meat are among the most expensive items in the market basket especially when eggs are at their higher prices. Other protein foods such as milk, cheese, peas and beans and the cereals are less expensive. In selecting the more perishable fresh fruits and vegetables, especially when these are out of season, we may pay very high for flavor. Watch these closely.

The actual edible material in any one food may prove expensive eating as the following figures show. They also show the wide range in the prices of the various cuts of meat and the different kinds of fish:

Six French chops at sixty-five cents per pound weighed 2¾ pounds and cost $1.80. Trimmed, ready for cooking, the weight was one pound five ounces. On further trimming off all but the edible portion, the weight was 12 ounces, bringing the actual cost of the meat to $2.40 per pound. Over 70 percent was waste material. In the butcher's trimmings there was some lean meat suitable for stew. How many ever order these sent home? There was below 2 percent of waste in 2 pounds of lean round steak at 50 cents per pound, bringing the real cost to about 60 cents per pound. A five-pound rib roast at 52 cents per pound yielded 45 percent waste, bringing the cost to about 95 cents per pound. There was a little over 31 percent waste in a four-pound haddock at 35 cents per pound, bringing the cost to about 50 cents per pound. Salmon at 65 cents per pound had 30 percent waste, bringing the cost to 92 cents per pound. All these foods are high in protein and therefore interchangeable in the diet as building material. We mention this, as it is misleading to attempt to compare the costs of foods that really can not be compared as to food value, for foods do differ widely in nutritive value. Only through such studies as these can the menu-maker gain definite information as to the real cost of food in trying to reduce her food budget.

Cereals play a leading part in low cost meals, so do cabbage, and the root vegetables such as carrots and turnips partly because their keeping qualities are so good that their transportation and storage are not expensive. The dried fruits and dried peas and beans should be used freely in low cost menus and canned fruits and vegetables hold an intermediate place in cost between dried and fresh fruits and vegetables.

If the larger size package can be used to advantage and without any waste, it is usually much cheaper than the smaller package, weight for weight.

The table below shows the comparative cost of the mineral elements and the protein in the various foods. We have not included starch, sugar or fat as these are usually the cheapest nutrients in our diet.

COMPARING THE COST OF NUTRIENTS IN AVERAGE SERVINGS OF FOOD

Foodstuffs arranged from the cheaper to the more expensive sources

Calcium	Phosphorus	Iron	Protein
Cabbage	Dried Beans	Cabbage	Dried Beans
Cheese	Cabbage	Dried Beans	Rice
Turnips	Oatmeal	Spinach	Macaroni
Milk	Cheese	Potatoes	Wheat Cereal
Dried Beans	Potatoes	Oatmeal	Bread
Cauliflower	Turnips	Raisins	Oatmeal
Carrots	Dried Peas	Dried Peas	Dried Peas
Oatmeal	Milk	Turnips	Corn Meal
Spinach	Spinach	Lettuce	Cheese
Celery	Fish	String Beans	Peanut Butter
Lettuce	Meat	Prunes	Eggs
Potatoes	Eggs	Eggs	Milk
String Beans	Carrots	Meat	Nuts
Oranges	Cauliflower	Bananas	Fish
Dried Peas	Lettuce	Canned Peas	Meat
Eggs	String Beans	Carrots	
Canned Tomatoes	Canned Tomatoes	Cauliflower	
Prunes	Prunes	Canned Asparagus	
Rhubarb	Bananas	Canned Tomatoes	
Bananas	Canned Peas	Cheese	
Canned Peas	Oranges	Apples	
Canned Asparagus	Celery	Fish	
Fish	Canned Asparagus	Oranges	
Meat	Rhubarb	Celery	

The above Table is Based on These Prices:

Eggs, 42 cents a dozen
Apples, 30 cents a dozen
Oranges, 48 cents a dozen
Peas, 20 cents a can (1¼ lb.)
Lean meat, 48 cents a pound
Fish, 35 cents a pound
Spinach, 10 cents a pound
Milk, 16 cents a quart
Strawberries, 21 cents a box (1¼ lb.)

Lettuce, 10 cents a pound
Potatoes, 4 cents a pound
Celery, 15 cents a bunch (¾ lb.)
Cauliflower, 25 cents a head (3 lbs.)
Cabbage, 6 cents a pound (4 lbs.)
Asparagus, 40 cents a can (30 oz.)
String beans, 10 cents a pound
Cheese, 40 cents a pound
Nut meats, $1.30 a pound

Planning meals ahead will greatly help in keeping down their cost. A week's menus on a sheet of paper gives one a general view of what is to be served and is one of the best ways to discover whether or not these menus make up a well-balanced selection as far as cost is concerned. If one of the main objects is to keep down costs, are the less expensive foods, mentioned above, well represented and in a variety and form that will whet the appetite? If a roast has been selected for one dinner, how and when is the left-over portion going to be used? Will fuel be used economically? If baking is being done for any one meal is the oven used to capacity for cooking other dishes to be served for the next meal or the next day? This is particularly important in using electricity. If the decision as to what to serve for dinner is left to the last minute this hit-and-miss method may prove expensive.

V. TIME AND STEP SAVING MEALS

1. Sunday Meals—Sunday dinners should be meals that can be prepared quickly after church and because it is a day for rest and relaxation it is much more healthful to keep the meals very simple. On this one day the luxury of a steak or chops might be considered. Mixed grills prepared in the frying-pan are inviting; sausages and sautéd apples or tomatoes, chops and sautéd bananas, bacon and sautéd bananas or tomatoes are all delicious combinations and can be served with a salad or simple dessert. Dishes prepared the day before and kept in the refrigerator until ready to cook or serve are excellent for Sunday. Among these will be the great variety of casserole dishes, which you will find by consulting the index to this book, stuffed peppers or tomatoes, cold sliced or jellied meats with a salad and a simple dessert. Ice cream can be made in the morning and packed ready for dinner.

For supper, a main-dish salad or dishes that can be made with a table grill or in a chafing dish, served with bread and butter or toast, make appetizing Sunday suppers. Here are some suggestive menus:

HOT WEATHER SUNDAY MEALS

DINNER
Orange or Pineapple Mint Cocktail
Pressed Chicken
Creamed Potatoes en Casserole
Fresh String-Bean Salad
Chocolate Cornstarch Pudding

SUPPER
Cucumber Salad with Salmon
Dressing
Brown Bread and Butter Sandwiches
Iced Tea   Cinnamon Cake

DINNER
Cream of Watercress Soup
Sliced Cold Lamb   Asparagus
New Potatoes with Butter Sauce
Peach Ice Cream   Sponge Cake

SUPPER
Stuffed Tomato Salad
Graham Bread
Cream Cheese Sandwiches
Blueberry Cake   Iced Fruit Punch

COLD WEATHER SUNDAY MEALS

DINNER	DINNER
Vegetable Soup	Cream of Tomato Soup
Lamb Chops Sautéd Bananas	Chicken en Casserole Steamed Rice
Buttered Carrots	Scalloped Onions
Orange Bavarian Cream	Baked Apple and Cream
SUPPER	
Lobster and Mushroom en Casserole	**SUPPER**
Brown Bread and Lettuce	Curried Eggs in Chafing Dish
Sandwiches	Hot Biscuits
Nut Cake Tea	Fruit Salad

2. **Dinners made after Business Hours or a Late Shopping Trip—** When you expect a shopping trip, club meeting or other engagements to keep you out late in the afternoon plan a dinner that can be made quickly, and that will include some dishes which can be made in the morning. Many business women and men too like to make their own dinners after business hours. The electric fireless cooker will prove valuable and the pressure cooker will cut down the time for cooking vegetables and other foods. Dishes that can be made the evening before or in the morning should also be planned for these dinners. Again we recommend the useful casserole. The quickly cooked steak and chops, although expensive meats, often meet an urgent need for saving time, when time may mean more to a busy woman than pennies. The mixed grill, broiled or cooked in the frying-pan, is also quickly prepared. (See Page 226.) We give below some suitable menus.

In the first menu the ham, sweet potatoes, and tomatoes are all broiled, as a mixed grill in the broiler oven, thus using only one utensil. The previous evening the potatoes were boiled and the cabbage was chopped and put in the refrigerator in ice water.

In the second menu the dried beef was frizzled in butter in a frying-pan and placed on the hot platter. Then the whole ripe bananas were sautéd in the same frying-pan using more butter or bacon dripping. The previous evening the beets were cooked, the salad green was washed, and the caramel tapioca pudding was made.

In the third menu the bread and cheese dish was prepared in individual casserole dishes in the morning before leaving the house. This required thirty minutes' baking at 350° F. upon coming home at night. The salad green was prepared with that for the previous night's meal.

In the fourth menu the Brussels sprouts were prepared the previous evening, as was the salad green. The rolls were purchased, cut in half and toasted in the electric toaster. ,In the fifth menu the celery and spinach were prepared the previous evening. In the sixth menu the cauliflower and romaine were prepared the night before. Canned tomato soup was used as the basis for the sauce, it being made in the same frying-pan in which the halibut steak was sauted.

Mixed Grill of
Broiled Ham, Broiled Sweet Potatoes,
and Broiled Tomatoes
Cole-Slaw   Cake

Frizzled Dried Beef   Sautéd Bananas
Whole Wheat Bread   Beet Salad
Caramel Tapioca Pudding

Calves' Liver and Bacon
Creamed Brussels Sprouts
Romaine Salad
Thousand Island Dressing
Toasted Rolls
Grapefruit with Grape Juice   Cake

Cheese Fondue
Stewed Canned Tomatoes
Apple and Nut Salad   Cake

Corn and Green Pepper Chowder
Buttered Spinach with Eggs
Celery
Camembert Cheese   Currant Jelly
Butter Crackers or Saltines

Sautéd Halibut Steak, Tomato Sauce
Rice   Cauliflower
Romaine Salad
Dates   Graham Crackers

3. **Dish-Saving Meals**—We are always interested in meals that save dishwashing, especially pots and pans. The casserole as both baking and serving dish is useful for this purpose. Consult the index and you will discover many suggestions for the casserole dishes that provide for one full course in one dish such as mixtures of meat, fish or eggs and vegetables. An extra vegetable may sometimes be advisable, depending upon the rest of the meal. A salad may often be substituted.

The club-plate service for luncheon or dinner is another dish saver, and insures hot food since the course is served directly from the kitchen on the individual plates. With the exception of a watery vegetable such as tomatoes almost any combination lends itself to club-plate service. Vegetable-dinners (see page 126) are particularly attractive served this way.

VI. SCHOOL LUNCHES AND PICNIC BASKETS

Lunch boxes go picnicking in the summer and return to school in the autumn. School lunches and picnic meals have much in common, as they must both lend themselves to easy packing and both should hold pleasant surprises for the lunchers.

School lunches are closely associated with child health. Uninviting paper-bag lunches, prepared without much thought for the interest which a variety of food brings to children, should be a thing of the past. An attractive box and paraffin paper for wrapping take the place of paper bags, while a vacuum bottle for carrying milk, hot cocoa or soup is most useful. Fortunately, many schools now serve good well-balanced hot lunches and mothers of the community should support all such undertakings through every possible cooperation with the school. These lunches may or may not be supplemented by a box lunch from home.

Sandwiches are the great staple for the lunch-box and Graham or whole wheat bread should be used freely. Many delicious fillings can be evolved from such foods as cheese, peanut-butter, jam, raisins, lettuce, dates, crisp celery, figs and chopped nuts, shredded cabbage, sliced tomatoes, hard cooked eggs and cold sliced or minced meat. These can be made into "spreads" with some mild salad dressing or a little cream when suitable to the mixture. Oranges, apples, pears and other fruit and whole tomatoes in paraffin paper carry well.

Glass and china individual baking dishes and paper cases make possible the baked custard or pudding, the plain cake or gingerbread and small molds of pressed or jellied meat, in a way that pleases the young luncher. All lunches should of course consider the age of the luncher. Here are some suggestions for the lunch box:

LUNCH-BOX MENUS FOR THE ELEMENTARY SCHOOL	LUNCH-BOX MENUS FOR THE HIGH SCHOOL
Egg and Celery Sandwiches Little Sponge Cakes Dates Milk	Cold Sliced Chicken Celery Graham Bread and Butter Sandwiches Date Blanc-Mange in Cup Plain Cookies
Chicken and Tomato Sandwiches Gingerbread Milk Apple	Tomato Soup Slice of Beef Loaf, Lettuce Sandwiches Caramel Cup Custard
Graham Crackers with Peanut Butter Baked Cup Custard Apple Milk	Nut and Cheese Sandwiches Tapioca Cream Celery Raisin Cake
Egg and Lettuce Sandwiches Caramel Cup Custard Milk	Salmon Salad Bread and Butter Grapes Milk Cookies

VII. COOKING FOR ONE OR TWO

The main problem here seems to be to avoid small quantities of left-overs and to use up such foods as a roast or a cake.   Food purchased ready in portions for serving is most convenient as chops, a small steak, tomatoes, potatoes, apples, and bananas for baking or sautéing, sausages and bacon.   Any fraction of the regular cake or muffin recipe can easily be prepared, and there are baking pans suitable for the small layer and loaf cake.   The smallest size can available, for any canned vegetable or fruit, although more expensive, weight for weight, than the larger can is often more economical in the end as it simplifies the problem of using left-overs.

It is a simple matter to cook enough of any vegetable for one or two and stews lend themselves to small quantity cooking.   The useful casserole, especially the individual size, lends friendly aid, and the mixed grill of chops, sausages, or bacon with sautéd fruit or vegetables will prove a great favorite.

Roasts need not be absent from the bill-of-fare. Small Delmonico roasts of two pounds or a little over cook well; so do the prime ribs. Similarly a small pot roast or a small piece of beef for braising can be used to advantage.

VIII. MENUS FOR A WEEK

We fully sympathize with those who grow tired of making out menus week after week, so we are giving here two sets of menus for a week for a family of six. The two given are more particularly suitable for the winter months, but all may be, with a few changes, adapted to any season. They are all "balanced meals" planned with our Daily Diets as a guide. (Page 220.)

A—First Week

SUNDAY

BREAKFAST
Sliced Oranges
Bread-Crumb Omelet
Graham Gems
Coffee   Milk

DINNER
Baked Ham   Raisin Sauce
Scalloped Potatoes Buttered Spinach
Stuffed Celery Salad
Apple Pie

SUPPER
Creamed Oysters
Pepper Sandwiches
Chocolate Cake   Tea

MONDAY

BREAKFAST
Stewed Prunes
Creamed Codfish
Brown Bread Toast
Coffee   Milk

LUNCHEON
Lima Beans en Casserole
Cabbage Slaw Baking-Powder Biscuits
Pineapple Sauce

DINNER
Ham Croquettes   Parsley Sauce
Riced Potatoes
String-Beans in Stewed Tomato Sauce
Orange Floating Island

TUESDAY

BREAKFAST
Baked Apples
Whole Wheat Cereal   Cream
Broiled Sausages   Toast
Coffee   Milk

LUNCHEON
Tomato Rarebit   Corn Cake
Celery
Caramel Junket

DINNER
Fish Chowder
Beet and Egg Salad   Graham Bread
Raisin Pie

WEDNESDAY

BREAKFAST
Grapefruit
Waffles   Bacon   Sirup
Coffee   Milk

LUNCHEON
Creamy Eggs on Brown Bread Toast
Scalloped Tomatoes
Pear Sauce   Cookies
Cocoa

DINNER
Green Peppers Stuffed with Meat
Potato and Onion Pie
Raw Carrot and Apple Salad
Snow Pudding Orange Custard Sauce

THURSDAY

BREAKFAST

Apple Sauce

Oatmeal   Cream
    Creamed Dried Beef   Toast
    Coffee   Milk

LUNCHEON

Casserole of Peas with Carrot Sauce
Popovers
Fruit Jelly

DINNER

Onion Soup au Gratin   .
Cauliflower Duchesse
                        Buttered Spinach
Shredded Lettuce and Egg Salad
Spanish Cream   Maple Sirup

FRIDAY

BREAKFAST

Sliced Oranges and Bananas
Ready-to-Serve Cereal.   Cream
Eggs Poached in Milk Graham Toast
    Coffee   Milk

LUNCHEON

Cream of Salmon Soup
Cabbage Salad Sandwiches
Gingerbread   Tea

DINNER

Clear Tomato Soup
One-Plate Fish Dinner of
Steamed Halibut
                    Drawn Butter Sauce
Rice   Buttered Beets
Chopped Celery with French Dressing
Peach Tapioca Pudding

SATURDAY

BREAKFAST

Cereal with Dates
Omelet   Spanish Sauce
Corn Cake
    Coffee   Milk

LUNCHEON

Macaroni, Italian Style
Brown Bread
Baked Bananas
Tea

DINNER

Lamb Chops   Glazed Sweet Potatoes
Creamed Turnips
Lettuce Salad
Caramel Bread Pudding

B—Second Week

These meals are planned to especially meet the needs of a mother with a small baby and other young children. We are assuming that the mother is busy with the baby during the half hour before dinner, and for this reason we have planned these menus to avoid last-minute preparation. Most of the meals are oven meals as they require less attention.

We have kept in mind the needs of the children in these menus, as these will also fit the adults' requirements. However, we realize that the adults may sometimes want foods which the children should not have. For Sunday dinner, therefore, we are giving father and mother individual apple pies and the children apple sauce. Also, for supper that night, the adults have Tomato Rarebit and the children Milk Toast. (See Page 26 for Milk Desserts.)

SUNDAY

BREAKFAST
Stewed Apricots and Raisins (adults)
Orange Juice (2 children)
French Omelet   Corn Muffins
(Cooked Wheat Cereal for children)
Coffee   Milk

DINNER
Bouillon
Roast Leg of Lamb
Baked Potatoes   Buttered Spinach
Celery and Carrot Salad
Individual Apple Pies (adults)
Apple Sauce (2 children)

SUPPER
Tomato Rarebit (adults)
(Milk Toast for 2 children)
Lettuce and Brown Bread Sandwiches
Pineapple and Orange Cup
Molasses Cookies
Tea   Milk

MONDAY

BREAKFAST
Grapefruit (adults)
Orange Juice (2 children)
Ready-to-Serve Cereal   Cream
Bacon   Toast
Coffee   Milk

LUNCHEON
Cream of Spinach Soup   Toast
Mashed Potatoes and Poached Egg
Date Marmalade   Milk

DINNER
Lamb and Vegetables en Casserole
Lettuce Salad
Maple Bread Pudding   Milk

TUESDAY

BREAKFAST
Apple Sauce
Cooked Cereal   Cream   Toast
Coffee   Milk

LUNCHEON
Creamed Minced Lamb
Peas   Celery Hearts
Graham Bread   Malted Milk

DINNER
Spanish Rice   Buttered String-Beans
Brown Bread   Date Custard

WEDNESDAY

BREAKFAST
Stewed Prunes
Soft Cooked Eggs   Graham Muffins
Coffee   Milk

LUNCHEON
Cream of Green Pea Soup
Lettuce and Brown Bread Sandwiches
Molded Cereal with Chopped Figs
Top Milk

DINNER
Meat Loaf   Baked Potatoes
Creamed Celery Tomato Jelly Salad
Sponge Cake   Peach Short Cake
(2 children)   (2 adults)
Sliced Canned Peaches

THURSDAY

BREAKFAST
Orange Juice (2 children)
Farina with Dates
Bacon   Toast
Coffee   Milk

LUNCHEON
Meat Loaf (small serving)
Spinach   Whole Wheat Bread
Milk Flavored with Cocoa
Stewed Prunes .

DINNER
Vegetable Plate consisting of
Mashed Potatoes with Poached Eggs
Buttered Beets   Cabbage Salad
Caramel Spanish Cream

FRIDAY

BREAKFAST
Orange Juice
Hominy Grits   Cream   Toast
Coffee   Milk

LUNCHEON
Scrambled Eggs
Lettuce and Peanut Butter Sandwiches
on Whole Wheat Bread
Milk   Apple Sauce

DINNER
Fish with Potato Stuffing and
Tomato Sauce
String-Beans
Bananas Baked in Skin
Tea   Milk

SATURDAY

BREAKFAST
Baked Apples
Creamy Eggs   Toast
Coffee   Milk

LUNCHEON (entire family)
Lima Beans with Tomato Sauce
Celery
Whole Wheat Bread
Steamed Rice and Raisins with Top
Milk

DINNER
Liver en Casserole   Baked Potatoes
Buttered Cabbage
Floating Island   Oatmeal Cookies

Menus for Special Occasions

NEW YEAR'S DINNER
Shrimps and Olives in Aspic
Cream of Mushroom Soup
Pulled Bread
Roast Capon   Southern Gravy
Riced Potatoes   Brussels Sprouts
with Hollandaise Sauce
French Bread   Scalloped Onions
Pickled Peaches
Endive and Malaga Grape Salad
Caramel Nut Ice Cream
Coffee   Chocolate Cake
Salted Nuts   After Dinner Mints

LINCOLN'S BIRTHDAY AFTER-
NOON TEA REFRESHMENTS
Mock Deviled Ham Sandwiches
Pimiento Sandwiches
Cherry and Cheese Salad
Checkermints   Salted Nuts
Tea
———
Crab Japanese in Ramekins
Brown Bread and Lettuce Sandwiches
Radish Roses   Celery Curls
Loganberry Ice   Cake
Tea
———
Fresh Shrimp and Celery Salad
Cream Cheese and Horseradish
Sandwiches
Nut Bread Sandwiches
Spanish Cream   Raspberry Sauce

WASHINGTON'S BIRTHDAY
LUNCHEONS
Oysters on Half-Shell
Southern Fried Chicken
Sliced Virginia Ham
Hot Baking-Powder Biscuits
Stuffed Celery Salad
Waffles   Maple Sirup
Cherry Ice   Sponge Cake
Coffee

Cherry Fruit Cocktail
Stuffed Pork Tenderloin
Grilled Sweet Potatoes
Peas   Spoon Bread
Celery   Olives
Lettuce Salad
Thousand Island Dressing
Strawberry Ice Cream
Cake   Coffee

COLONIAL LUNCHEONS
Cherry Cocktail
Shrimps à la King
Toast Point Garnish
Tiny Buttered Rolls
Radishes   Stuffed Olives
Grape Bavarian Cream
Hatchet Cookies   Coffee
———
Cream of Beet Soup   Crisp Crackers
Boiled Salmon   Drawn Butter Sauce
Mashed Potatoes sprinkled with
Paprika
Celery Curls   Mixed Pickles
Pimiento and Asparagus Salad
Loganberry Ice
Patriotic Cake (Pink Icing)
Coffee

COLONIAL TEAS
Red Cherries Stuffed with Cream
Cheese Salad
Small Graham Rolls
Tea or Coffee   Salted Nuts
Maple Nut Ice Cream
Sugar Cookies cut in Hatchet Shapes
———
Creamed Oysters in Patty Shells
Pepper Sandwiches
Rolled Celery Sandwiches
Tea or Coffee   Salted Nuts
Cranberry Milk Sherbet
Pound Cake   Bonbons

VALENTINE LUNCHEONS

Tomato Bouillon
Jellied Chicken Salad
Clover Biscuits
Pineapple Ice   Cake
Nuts   Coffee

_____

Fruit Cocktail
Veal Croquettes with Tomato Sauce
Baking-Powder Biscuits
Celery stuffed with Cheese
Strawberry Ice Cream in Heart Molds
Cake

_____

Chicken Bouillon
Creamed Scallops and Mushrooms in
Timbale Cases
Pimiento Sandwiches
Radish Roses   Celery Hearts
Red Cherry Salad   Sponge Drops
Candied Hearts   Coffee

_____

Cream of Celery Soup
Croûtons cut in Heart Shapes
Ham Mousse   Green Peas
Mashed Potato Hearts
Molded Beet Salad
Raspberry Ice Cream   Cake
Coffee

VALENTINE BRIDGE OR TEA MENUS

Creamed Minced Ham with Mush-
rooms
Heart Shaped Bread and Butter
Sandwiches
Peppermint Ice Cream   Cake
Salted Nuts   Coffee

_____

Stuffed Cherry Salad
Pimiento Sandwiches
Chopped Ham Sandwiches
Mints   Salted Nuts
Coffee

VALENTINE DINNER

Cream of Pimiento Soup
Baked Ham   Mashed Potato Cones
(Sprinkled with Paprika)
Creamed Cauliflower
Tomato Jelly Salad
Loganberry Ice Cream   Coffee

ST. PATRICK'S DAY DINNER

Cream of Spinach Soup
Crisp Crackers
Crown Roast of Pork filled with Green
Peas
Potato Balls with Chopped Parsley
Apple or Watercress Salad
Pistachio Ice Cream
Decorated Cakes (Green Icing)

ST. PATRICK'S DAY LUNCHEON

Cream of Pea Soup
Jellied Chicken with Green Coloring in
Jelly
Creamed Potatoes   Green Olives
Celery Curls   Clover Leaf Rolls
Coffee
Stuffed Green Pepper Salad
Mint Ice   Cake with Green Frosting

_____

Cream of Spinach Soup
Creamed Chicken in Pepper Cases
Green Olives   Green Pickles
Lettuce Sandwiches   Asparagus Rolls
Pistachio Ice Cream
Bonbons   Salted Nuts
Coffee

SIMPLE EASTER DINNERS

(Yellow and Green)

Cream of Spinach Soup
Crown Roast of Lamb
Pan Roasted Potatoes
Fresh Asparagus with Hollandaise
Sauce
Grapefruit and Green Pepper Salad
Pistachio Ice Cream   Lady Fingers
Candied Orange Peel   Coffee

_____

Mint Orange Cocktail
Meat Loaf   Mashed Potatoes
Buttered Carrots with Green Pea
Sauce
Lettuce Salad
Tiny Parker House Rolls
Rhubarb Meringue Pie   Coffee

SIMPLE EASTER LUNCHEONS

Creamed Stuffed Eggs on Toast
Buttered Diced Asparagus
                    Hot Cross Buns
Easter Salad (cabbage, apple, celery
        and pineapple)
Lemon Ice   Sponge Cake
            Tea

Molded Chicken Salad on Watercress
Celery Stalks Stuffed with Cheese
    Nut Baking-Powder Biscuits
Orange Fruit Jelly   Custard Sauce
    Cake   Tea

MAY DAY BREAKFASTS

Bouillon   Wafers
Salmon Cutlets   New Peas
    Parker House Rolls   Coffee
Strawberries in Angel Cake Baskets

Strawberries au Naturel
Broiled Chicken
            Creamed New Potatoes
    Waffles   Maple Sirup
            Coffee

EARLY WEDDING BREAKFASTS

Fruit Cocktail in Fruit Shells
Creamed Chicken in Toast Patties
    Hot Baking-Powder Biscuits
    Jam or Marmalade
Hot Coffee   Cream

Halves of Grapefruit or Melon
Halves of Broiled Chicken (or squab)
    on Buttered Toast
    Corn-Bread Sticks
Currant Jelly or Currant Preserves
    Coffee   Cream

Orange Baskets filled with orange
        sections
    Creamed Fish
(scallops, crab flakes, or salmon)
Popovers   Strawberry Jam
    Coffee   Cream

Grapefruit filled with white grapes
Southern Fried Chicken
            Grilled Sweet Potatoes
    Waffles   Maple Sirup
        Coffee   Cream

ELEVEN O'CLOCK WEDDING BREAKFASTS OR LUNCHEONS

Fruit Cocktail
Olives   Celery   Nuts
    Lobster Patties   Peas
Buttered Parker House Rolls   Coffee
Asparagus Tip Salad   Cheese Sticks
    Chocolate Ice Cream with
        Mint Candy Sauce
Cakes   Bonbons

Vegetable Cocktail
    Browned Saltines
Salted Nuts   Radishes
    Filet Mignon on Toast
    Mushroom Sauce
Potato Balls in Parsley Butter
Maple Ice Cream   Macaroons
        Bonbons

Chilled Bouillon   Celery
Whole-Wheat Buttered Crackers
        Salted Pecans
Chicken à la King on Toast
    Potato Croquettes
Tomato Cups filled with
    Cream Cheese and Olives
Pineapple Ice Cream   Cakes
        Coffee

Consommé
Sweetbread and Mushroom Patties
Fruit Salad   Assorted Sandwiches
Frappé or Ice Cream   Sweet Wafers
    Fancy Cakes   Bonbons
        Coffee

Iced Bouillon   Saltines
    Molded Jellied Chicken
Fruit Salad   Sandwiches
    Pineapple Ice   Cakes
        Bride's Cake
Coffee   Bonbons   Nuts

Consommé   Crisped Wafers
Creamed Chicken in Timbale Cases
    Ham Mousse
Green Peas   Potato Roses
    Cucumber Jelly Salad
    Strawberry Ice Cream
Nuts   Coffee   Cakes

Fruit Cocktail
Scalloped Shrimp in Ramekins
Filet of Beef (Individual Service)
Mushroom Sauce
Hot Rolls
French Fried Potatoes
Asparagus Salad
Toasted Crackers
Fruit Ices, Assorted Flavors
Cakes
Candied Fruits   Coffee

BRIDE-TO-BE LUNCHEONS

Pineapple Cocktail
Creamed Fresh Shrimps with Green
Peas
Heart-Shaped Baking-Powder Biscuits
Molded Beet Salad
Loganberry Ice Cream   Bride's Cake

Cream of Cauliflower Soup
Sliced Tongue   New Potato Salad
Buttered Asparagus and Peas
Parker House Rolls
Fresh Fruit Ice Cream

Mushroom Timbales   Celery
Lettuce Sandwiches
Pineapple Bavarian Cream
Chocolate Cake   Coffee

Haddock in Tomato Cups
Cheese Sauce
String Beans
Buttered Rolls with Cress
Cucumber Salad   Radish Dressing
Individual Strawberry Shortcakes

Orange Cocktail
Pressed Veal   Tomato Slaw
Stuffed Celery
Pineapple Ice Cream   Pecan Cookies

WEDDING SUPPERS

Creamed Mushrooms in Timbale Cases
Celery
Lettuce Sandwiches
Pineapple Bavarian Cream
Chocolate Cake   Coffee

Chicken Bouillon
Wafers
Sliced Tongue and Grape Jelly
New Potatoes in Parsley   Peas
Cucumber Salad   Cheese Straws
Strawberry Charlotte Russe
Coffee

Chicken à la King
Olives, Ripe and Green   Rolls
Molded Beet Salad
Brown Bread Sandwiches
Grape Juice Ice
Coffee   Stuffed Dates and Prunes
Fancy Cakes

Chicken Jelly Salad
Sweet Pickles   Hot Rolls
Raspberry Ice with Whipped Cream
Bride's Cake
Salted Nuts   Coffee

Creamed Oysters garnished with
Toast Points
Tiny Buttered Rolls
Club Celery
Banana Ice Cream garnished
with Candied Violets
Iced Cakes   Bonbons
Bride's Cake
Coffee

Chicken Salad
Olives   Pickles   Cheese Sticks
Coffee   Cream
Orange Ice
Cakes with Orange Frosting
Salted Almonds   Green Mints

Green Pepper Rings Stuffed with
Olives and Nuts and Cream Cheese
Buttered Bread Rolls   Pickles
Coffee   Pistachio Ice Cream
Cakes with Green Frostings

Oyster Patties
Olives   Cucumber Salad
Salted Pecans
Bread and Butter Rounds
Coffee   Cream
Lemon Water Ice
Cakes   Bonbons

Lobster or Crab-Flakes Creamed and
Served in Ramekins
Celery   Pickles
Olives   Salted Almonds
Cucumber Sandwiches
Pimiento and Egg Sandwiches
Coffee   Cream
Chilled Fruit in Fruit Baskets
Cakes   Bonbons

WEDDING ANNIVERSARY— EVENING COLLATIONS

GOLDEN ANNIVERSARY

Sweetbread and Mushroom Patties
Assorted Sandwiches
Orange Ice   Salted Almonds
Yellow Frosted Wedding Cake
Yellow Bonbons   Lemonade

SILVER ANNIVERSARY

Tuna Fish à la King in Mashed Potato
Nests
Celery Sticks Stuffed with Cream
Cheese
Parker House Rolls
Vanilla Ice Cream in Wedding Bell
Shaped Molds
Wedding Cake with White Icing and
Silver Dragées
Bonbons wrapped in Silver Foil
Nuts   Coffee

FOURTH OF JULY DINNERS

Cantaloupes Filled with Raspberries
Broiled Fresh Salmon
New Potatoes   Green Peas
Clover Leaf Rolls
Cucumber Salad   Toasted Crackers
Vanilla Ice Cream with Crushed
Strawberries
Sponge Cake

Jellied Canned Tomato Soup
Broiled Lobsters   Stuffed Potatoes
Luncheon Rolls Fresh Asparagus
Stuffed Green Pepper Salad
Cherry Pie

HALLOWE'EN FESTIVITIES

Chicken Almond Sandwiches
Cream Cheese and Pineapple
Sandwiches
Individual Pumpkin Pies
Whipped Cream
Cider

Piquant Sandwiches
Orange-Pecan Salad   Gingerbread
Coffee

Curried Eggs on Toast
Baking-Powder Biscuits
Cider Ice   Sponge Cake
Coffee   Salted Nuts

Creamed Shrimps with Eggs
Bread and Butter Strips
Spook Salad   Cakes
Coffee

THANKSGIVING DINNERS

Cream of Tomato Soup
Roast Turkey
Southern Giblet Gravy
Potato Croquettes
Brussels Sprouts
Cauliflower with Hollandaise Sauce
Cranberry Jelly
Romaine Salad   French Dressing
Individual Pumpkin Pies
Whipped Cream   Cider Ice
Nuts   Raisins

Halves of Grapefruit
Roast Duck   Apple Stuffing
Baked Sweet Potatoes
Creamed Turnips   Cole-Slaw
Baked Squash   Cider
Indian Pudding   Foamy Sauce
Nuts   Coffee

Fruit Cocktail
Chicken Fricassee   Riced Potatoes
Celery   Buttered Onions
Squash Pie

CHRISTMAS DINNERS

Grapes in Orange Juice Cocktail
Cream of Oyster Soup
Crown Roast of Pork
Grilled Sweet Potatoes
Stuffed Apples   Buttered Spinach
Tomato Jelly Salad   Cheese Straws
Plum Pudding
Foamy and Hard Sauce
Salted Nuts   Mints
Coffee   Cider

———

Scallop Cocktail
Roast Turkey   Giblet Stuffing
Sweet Potato Croquettes
Creamed Green Peppers   Squash
Cranberry Jelly
Lettuce Salad
Roquefort French Dressing
Mince Pie   Coffee
Nuts   Raisins

BUFFET LUNCHEONS

Chicken Pie
Cranberry Jelly in Molds
Lettuce Sandwiches
Orange Ice   Drop Cookies
Coffee

———

Hors d'Oeuvres
Crabmeat in Mushroom Sauce
Tiny Baking-Powder Biscuits
Stuffed Cherry Salad

BUFFET SUPPERS

Fruit Cocktail in Glasses
Sliced Ham   Scalloped Tomatoes
Celery   Stuffed Olives
Pepper Sandwiches
Small Mince Turnovers

———

Grapefruit Cups
Scalloped Scallops   Baked Tomatoes
Stuffed Celery   Salad Rolls
Chocolate Layer Cake

BRIDGE LUNCHEONS

(Also see P. 235)

Chicken Mousse
Tomato Cream Salad
Bread and Butter Sandwiches
Fresh Raspberry Tarts   Coffee

———

Stuffed Peppers Supreme
Olives, Celery and Radish
on Watercress
Cream Cheese and Horseradish
Sandwiches
Peach Cottage Pudding

———

Ham Piquant
Cucumber Jelly Salad
Baking-Powder Biscuits
Apricot Ice
Sugar Cookies

———

Meat Roll Sandwich with
Tomato and Mushroom Sauce
Fresh Peas
Strawberry Ice   Sour Cream Cake

BIRTHDAY PARTY SPREADS

Rolls filled with Chicken Salad
Olives   Curled Celery
Watermelon Pickle
Salted Nuts   Coffee
Peach Ice Cream
Decorated Birthday Cake
Bonbons

———

Creamed Shrimp and Fresh Green
Peas in Patty Shells
Rolled Celery Sandwiches
Rolled Asparagus Sandwiches
Coffee
Vanilla Ice Cream
Decorated Birthday Cake
Bonbons wrapped in Silver foil

BIRTHDAY LUNCHEON

Consommé
Chicken à la King Toast point garnish
Tiny Buttered Rolls
Fruit Salad
Hot Chocolate   Whipped Cream
Peppermint Ice Cream
Birthday Cake
Bonbons

CHILDREN'S BIRTHDAY PARTIES

(Suitable for Children Between
6-12 yrs.)
Minced Chicken Sandwiches
Whole Wheat Bread and Butter
Sandwiches
Vanilla Ice Cream or Junket
Lady Fingers   Cocoa
Opera Sticks

Creamed Chicken on Toast
Bread and Butter Sandwiches
Peppermint Ice Cream   Sponge Cake
Hard Candy

Creamed Oysters
Lettuce Sandwiches
Baked Custard
Chocolate Covered Animal Crackers

Peanut Butter Sandwiches
Bread and Butter Sandwiches Spread
with Honey
Cocoa   Animal Cookies
Diced Oranges
Lollypops

LITTLE TOTS' BIRTHDAY PARTY

Graham Crackers   Zwiebach
Cooked Prune Pulp
or
Tapioca Cream
Plain Cookies   Milk

SMALL AFTERNOON TEA

Rolled Celery Sandwiches
Roquefort Cheese Sandwiches
Candied Orange Peel   Tea

Domino Sandwiches
Orange Marmalade and Cream Cheese
Sandwiches
Toasted Pound Cake
Salted Nuts   Tea

Sweet Pepper Sandwiches
Cream Cheese Crackers   Jelly Tarts
Mints   Tea

Rolled Asparagus Sandwiches
Chilaly Sandwiches
Chocolate Cookies   Tea

SUBSTANTIAL AFTERNOON TEAS

Savory Sandwiches
Asparagus and Egg Salad
Mayonnaise
Orange Cream   Pecan Cookies
Coffee

Mexican Relish
Tomato Salad   Mayonnaise
Buttered Tea Biscuits
Plain Layer Cake with Chocolate
Whipped Cream Filling   Coffee

Mock Lobster Salad
Brown Bread Sandwiches
Olives
Chocolate Ice Cream
Assorted Cakes   Tea

Oysters in Golden Sauce
Hot Toast
Stuffed Egg and Pimiento Salad
Salted Nuts   Candied Orange Peel
Coffee Sponge Baskets
Tea

Shrimp Newburg
Red Cabbage Slaw   Celery Curls
Nut Bread Sandwiches
Orange Snow Pudding
Boiled Sponge Cake   Coffee

Table Service

Serving Dinner Without a Waitress

I. SUGGESTIVE DINNER MENU

Clam Soup   Crisped Crackers
Roast Lamb   Pan Roasted Potatoes
Brown Gravy
Buttered Peas   Mint Jelly
Bread   Butter
Grape Fruit Salad
Apple Pie   Cheese
Coffee

II. SETTING TABLE

Arrange table pad, tablecloth, centerpiece of flowers, fruit or a plant and candlesticks, and set table following diagram on P. 242. Always set forks with tines up and cutting edge of knife towards plate.

III. SERVING

1. Just before dinner is announced, place the filled individual soup plates on the service plates at each cover. Also place a plate of crisped crackers on the table.

2. In seating the family and guests, place guest of honor at host's right, and the guest second in importance to his left.

3. The hostess or one of the children can serve and remove, as is necessary.

4. After family is seated, pass crackers from one to another, letting the hostess help herself first, and then to her right around the table.

5. The soup course finished, remove cracker plate. Then beginning with hostess, go to her left, remove the soup plate with left hand, change it to right hand, and remove soup plate of person sitting to hostess' right, with left hand. So on around table.

6. The service plates are used as dinner plates. Place roast before host. Place vegetables as diagram. (See P. 242.) It helps to have the vegetables that are to be on same plate with meat, served by one who sits near carver.

241

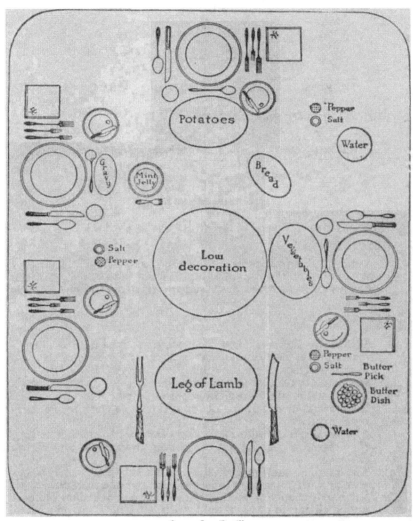

Courtesy Lucy G. Allen

Diagram of Table Laid for Home Service Without Service of Maid.

7. Host places serving of meat on plate, as well as the vegetables if they are near him. Otherwise he passes plate to those serving vegetables. The filled plate is then passed to hostess. She changes it for her empty plate, which she passes to the nearest person, and then on to the host.

8. Host then serves those to right of hostess in turn around the table.   If preferred, host may simply place meat on plate.   Then vegetables may be passed from one to another in serving dish.

9. Another method of using dinner plates is to remove soup and service plates together.   Then bring in six warm dinner plates and place before carver.

10. Relishes, bread and butter should be passed as the crackers were.

11. With main course completed, remove platter with carving knife and fork on it.   Then the vegetables, gravy, relishes and last the plates.   (Remove the latter in same order as soup plates.)

12. Next bring in two individual plates of salad.   Place one before hostess with left hand, change the one in right hand to left and place before person to hostess' right.   Repeat until all are served.

13. Remove from each cover the salad plate with one hand, and bread and butter plate with other hand and take both to kitchen.   Repeat until all plates are removed.

14. Remove on a small tray, salts and peppers and any unused silver.

15. Remove crumbs using napkin and plate.

16. Next bring in two individual servings of pie arranged on dessert plates, with a small piece of cheese on each plate.   Place one before hostess with left hand, change the one in right hand to left and place before person to hostess' right.   Repeat until all are served.

17. Next serve the coffee, bringing in two cups at a time, arranged on saucers with the spoons in position on the saucers.   Place at covers, as in case of salads, repeating until all are served. Sugar and cream may be passed as above, or placed on table, and passed from one to another.

18. If preferred, the dessert and coffee service may be arranged on a tea wagon and drawn to the hostess.   Then the hostess places the plates, pie and serving silver on the table before her.   She serves, passing the plate to the guest of honor, then to the one at the guest's right, and so on around the table.   Cheese is passed from one to another, started by the hostess, who takes it from tea wagon.   She also pours coffee from tea wagon, preparing it with cream, sugar, as persons fancy, and passes it as above.

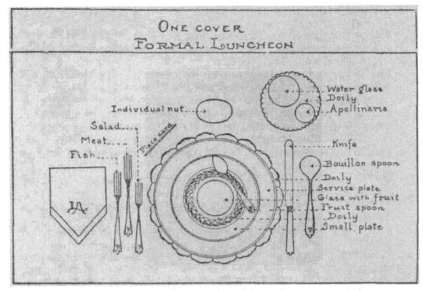

Above is shown the arrangement of the china, silverware and glassware
for each cover at a formal luncheon.

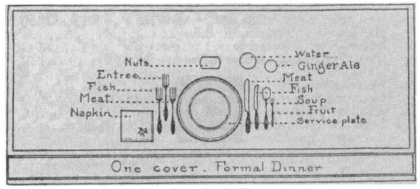

Courtesy Lucy G. Allen

The illustration above shows the formal dinner cover in detail with the
correct placement of the china, silverware and glassware.

Serving Luncheon with One or Two Waitresses

I. SUGGESTIVE LUNCHEON MENU

Pineapple Cocktail
Cream of Cucumber Soup
Sliced Tongue   Potato Croquettes
Buttered Asparagus
Parker House Rolls
Hearts of Lettuce   Russian Dressing
Loganberry Ice Cream   Cake
Nuts   Coffee   Bonbons

II. SETTING TABLE

1. Lay table with luncheon cloth which comes to edge of table or hangs about 6 inches below.   Or use a luncheon set consisting of center runner and individual plate doilies.

2. Arrange centerpiece of flowers, etc.   Use candlesticks if desired. Set table following diagram for one cover at formal luncheon (P. 244). Use 10-inch service plates and luncheon napkins 13 to 17 inches square. Place salts and peppers between each two covers. Dessert silver is placed when dessert is served.

III. SERVING

1. Before luncheon is served, have these items in readiness on serving table.

   a.   Finger bowls ¼ full of warm water, arranged on plates with doilies between.

   b.   Serving silver including meat fork, serving fork and spoon for asparagus, salad serving fork and spoon, ice cream spoons, dessert plates, coffee service, 2 small napkins and plates for removing crumbs, serving napkins, water pitchers, bowl of chopped ice with spoon, olives, pickles, etc., if served.

2. When luncheon is announced have fruit cocktail on service plates.   Arrange each cocktail glass on a small plate with doily between glass and plate, and a spoon on right hand side of plate, and place on service plate. Also have water glasses ⅔ full of water.

3. If hostess alone is entertaining, place guest of honor at her right, with second guest of importance at her left. If both host and hostess are entertaining, let them sit at opposite ends of table. The lady guest of honor, who is led in by host, sits

at his right, the second lady of importance sits at host's left. If there is a gentleman guest of honor, he sits at hostess' right.

4. If 1 waitress is serving, let her serve hostess first, then person to her right and so on around table in succession.

5. If 2 waitresses are serving, service is more prompt if two dishes of each course, one for each waitress, are prepared. When hostess only is entertaining, one waitress serves hostess first, and in turn to right going half way around table. The second waitress serves person directly opposite hostess first and proceeds to right. If both host and hostess are entertaining, one waitress serves hostess first and then to the right around table including host. Second waitress serves lady guest of honor and to her right in turn.

5. If 2 waitresses are serving and hostess does not wish to prepare 2 dishes of everything, let one waitress serve meat course, starting with hostess and proceeding to her right around table. Second waitress follows with potatoes, serving in same manner. First waitress follows with peas, and so on. The same order may be followed in serving salad and dessert.

7. Everything should be passed and served from left, with exception of extra silver and beverages, which are placed at right, from right.

8. After cocktail course is completed, following order for serving given above, let waitresses remove with left hand, one at a time the cocktail service which includes cocktail glass, doily, small plate and spoon, leaving the service plates.

9. Bring in cream soup cups and saucers, one at a time and place on each service plate.

10. Pour ginger ale from right hand side of each person with right hand.

11. Remove entire soup service including service plate with left hand, and place a warmed luncheon plate with right hand.

12. Next, serve sliced tongue, potato croquettes, vegetables and rolls in turn to those at the table, with left hand. In serving, have necessary silver in place on each serving dish and present the side of each serving dish. Place a napkin under each serving dish.

13. Next remove each luncheon plate with left hand and replace with salad plate with right hand. Then serve salad with left hand.

14. Remove salad plates one at a time. Remove salts and peppers, using a tray. Crumb table using small napkin and plate.

15. Place ice cream plates with spoon at right of each plate, one at a time from left. Then serve ice cream with serving silver in position and napkin under serving dish. Pass cake.

16. Remove each ice cream plate with left hand. Place finger bowl service with right hand.

17. Place filled coffee cup and saucer with spoon in place at right of each guest. Serve sugar and cream from tray.

18. Fingerbowl is removed by guest, and plate used for bonbons passed last by waitress.

Serving Buffet Luncheon

I. SUGGESTIVE MENU

Fruit Cocktail in Glasses
Sliced Ham   Scalloped Potatoes
Celery   Stuffed Olives
Lettuce Sandwiches
Small Mince Turnovers

NOTE: Select dishes that can easily be eaten with a fork or spoon. Knives have no place at a buffet meal.

II. SETTING TABLE

1. Arrange luncheon cloth, centerpiece and candles.

2. Arrange food, china, silver and napkins on table.

3. Prepare fruit cocktail in glasses on small plates with doilies between, and group on one side of the buffet table. The spoons may be grouped near glasses or placed one on each cocktail plate.

4. On opposite side of table place sliced ham arranged on platter with serving fork in position. Arrange desired number of forks in row on table above platter.

5. To left of platter arrange in a pile the desired number of luncheon plates.

6. The napkins in piles of not more than six each should be arranged one pile at left of plates, and the other near the fruit cocktail glasses on opposite side of table.

7. At one end of table arrange the casserole of scalloped potatoes, with serving spoon at right.

8. At opposite end place dish of mince turnovers. To the left place a pile of tea plates with necessary forks for turnovers.

9. At opposite corner place a dish of celery and a platter of sandwiches.

10. If ice cream is selected as dessert, it should be brought in after first and second courses are served and removed.

11. Serve coffee from urn at small side table or the filled cups may be served on a tray from kitchen.

12. Generally it is necessary for only two people to sit at table and serve the guests as they present their plates.

13. If there is plenty of maid service, and the guests are few, chairs and small tables may be arranged for seating the guests.   Then the waitresses may serve each guest.

Purchasing Guide of Kitchen Utensils

The Large Equipment

Refrigerator
Kitchen Cabinet
Extra Storage Units

Range
Sink with Drainboards
Serving Table

At Kitchen Cabinet or Work Table

1 set storage jars
5 mixing bowls, nested, ½ pt. to 2 qts. capacity
1 lemon squeezer, glass, wide juice rim with lip
6 custard cups
1 flour sifter
1 grater
2 standard measuring cups
1 biscuit cutter
1 set of muffin pans, 6 or 8 in a set
1 casserole, 1 qt.
1 egg-beater, wheel type
1 scissors, 8″
1 knife sharpener
1 paring knife
1 slicing knife, 9″ blade
1 bread knife
1 case knife
1 spatula, 7″ blade
1 broad spatula, blade 2½″ wide x 6″ long
1 fork, two tined, 4″
1 fork, two tined, 6″
2 teaspoons
2 wooden spoons, 10″ and 14″
1 apple corer
1 corkscrew and bottle opener
1 wire strainer
1 utility plate, 12″ diameter
2 sets measuring spoons, ¼ tsp., ½ tsp., 1 tsp., 1 tbsp.
1 can opener

1 workboard for mincing, etc., 12″ x 8″
1 chopping bowl and knife
1 breadbox
1 cakebox
1 breadboard

Near or at Range

1 ladle
1 salt and pepper shaker
1 potato masher
1 coffee-making appliance
1 teapot
2 frying-pans, 4″ and 8″ or 10″
1 double-boiler, 1½ qts.
3 lipped saucepans, 1 pt., 1½ pts. 1 qt.
1 basting spoon
1 toaster
1 flour dredger, ½ pt.
1 oven thermometer
1 fat thermometer
1 candy thermometer
1 kettle

At Sink

1 towel rack
1 funnel
1 sink strainer
1 soap dish
1 soap shaker
1 dishpan, about 12 qts. capacity
1 vegetable brush

249

At Sink (Continued)

2 straight-sided covered vegetable pans, 3½ qts. each
1 garbage can
1 colander
1 dish drainer

Storage Cabinet

1 square cakepan, 10" x 10"
1 oblong cakepan, 10" x 5"
2 layer cake pans, 9"
1 cooky sheet, 12" x 12"
1 griddle, 10"
2 pie plates, 10"
1 roasting pan, 15" x 10"
1 Berlin pan with cover, 6 qts.
2 wire cake coolers
1 food chopper
1 potato-ricer
1 rolling-pin
1 steamer

For Refrigerator

1 butter jar
3 refrigerator dishes for left-overs
1 ice pick

Optional Equipment

Household scales
1 quart measure
1 or more jelly molds
1 grapefruit knife
1 tube cakepan
1 doughnut cutter
1 ice-cream freezer
1 wooden mallet
1 heavy ice-bag
1 waffle iron
1 timbale iron
1 deep fat frying kettle with basket to fit
1 set cooky cutters
2 butter-ball paddles
1 bean pot
1 fireless cooker
1 steam pressure cooker
1 electric mixing and beating machine

Household Tools

1 screw-driver
1 hammer
1 monkey wrench
1 pair pliers
1 folding foot-rule

All kitchen equipment tested and approved by Good Housekeeping Institute will be found in our List of Tested and Approved Devices which may be secured from our Bulletin Service for 15 cents. (See P. 211.)

Good Housekeeping Institute

Cooking Temperature Chart

Cooking by Temperature Eliminates Food and Fuel Waste

Baking Temperatures

Kind of Food	Temperature Fahrenheit	Time	Kind of Food	Temperature Fahrenheit	Time
BAKED APPLES	400°	Until tender	MERINGUE	300°	15 min.]
BAKED BEANS	350°	6 to 7 hrs.	PIES:		40 min. (re-
			Apple or any *double-crust*		duce the
BISCUITS			pie, having raw filling	450°	h e a t
Baking-Powder	450°	12 to 15 min.			slightly
Raised	400°-425°	20 min.			d u r i n g
					l a s t 10
BREADS:					min.)
White	375°	60 min.	Custard, Pumpkin, or sim-		
Corn	400°	20 to 25 min.	ilar *open* pies	450°	10 min.
Muffins	400°	25 min.		and then	
Popovers	450°	30 min.		325°	30 min.
	and then		Cranberry, or similar *open*		
	350°	15 min.	*cross-cut* pies	450°	20 min.
Nut	350°	45 min. to 1	"Fruit Deeps," like apple		40 min. (re-
		hr.	or other deep fruit pies,		duce the
CAKES:			having a top crust only	450°	h e a t
Angel	320°	1 hr.			slightly
Fruit, Small	325°	1¼ hrs.			d u r i n g
Fruit, Large	275°	3 to 4 hrs.			l a s t 10
Gingerbread	325°	35 min.			min.)
Plain (sheet or cup)	375°	30 min.	Mince Pie, or any *double-*		
Plain (loaf)	350°	45 min.	*crust* pie, with a pre-		
Plain (layer)	375°	20 min.	viously cooked filling	450°	30 min.
Pound	350°	1 to 1¼ hrs.	Open Pies, having a souf-		
Sponge	320°	1 hr.	flé filling	375°	30 min.
			Pastry Straws	500°	10 min.
COOKIES:			Pie Shells	500°	12 min.
Drop, Bran	425°	12 min	Puff Paste	500°-550°	12 min.
Filled	450°	11 min.	Tart Shells	500°	10 min.
Ginger Snaps	350°	7 min.	Turnovers	450°	15 min.
Macaroons	350°	20 min.			
Rolled Vanilla	450°	10 min.	POTATOES:		
Soft Molasses	375°	18 min.	Baked, Small White	500°	25 min.
			Baked, Medium White	500°	40 min.
CREAM PUFFS AND ÉCLAIRS	400°	35 min.	Baked, Large White	500°	1 hr.
			Baked, Sweet	500°	35 min.
CUSTARDS:			Scalloped	350°	45 min.
Individual	325°	40 min.	PUDDINGS:		
Large, one-quart	325°	75 min.	Bread	350°	1 hr.
			Rice	320°	2 to 3 hrs.
MEATS AND FISH:			SCALLOPED DISHES (previ-		
Meat Loaf	400°	45 min.	ously cooked materials		
Meat Pie (Baking-Pow-			used)	500°	12 min.
der Biscuit Crust)	450°	30 min.	SOUFFLÉS	375°	20 to 30 min
Meat Casserole	350°	2½ to 3 hrs.			
Fish	425°-450	20 to 60 min.	TIMBALES:		
Sliced Ham	450°	20 min.	Individual	325°	40 min.
			Large	325°	75 min.

251

Roasting Temperatures

Kind of Food	Temperature Fahrenheit	Time	Kind of Food	Temperature Fahrenheit	Time
Beef (uncovered roaster) Rare	500° for 20 min. and 400° for remaining time	15 min. to the pound, plus 15 min.	Lamb, Spring (uncovered roaster)	500° for 30 min. and 450° for remaining time	15 min. to pound
Medium	500° fo 20 min. and 400° for remaining time	18 min. to the pound, plus 15 min.	Lamb, Spring (covered roaster)	550° for 30 min. and 450° for remaining time	15 min. to pound
Well Done	500° for 20 min. and 400° for remaining time	24 min. to the pound, plus 15 min.	Lamb, Leg (uncovered roaster)	500° for 30 min. and 450° for remaining time	20 min. to pound
Beef (covered roaster) Rare	550° for 30 min. and 450° for remaining time	10 min. to the pound, plus 15 min.	Lamb, Leg (covered roaster)	550° for 30 min. and 450° for remaining time	20 min. to pound
Medium	550° for 30 min. and 450° for remaining time	12 min. to the pound, plus 15 min.	Veal, Loin (uncovered roaster)	500° for 30 min. and 450° for remaining time	20 min. to pound
Well Done	550° for 30 min. and 450° for remaining time	15 min. to the pound, plus 15 min.	Veal, Loin (covered roaster)	550° for 30 min. and 450° for remaining time	20 min. to pound
Ham, Fresh or Pork (uncovered roaster)	500° for 30 min. and 450° for remaining time	30 min. to pound	Poultry (uncovered roaster)	500° for 15 min. 450° for 10 min. and 400° for remaining time	20 min. to pound (wgt. after bird is cleaned and dressed)
Ham, Fresh or Pork (covered roaster)	550° for 30 min. and 450° for remaining time	30 min. to pound	Poultry (covered roaster)	550° for 20 min. 500° for 10 min. and 400° for remaining time	20 min. to pound (wgt. after bird is cleaned and dressed)

Deep Fat Frying Temperatures

Kind of Food	Temperature Fahrenheit	Time	Kind of Food	Temperature Fahrenheit	Time
Croquettes, Fish Balls, and all previously cooked food	390°	Until brown	FISH AND MEAT: Butterfish and other medium-sized fish	390°	3 min.
Doughnuts, Fritters and all raw dough mixtures	360°-370°	Until brown	Cod Steaks and fillets of large fish	375°	4 min.
			Oysters and soft clams	390°	1 min.
			Scallops	360°	2 min.
French Fried Potatoes (strips ¼ inch thick and ¼ inch wide)	395°	About 4½ min.	Smelts and other small fish	390°	3 min.
			Veal Cutlets	400°	3 min.

To assist the housewife in following recipes not giving oven temperatures, this table will prove helpful: A Slow Oven ranges from 250° F. to 350° F., a Medium Oven from 350° F. to 400° F., a Hot Oven from 400°F. to 450° F. and a Very Hot Oven from 450° F. to 550° F.

© 1927
Good Housekeeping

INDEX

253

251

256

stuffed eggs on toast

9 781013 940835